Y0-ARD-473

Russia and Italy Against Hitler

Recent Titles in
Contributions to the Study of World History

Young Guard! The Communist Youth League, Petrograd 1917-1920
Isabel A. Tirado

Engine of Mischief: An Analytical Biography of Karl Radek
Jim Tuck

Central America: Historical Perspectives on the Contemporary Crises
Ralph Lee Woodward, Jr., editor

The Free Germany Movement: A Case of Patriotism or Treason?
Kai P. Schoenhals

Victims and Survivors: Displaced Persons and Other War Victims
in Viet-Nam, 1954
Louis A. Wiesner

Tsar Paul and the Question of Madness: An Essay in History and
Psychology
Hugh Ragsdale

The Orphan Stone: The Minnesinger Dream of Reich
Richard J. Berleth

American Constitutionalism Abroad: Selected Essays in Comparative
Constitutional History
George Athan Billias, editor

Appeasement in Europe: A Reassessment of U.S. Policies
David F. Schmitz and Richard D. Challener, editors

Ritual and Record: Sports Records and Quantification in Pre-Modern
Societies
John Marshall Carter and Arnd Krüger, editors

Diverse Paths to Modernity in Southeastern Europe: Essays in National
Development
Gerasimos Augustinos, editor

The Chinese Revolution in Historical Perspective
John E. Schrecker

Cities and Caliphs: On the Genesis of Arab Muslim Urbanism
Nezar AlSayyad

The French Revolution in Culture and Society
David G. Troyansky, Alfred Cismaru, and Norwood Andrews, Jr., editors

RUSSIA AND ITALY AGAINST HITLER

The Bolshevik-Fascist Rapprochement of the 1930s

J. Calvitt Clarke III

FOREWORD BY Clifford Foust

Contributions to the Study of World History
Number 21

Greenwood Press

New York
Westport, Connecticut
London

DK
67.5
I8
C53
1991

Copyright Acknowledgment

The author and publisher are grateful for permission to reprint the following:

"Manifestations of cordiality." Copyright © 1989 U.S. Naval Institute. Reprinted by permission from the Spring 1989 issue of *Naval History.*

Library of Congress Cataloging-in-Publication Data

Clarke, Joseph Calvitt.
     Russia and Italy against Hitler : the Bolshevik-Fascist
rapprochement of the 1930s / Joseph Calvitt Clarke III ; foreword by
Clifford Foust.
          p.   cm. — (Contributions to the study of world history, ISSN
0885–9159 ; no. 21)
     Includes bibliographical references and index.
     ISBN 0–313–27468–1 (alk. paper)
     1. Soviet Union—Foreign relations—Italy.   2. Italy—Foreign
relations—Soviet Union.   3. Soviet Union—Foreign
relations—1917–1945.   4. World politics—1933–1945.   I. Title.
II. Series.
     DK67.5.I8C53   1991
     327.45047—dc20   90–43372

British Library Cataloguing in Publication Data is available.

Copyright © 1991 by J. Calvitt Clarke III

Library of Congress Catalog Card Number: 90–43372
ISBN: 0–313–27468–1
ISSN: 0885–9159

First published in 1991

Greenwood Press, 88 Post Road West, Westport, CT 06881
An imprint of Greenwood Publishing Group, Inc.

Printed in the United States of America

The paper used in this book complies with the
Permanent Paper Standard issued by the National
Information Standards Organization (Z39.48–1984).

10 9 8 7 6 5 4 3 2 1

Contents

Illustrations   *vii*
Foreword by Clifford Foust   *ix*
Preface   *xiii*

I Background to the Italo-Soviet Rapprochement of 1933 and 1934

Introduction: Russia and Italy   3

1 Tripartite Rapprochement: Moscow, Rome, and Berlin   9

2 The USSR and Italy Respond to Hitler   39

3 The Four Power Pact   59

II The Italo-Soviet Rapprochement of 1933 and 1934

4 Ideological Rapprochement   77

5 Economic Rapprochement   99

6 Political Rapprochement   111

7 The Italo-Soviet Pact of Friendship, Neutrality, and Nonaggression,
  September 2, 1933   123

8 Military Contacts   145

9 Successful Collective Security?   163

Epilogue   *185*
Selected Bibliography   *201*
Index   *209*

Illustrations

Figure 1 Soviet-Italian Trade   20

Table 1   Flag Carriers at Novorossiisk in 1933   106

Table 2   The Italian Flag in the Port of Novorossiisk in 1934   106

Table 3   The Italian Flag in the Port of Odessa in 1934   107

Foreword

Let the reader take care. This is a book easily misjudged. On the surface, it is a close study of the diplomatic and commercial ties binding Stalin's Russia and Mussolini's Italy in 1933 and 1934. These years of improved relations were made palpable in the commercial agreement of May 1933, the political Pact of Friendship of September, and the increasing military contacts spanning the first half of the decade. A brief era of good feeling ensued, which eroded after 1935 with Italy's invasion of Abyssinia and the participation of both nations in the Spanish Civil War. Ultimately, of course, Mussolini joined Hitler in the attack on the Soviet Union in 1941.

Narrowly focused, there may not appear to be very much very remarkable in this tale even though the rapprochement of two such ideologically different governments might seem odd. Italian-Russian relations had, after all, been cordial enough before the Revolution and again during the New Economic Policy period, and by 1930 signs of improvement could be seen in their cooperation with Germany against France. Commerce between these two medium-weight powers leaped forward in 1931.

But the events that Clarke richly describes, when set against a larger canvas, take on greater significance. Hitler's assumption of power and the rise of German economic and military power, to say the least, upset the European state system and threatened to reshape or destroy the rough power balance achieved by between-the-wars Europe. It took some time for politicians to appreciate fully the new dangers, but more quickly than most, those in Moscow and Rome sensed that a veritable "Diplomatic Revolution" was underway. For Moscow, the changes in Germany marked the beginning of the decline of the centerpiece of their NEP foreign policy, the German connection that evolved after Rapallo. For Rome, the changes threatened

Austria, the Alto Adige region, and Italian aspirations in the Balkans. Hitler and Nazism were not the only catalysts to the improved Moscow-Rome connection, but they were critical.

Further, both countries sorely needed economic stimulus and succor. Both undertook state-sponsored industrial and commercial programs intended to lift their economies by their own bootstraps. The Great Depression made inroads on both economies, and both strove centrally and autarkically to mitigate them. Both could profit from augmented trade: The Italians desired Soviet grains for pasta, timber, metals, and raw and semiprocessed materials; the Soviets needed ships, military goods, automobiles, electrical equipment, and so forth.

Finally, the seeming incompatibility, even adversarial character, of their respective cherished ideologies presumably should have blocked profitable relations. Both overcame this disability, and, as Clarke tells us, ideology and political differences did not inhibit the rapprochement. Indeed, the Soviets had already made it amply clear as early as Brest-Litovsk that they would not tolerate the imperatives of ideological purity impinging on the practical needs of the economy or government. Witness their gymnastics in treating the rise of Nazism before 1933 as a boon to the communist movement. Fascism had not come to terms, perhaps, quite as decisively as had the Soviets with this issue, and hence Italy was treated to an extended, public, and important debate in the early thirties, especially in *Critica Fascista*. This debate included a compelling articulation of a doctrine of convergence, even merging, of the two political ideologies and systems.

The lessons and contributions of Clarke's study are several. Particularly important, especially in this era of the comparative decline of super-powers and their empires, is the simple but easily forgotten notion that "great powers" never operate in a vacuum; they swim along as large whales in a sea filled with lots of smaller fish, and, after all, take on some of their definition as great from the lesser fry. It is all too easy to take seriously only the whales; smaller creatures also contribute to marine ecology, and indeed are crucial as food and supportive companions to the big mammals.

Excluded from the perquisites and "responsibilities" of great-power status, neither the Soviet Union nor Italy was truly a great power, but both aspired to be. They were relatively benign porpoises who would have liked to be large, fearsome sharks, as Germany was quickly becoming. This monograph illustrates the importance of studying these lesser powers and their interrelations, rather than fixing exclusively on British, French, and German politics. A good deal of light can thus be shed on great power politics. Clarke reveals to us the degree to which Italy apprehensively regarded German motives and succeeded in influencing, however temporarily, the German agenda and its timing. By the same token, the Soviet Union played a far greater role in the Diplomatic Revolution of the early thirties than initially appears obvious.

Furthermore, in the light of the "Soviet accord with fascism" in 1933 and early 1934, the Soviet pact with Hitler in 1939 should not have come as the shocking surprise most of the world pretended it was. The righteous indignation expressed by so many in the West, then and later, is not entirely warranted. It is instructive here to note what Clarke tells us, that improved relations between Moscow and Rome in the early thirties were not intended on either part to alienate Berlin, so much as they were to persuade German authorities of the utilities that could flow from deemphasizing ideological differences and focusing pragmaticly on national and transnational security and economic uplift. The Soviets wanted the intimacy of Rapallo, not the isolation of Germany. Similarly, the Italians desired to show Berlin the values of renewed accord with Moscow, in part at least to deflect her attention from the south. The conduct of this Soviet-Italian diplomacy for concrete and mundane ends of perceived national interest speaks to how easily we can be misled by the ballyhoo and glitz of ideological and fundamentalist imperative. Soviet international politics (as distinct from proletarian internationalism) had been pragmatic all along, willing to risk temporary impurity for ultimate triumph. Fascism seems to have taken much the same approach. By contrast, Nazism, at least as it was interpreted and applied by psychotics like Hitler, took on a peculiarly virulent and dangerous mien.

We can eagerly look forward to J. Calvitt Clarke III carrying this study beyond 1935 to examine the mechanism of bilateral relations that led these two to meet on the field of battle in 1941.

Clifford Foust

Preface

Soon after the start of the Second World War in 1939, Augusto Rosso, the last of Italy's prewar representatives in Moscow, tried to explain to Rome why the Soviets had allied with the Nazis, their potential enemies. Militarily unprepared, he argued, Moscow hoped to unleash an exhausting war that would spur the revolutionary goals of the Communist International (Comintern). Rosso closed, "I . . . hold this opinion because if I found myself in the shoes of a Politburo member I would not reason otherwise."[1]

Clearly, in nailing down an argument, Rosso's closing was a weak bit of pot metal, easily bent or broken in the attempt to hammer it home. But what else could he say? Given the lack of dependable information, untainted by Moscow's public propaganda needs, his alternative was to declare that Soviet policy was irrational or, at least, inexplicable.

Such explanations do not long satisfy ministers back home. A critical part of an ambassador's charge is to take the best information available and draw from it rational conclusions usable to his government. In Joseph Stalin's Russia, with the impossibility of forming useful personal relationships with Soviet leaders, an ambassador's job was particularly trying.

The problems confronting today's historians have little changed. How many have lamented, "Until the Soviet archives are opened. . . . " Until then, we can do little more than what Rosso did—gather the best information available; examine it dispassionately; and draw credible conclusions based on the assumption that the Kremlin, by its own lights, operated on the same data in a rational, self-serving way. Because Stalin was always the final arbiter of policy, the historian must be presumptuous enough to sit himself in the dictator's seat and conclude, "This is what Stalin thought, because if I were he, I could do no other."

The bulk of my research comes from the embassy and consular reports now preserved in the Foreign Ministry Archives in Rome. These files covering the years 1924 to 1941 have hardly been touched in the effort to understand Stalin's Russia. This is an undeserved slight, for therein lies a wealth of information compiled by a long list of outstanding observers on all aspects of Soviet foreign and domestic policy events and conditions. Although many of these reports do little more than emphasize themes already illuminated elsewhere—the importance, however, of confirmation should not be underestimated—also lurking in the archives are valuable new insights and twists.

Of course, in relying heavily on the Italian perspective in defining the USSR, I have also said a great deal about Italy. And beyond that, the complex of relations developing in the 1930s between the fascist Royal Kingdom and the bolshevik Union of Soviet Socialist Republics was played out against the backdrop of the many important events of Europe's interwar diplomacy.

Relations between the Soviet Union and Italy from the time of formal diplomatic recognition in 1924 were substantive, active, varied, and generally reflected prewar traditions. For the most part, both the communist and fascist ideocracies felt the other's revolutionary militancy to be rather benign. It would have been alarmist beyond belief for Stalin to have feared anything emanating from Italy, and Mussolini had had little trouble in rounding up Italy's communists. Ideology, therefore, played no significant role in Italo-Soviet relations, except for those times when, for other reasons, they already were strained—and that was infrequent enough until after 1936. Only then did each wield the ideological club to bludgeon the other. Fascism and communism rationalized rather than initiated policy.

Practical politics gathered new urgency with Adolf Hitler's rise to power in Germany in January 1933—an event that overturned all previous European diplomatic possibilities. Buffeted by the forces unleashed, Moscow and Rome sought ways to contain the resurgent Germany. Both came to reject parts of their anti-Versailles revisionism and began to support the status quo, to the extent that it could block German expansion in directions harmful to themselves. In economic, political, ideological, and military matters, each turned to the other for support, especially in Southeast Europe, where their self-interested cooperation and competition met head on.

I maintain that the Soviets were attempting, and the Italians for a brief while were not unwilling, to put Germany "in a straitjacket of peace" through a complex and interlocking alliance system binding Rome, Moscow, Paris, and the capitals of the Little and Balkan ententes "in a chain of agreements designed to girdle Europe."[2] In many ways, Rome was the key, because only through the Italians, if at all, could the defeated and anti-Versailles Budapest and Vienna be brought to cooperate with the satisfied and strongly antirevisionist Belgrade, Bucharest, and Prague. And Italy's help was most important in bringing Sofia to cooperate with Ankara, Athens, Belgrade, and

Bucharest. Further, Italy was the one power both willing and geographically able to stop Nazi aggression with its first step in Austria.

Despite the important diplomatic roles that the Soviet Union and Royal Italy played in the 1930s, until now, with only one exception, no work has dealt comprehensively and directly and with their government-to-government relationship.[3]

A brief word about organization. Part I attempts to describe the background of the move toward serious cooperation in 1933 and 1934. The Introduction builds a foundation to the story by demonstrating how little the new ideologies and dictators changed the basic conundrums facing the two states.

Chapter 1 discusses the working out in 1929 and 1930 of the tripartite Italo-Soviet-German cooperation directed against France. The flight of an Italian air wing to Odessa in 1929 is a significant case study of the flirtations between the two states, which presaged the more extensive military contacts to take place in 1933 through 1935. Given the political importance that Moscow attached to any agreement in any field, a discussion of economic relations is especially appropriate. Although in terms of world totals Italo-Soviet trade was not terribly important, in specific areas such as oil and naval construction it proved significant.

Chapter 2 describes the Italian and Soviet responses to Hitler's rise to power. Clearly, although both Rome and Moscow wished to see continued their tripartite cooperation with Berlin, Hitler was determined to move against Italy's influence in Austria and against the USSR in the East. Hitler was a strong rope potentially binding Rome and Moscow together. The chapter closes with the ideas on fascism of Ernst Henri, a popular Soviet publicist of the 1930s.

The most significant of Italy's diplomatic initiatives before the Italo-Abyssinian War was Mussolini's Four Power Pact negotiated and signed in 1933. A realistic attempt to tie up the loose ends left over from the Great War, its potential was undermined from the start by France and its allies. Portending the Kremlin's concern five years later over its exclusion from the Munich Conference, Chapter 3 describes how even this weakened pact threatened the Soviet Union with isolation in the face of a hostile Germany bound to France, Britain, and Italy.

The USSR was in a difficult spot. Part II describes Moscow's attempt to break out of its isolation. Rapprochement, however, was a matter of linkage— to be successful it had to cover many areas of national and international life. To clear the decks of encumbrances, the matter of competing ideologies had to be dealt with. Chapter 4 makes clear that for neither the fascists nor the communists was ideology an insuperable obstacle. In Chapter 5 the economic rapprochement, especially the accord of May 6, 1933, cleared the way for the political talks described in Chapter 6. These negotiations culminated with the Pact of Friendship, Neutrality, and Nonaggression of September

2, 1933, and Foreign Commissar Maxim Litvinov's visit to Rome described in Chapter 7. Much of this drawing together took place in the arena of extensive military contacts. As Chapter 8 shows, these were important not only as a public symbol of diplomatic rapprochement, but also because they implied the possibility of military coordination to back up political arrangements.

Chapter 9 looks beyond bilateral Italo-Soviet relations to view collective security, that "strait jacket of peace" being strapped together to keep Germany subdued. I use the term "collective security" as I think the Soviets might have in their private councils. For them, the League of Nations was but a tool, perhaps useful, in containing German aggression against the Soviet Union. This was the extent of their international altruism. The key was protection of the USSR—whether they found it within the League or through some other mechanism of collective action was unimportant.

Collective security seemingly had its one grand triumph in Austria, and Soviet policy to include Italy as an important component appeared completely justified. Then what happened? Why did Italy within two short years throw over its old policy to join with Germany against the Soviet Union? That both Italy's role in collective security and collective security itself ultimately were dashed on the rocks of the Italo-Abyssinian War of 1935 and 1936 was not for want of effort by the Soviet pilots. The Epilogue tries to explain this turn of events.

If the present story, although self-contained, appears to end overly abruptly, I hope that its readers will be forgiving. In the near future I intend to carry it forward to 1943 in another volume.

Any author of a work such as this would be remiss not to thank those without whose support it could never have been completed. While many have read parts of my manuscript at its various stages, Clifford Foust, George L. Yaney, John Lampe, George O. Kent, and Jon T. Sumida, all of the University of Maryland; William I. Shorrock and Jeanette E. Tuve of Cleveland State University; James J. Sadkovich of the General Motors Engineering & Management Institute; H. James Burgwyn of West Chester University; George Rhyne of Dickinson College; Anique van Ginneken of Katholieke Universitet, Nijmegen, the Netherlands; and Karen Carroll and Martha and Michael Moreno deserve special thanks. I am also indebted to Dr. Enrico Serra and his assistants in the historical archives at the Foreign Ministry in Rome for their kindness. And lastly, the many unsung workers at the Library of Congress in Washington, D.C., and the National Library in Rome made possible my research. Of course, I alone am responsible for any mistakes of fact or interpretation.

NOTES

1. Italy. Ministero degli Affari Esteri. Commissione per la pubblicazione dei documenti diplomatici, *I documenti diplomatici italiani* (abbreviated as DDI) (Rome, 1953–86), 9th ser., vol. 2, no. 207.

2. Grandi to Rome, 9/5/33: Ministero degli Affari Esteri, Direzione Generale degli Affari Politici, URSS (Rome), (abbreviated as AP URSS) b(usta) 10 f(oglio) 1.

3. See Mario Toscano, *Designs in Diplomacy: Pages from European Diplomatic History in the Twentieth Century*, trans. and ed. George A. Carbone (Baltimore, 1970), pp. 48-304, which deal with the period from 1939 to 1943. The slight volume by Carlo Lozzi, *Mussolini-Stalin: Storia delle relazioni italo-sovietiche prima e durante il fascismo* (Milan, 1983), makes no pretense of being other than a popular work.

I

Background to the Italo-Soviet Rapprochement of 1933 and 1934

Introduction: Russia and Italy

The First World War was an unmitigated catastrophe for Europe. Out of its carnage arose many new and freshly invigorated movements offering solace for the earlier certainties now destroyed. Wilsonianism, nationalism, bolshevism, fascism, and Nazism—all attempted to address the material and spiritual vacuums that convulsed the interwar period. The competition between them led to the Second World War.

One provocative yet insufficiently studied aspect of these larger struggles concerns the state-to-state relations between bolshevik Soviet Russia and the fascist Italian Kingdom. Worth studying on their own merits, they assume particular importance because around them swirled many of the critical events of the peacetime hiatus. These relations also shed light on the inner natures of both the Soviet and fascist regimes.

EARLY ITALO-RUSSIAN RELATIONS

Russian and Italian interests often came into contact in ways that affected all of Europe. Tsarist machinations in the 1850s, in fact, had been crucial in the very formation of the Italian Kingdom.[1] The critical area of their volatile mixture of self-interested cooperation and competition was Southeast Europe. After 1875, Italy hoped that the Three Emperors' League would break apart under Balkan stresses, thus creating opportunities for Rome to assert itself in that region. At the 1878 Congress of Berlin, however, Italy was disappointed, and by 1882 Rome had left France to join the Triple Alliance as a junior partner.[2] And within a decade many Italians had come to believe that Austria's preservation was necessary to prevent Russia's national and panslavic penetration of the Balkans, which would have been to

Italy's detriment.[3] Reflecting this trend, Russia was particularly active in supporting Abyssinia in the period leading up to Italy's traumatic defeat at Adowa in 1896.[4]

Although the Triple Alliance was renewed five times, by 1914 it was clear that Austria and Germany could no longer rely on Italian help in a general war.[5] Certainly Rome's improving relations with Russia provided much of the evidence for that conclusion. At Russian encouragement, the future king, Vittorio Emanuelle, married the goddaughter of Tsar Alexander III.[6] After his coronation, he visited St. Petersburg in 1902. Italy was just as upset as was Russia with Austria's machinations during the Bosnian-Herzegovinian Crisis of 1908 and 1909.[7] One outgrowth was Tsar Nicholas II's long-delayed return visit with Vittorio at the royal hunting lodge near Turin.[8]

With the resulting Racconigi Agreement of October 1909, the Russians turned to Rome to mediate their diplomatic isolation. Italy recognized Russia's interest in the Straits, while the tsarist regime acknowledged Rome's claim to Tripoli. Having agreed to maintain the Balkan status quo and to contain any further Austrian expansion, the pact proved its worth, to Italy at least, during the Italo-Turkish War of 1911 and 1912. As the war was breaking out, the Russian foreign minister who had negotiated the pact described the deal by which Russia promised

not to hinder Italy's freedom of action in Tripoli, in return for which Italy . . . promised us a favorable attitude . . . toward the Straits. . . . On the assumption that Italian action is inevitable . . . we ought to concern ourselves not only with the best way to preserve peace and order in the Balkan Peninsula, but also with the possibility of extracting from the impending events the most profit.[9]

Despite Italy's support, St. Petersburg was unable to use the war as an excuse to reexamine the Straits Question.

Rome's neutrality at the onset of the Great War and the negotiations scramble to provoke Italy to intervene graphically demonstrated the complex web of interdependence and antagonism marking Italo-Russian relations in the Balkan arena.[10] In short, Italy wanted to expand its influence and, to find room to maneuver, carefully tried to balance Austro-German and Russo-Slavic influences. For its part, St. Petersburg wanted Italy's help only when Russian armies were retreating and spurned it when things looked promising—the Russians saw no advantage in replacing Austria's hegemony with Italy's. In the confused situation, it was difficult for anyone to decide exactly where self-interest lay. After tortuous negotiations, the Allies bribed Rome to enter the war with the London Treaty of April 1915.[11] Ironically, however, Italy had entered at the worst moment, when the Entente had lost the initiative. Nor did Rome, as had been hoped, drag in the Balkan States against the Central Powers. Italy became mired in a frustrating war of attrition, made all the more dangerous by the October Revolution of 1917 in Russia.[12]

That war ended in a series of peace settlements that further frustrated the nominally victorious Italians. To distract them, London suggested that they occupy Georgia, which had broken away from the newly formed bolshevik government in Moscow.[13] Briefly tempted, the Italians allowed cooler heads in Rome to prevail, spurred in part by advice from one statesman, who wrote: "An Italian occupation of Georgia . . . would one day change into the cause, or pretext, for a Russo-German agreement directed against the western world. And we Italians would suffer first, in the Black Sea."[14]

ITALO-SOVIET RELATIONS IN THE 1920s

The postwar relationship between communism and fascism produced a fascinating interplay of ideology, pragmatism, and personal idiosyncrasies. And self-justification played no small role, especially as Moscow tried to explain away the failed socialist revolution in Italy.[15]

Pragmatism generally prevailed on both sides, as was amply demonstrated by the Comintern's crass treatment of the Italian Socialist Party (PSI). Basically, V. I. Lenin insisted that all revolutionary parties be cast in the bolshevik image.[16] When the PSI refused, he forced it to split, with the left wing becoming the Italian Communist Party (PCI). Casting about for a pliable leader for the PCI, he ultimately hooked Antonio Gramsci, who bolshevized the Italian party.[17] The Soviets thus destroyed whatever revolutionary potential remained on the Italian left. By 1926 the PCI was dead as a political force, but no matter. It was dancing obediently to Moscow's tune.

As with the other great powers, Italy had broken formal diplomatic relations with Lenin's revolutionary regime. And again, as with the other great powers, when the new government did not fall, Italy pragmatically worked to reestablish cordial relations. Difficult negotiations throughout 1921 culminated in two provisional trade agreements along the lines of the ones recently signed between London and Moscow. In effect, Italy had recognized the Soviet government, although the road to *de jure* recognition remained rough.[18]

Common interests, however, were sufficient to overcome these difficulties, including the PCI's objections. Moscow wanted to draw Rome into the Rapallo front with Berlin, as Lenin suggested to his foreign commissar, G. V. Chicherin:

Considering the importance of the Russo-German treaty, its acceptance by Germany, its influence on Italy, and the dogfight between the powers over oil concessions, we arrive at the conclusion that it would be most correct for us now to build up all our foreign policy on everything resting, over a certain period of at least a few months, only on the Russo-German treaty.[19]

For its part, Rome wanted to expand its commercial relations with the Soviets. Further, Benito Mussolini, the Italian premier and Duce, did not want to be left behind in any initiative that Britain might make. Recognition ended in an unseemly squabble over whether, of the great powers, Britain or Italy had recognized the USSR first.[20] In either case, on February 7, 1924, Rome and Moscow signed protocols exchanging formal recognition and recodifying commercial relations.

Although Rome's expectations of significantly expanded trade languished, overall formal relations between the two states proved satisfactory, even if not effusively friendly. The Soviets did not even protest the 1924 murder of the socialist opposition leader, Giacomo Matteoti. In fact, the Soviet plenipotentiary representative, K. K. Iurenev, despite Gramsci's vigorous protests in L'Unità, ostentatiously refused to cancel a previously issued invitation to Mussolini to dine at the Soviet embassy.[21] Even Italy's ratification of the Locarno Accords of 1925 raised hardly more than a small bump in the road.

The only major disturbance occurred in 1927 with Italy's ratification of the Bessarabian Protocol, which internationally sanctified Romania's postwar annexation from Russia of the Bessarabian region. Neither Italy nor the USSR, however, desired to break relations. In December 1928, the Duce went so far as to tell the Soviet plenipotentiary representative to Rome, D. I. Kurskii, of his conviction that sooner or later Italy and the Soviet Union would have to come to a political agreement to match the one already achieved in the economic field.[22] Pressing the point, he suggested a friendship pact of such a vast scope that it would have allowed Italy to break with England and France. Kurskii rejected the idea.

Mussolini's suggestion, however, remained as a portent for the future.

NOTES

1. As a small sample of the vast literature, see Giuseppe Berti, Russia e stati italiani nel Risorgimento (Turin, 1957) and Vladimir Efimovich Nevler, La Russia e il Risorgimento, ed. Vittorio Frosini and Mario Condorelli (Catania, 1976).

2. Cedric James Lowe and Frank Marzari, Italian Foreign Policy, 1870–1940 (London, 1975), pp. 13-54; Luigi Salvatorelli, La Triplice Alleanza: Storia diplomatica, 1877-1912 (Milan, 1939), pp. 23-71.

3. Ibid., pp. 73-206.

4. For the intense Russian activity in Northeast Africa before 1900, see, e.g., Bliuma Abramovna Val'skaia, Puteshestviia Egora Petrovicha Kovalevskogo (Moscow, 1956) and Carlo Zaghi, I russi in Etiopia, 2 vols. (Naples, 1972).

5. Enrico Decleva, Da Adua a Sarajevo: La politica estera italiano e la Francia, 1896–1914 (Bari, 1971), pp. 45-60, 161-87, 354-58, 416-28; Problemi italiani (Milan, 1915); Salvatorelli, La Triplice Alleanza, pp. 215-357.

6. Carlo Lozzi, Mussolini-Stalin: Storia delle relazioni italo-sovietiche prima e durante il fascismo (Milan, 1983), pp. 9-11.

7. Bernadotte Everly Schmitt, The Annexation of Bosnia 1908–1909 (Cambridge, 1937; reprint, New York, 1971).

8. Guido Donnini, *L'accordo Italo-Russo di Racconigi* (Milan, 1983). A Russian naval squadron visited Naples in February 1908 as a prelude to the agreement; see pp. 15-22.

9. Pavel Nikolaevich Efremov, *Vneshniaia politika Rossii (1907-1914 gg.)* (Moscow, 1961), p. 134. See also pp. 134-40 and William Clarence Askew, *Europe and Italy's Acquisition of Libya, 1911–12* (Durham, NC, 1942).

10. Revekha Abramovna Averbukh, *Italiia v pervoi i vtoroi mirovykh voinakh* (Moscow, 1946), pp. 18-34; V. V. Gotlib [Wolfram Wilhelm Gotlieb], *Tainaia diplomatiia vo vremia pervoi mirovoi voiny*: (Moscow, 1960), pp. 189-562; Valentin Alekseevich Emets, *Ocherki vneshnei politiki Rossii v period pervoi mirovoi voiny: Vzaimootnosheniia Rossii s soiuznikami po voprosam vedeniia voiny* (Moscow, 1977), pp. 25-170.

11. Mario Toscano, *Il Patto di Londra: Storia diplomatica dell'intervento Italiano (1914–1915)*, preface by Arrigo Solmi (Pavia, 1931); Anatolii Vasil'evich Lunacharskii, *Italiia i voina* (Petrograd, 1917).

12. See Giorgio Petracchi, *Diplomazia di guerra e rivoluzione: Italia e Russia dall'ottobre 1916 al maggio 1917* (Bologna, 1974).

13. Marta Petricioli, *L'occupazione italiana del Caucaso: "Un ingrato servizio" da rendere a Londra*, introduction by Rodolfo Mosca (Milan, 1972); Enrico Serra, *Nitta e la Russia* (Bari, 1975); Giorgio Petracchi, *La Russia rivoluzionaria nella politica Italiana: La relazioni italo-sovietiche 1917-25*, preface by Renzo de Felice (Bari, 1982).

14. Lozzi, *Mussolini-Stalin*, p. 55.

15. Many works have covered the revolutionary situation in Italy prior to Mussolini's takeover. See, e.g., Zinaida Pavlovna Iakhimovich, *Rabochii klass italii protiv imperializma i militarizma konets XIX-nachalo XX vv.* (Moscow, 1986); and Stefano Caretti, *La rivoluzione russa e il socialismo italiano (1917-1921)* (Pisa, 1974).

16. George Rhyne, "Legitimizing the Russian Revolution: Lenin and the Italian Left," unpublished paper delivered at the Mid-Atlantic Slavic Conference of the American Association for the Advancement of Slavic Studies, Albany, NY, Apr. 16, 1988.

17. For one example of the immense and often idolizing bibliography on Gramsci, see John M. Cammett, *Antonio Gramsci and the Origins of Italian Communism* (Stanford, CA, 1967). For the development of the PSI and PCI, see, e.g., Mikhail Alekseevich Dodolev, *Demokraticheskaia opozitsiia i rabochee dvizhenie v Italii, 1922-1926 gg.* (Moscow, 1975) and Joan Barth Urban, *Moscow and the Italian Communist Party: From Togliatti to Berlinguer* (Ithaca, NY, 1986), pp. 23-110.

18. Norbert H. Gaworek, "From Blockade to Trade: Allied Economic Warfare against Soviet Russia, June 1919 to January 1920," *Jahrbücher für Geschichte Osteuropas* 23, no.1 (1975): 65-67; Giorgio Petracchi, "La cooperazione italiana, il Centrosojuz e la ripresa dei rapporti commerciali tra l'Italia e la Russia sovietica (1917-1922)," *Storia Contemporanea* 8 (June 1977): 231-33; V. A. Buriakov, "Missiia V. V. Vorovskogo v Italii v 1921 godu," *Voprosy istorii* (Nov. 1971): 131-42.

19. Vladimir Il'ich Lenin, *Collected Works*, 45 vols. (Moscow, 1970), 45: no. 720; see also no. 717. Georgi Vasilevich Chicherin, 1872-1936. The son of a nobleman, he entered the tsarist foreign service but in 1904 joined the revolutionary movement and lived in exile in France, Germany, and England. From May 1918 to 1930 he was foreign commissar.

20. Lozzi, *Mussolini-Stalin*, pp. 94-95.

21. Alexandre Barmine, *One Who Survived: The Life Story of a Russian under the Soviets*, 5th ed. introduction by Max Eastman (New York, 1945), pp. 154-56. The bolsheviks had rejected the appellation of "ambassador" as part of the old, bourgeois diplomacy and insisted on using the term "plenipotentiary representative." In 1924 and 1925, Konstantin Konstantinovich Iurenev served in Italy as the plenipotentiary. He was later arrested by the Soviet secret police and died in prison in 1938.

22. Giampiero Carocci, *La politica estera dell'Italia fascista (1925–1928)* (Bari, 1969), pp. 57-58, 358 n.124; Union of Soviet Socialist Republics. Ministerstvo inostrannykh del SSSR. *Dokumenty vneshniaia politika SSSR* (abbreviated as *DVP*), (Moscow, 1970-1973), vol. 11: no. 376. From 1918 to 1928 Dmitrii Ivanovich Kurskii served as commissar of justice. Replacing Lev Borisovich Kamenev, he was the Soviet plenipotentiary in Italy from 1928 until his death in December 1932.

1

Tripartite Rapprochement: Moscow, Rome, and Berlin

Mussolini, of course, had made his proposal to Kurskii for a political pact within the context of his perceptions of Italian necessities. What were Italy's vital interests under the Duce? He maintained that his foreign policy was not original. For him, Italy was preeminently a Mediterranean power—an "island" in contact with Europe. In the mid–1930s, Italy received 86 percent of its imports by sea, and of these, 13 percent passed through the Dardanelles, 17 percent through Suez, and 70 percent through Gibraltar. Hence the fascist conviction that Italy must either dominate or be the prisoner of its *Nostro Mare*, the Mediterranean. Nor could Italy willingly concede to any other power hegemony in the Mediterranean's hinterland—the Danubian (including Austria and Hungary) and Balkan areas.[1]

AGAINST FRANCE AND ITS ALLIES, 1929-1932

Common Interests

Toward that end of maintaining its position in the Balkans, Italy sought to oust French political, economic, and cultural influences from Southeast Europe and struggled to prevent the spread of either German or Slavic predominance in the region. The fundamental Italian policy, like the British, was to prevent any single power from dominating the continent. With hearty ambitions in the Adriatic Sea, North Africa, the Levant, and along the shores of the Red Sea and Indian Ocean, fascist Italians wanted to resurrect the Roman Empire.[2]

How did this affect Rome's policies toward the USSR? Far from one another, no border or colonial controversies troubled their relations. Further, since recognition neither had tried to subvert the other. The decline of Italo-French relations following the war and the Italo-German rapprochement could not but draw the USSR and Italy closer together.[3]

Sundry aggravations, nonetheless, continued to prick at their relations. In early 1929, for example, Kurskii informed the foreign commissariat (NKID) that in 1921 and 1922 a delegate of the Italian parliament, Enrico Insabato, had joined the anti-Soviet and Ukrainian nationalist Petliura delegation in Rome, and that he had worked on the editorial board of its press for 3,000 lire a month.[4] Insabato, Kurskii continued, recently had revealed plans to organize Italy's "social and cultural ties" with the Ukraine. Taking his time to respond, on December 10 Deputy Foreign Commissar M. M. Litvinov charged that because Italy apparently was prepared to support attempts to rip the Ukraine from the Soviet Union, any wish to establish direct cultural ties with it was more perfidious than it might otherwise appear.[5] He told Kurskii to remind Italians that all contacts had to be made through the Union government and not its separate parts—thereby belying the Ukraine's technical independence and voluntary accession to the USSR.

By 1930, nonetheless, the Soviet Union, Italy, and Germany were tending to cooperate against France and its allies.[6] Like communist Russia, fascist Italy felt itself an outlaw victimized by a hypocritical world "democratic" conspiracy organized by France. Mussolini, with his typical braggadocio, told the crowds in Florence in May 1930:

There are sects, groups, parties, people organized in a cooperative for exploiting the immortal principles [of the French Revolution]—the greatest, most monstrous, most refined humbug. . . . For all their democracy and pacifism, they would not be adverse to unleashing a war, perhaps at second-hand, against the Italian people, guilty [only] of identifying itself with the Fascist regime.[7]

If spoken of Russia and communism, there was nothing here with which a good bolshevik could disagree.

In a press interview in mid–1930 upon his rise to leadership of the NKID, Litvinov explained the tripartite alignment, saying that the powers that had imposed the peace treaties were the more aggressive toward the Soviet Union and that there "had come about a certain community of interests between the Soviet Union and the States which had suffered through the war."[8] Litvinov thereby acknowledged Italy as one of the sufferers, and many regarded the friendship between Rome and Moscow as proving that the Soviet Union was ready to be on good terms with all countries, especially Germany, regardless of the treatment of domestic communists.[9]

Yet paralleling its schizophrenic German policy, the Comintern still, however pathetically, called for revolution in Italy.[10] For example, in 1932 the Executive Committee of the Communist International resolved that the PCI must come out from the deep underground by developing a mass struggle against the fascist dictatorship on the basis of the defense of the everyday interests of the toilers, utilizing fascist meetings, organizing impromptu meetings in the factories, penetrating into the fascist trade-unions and into cultural and cooperative organizations, preparing and carrying out strikes and demonstrations; strengthening in every way mass illegal work.[11]

Although the Great Depression had increased the PCI's underground support, the attempt to return its operational headquarters to Italy proved disastrous. Nor could the communist press widen its influence in Italy. Palmiro Togliatti's speech of March 1934 to the Comintern marked the pitiful nadir of communist activities in Italy. What was supposed to celebrate communist resistance was more a sad recital of a few pseudo, impotent, and would-have-been events clearly demonstrating the non-role played by communism and a eunuch PCI in Italy.[12]

Litvinov and Grandi

Litvinov: The New Foreign Commissar. Italy's representatives closely followed Litvinov's troubled rise to head the NKID in 1930, and they reported rumors that he had threatened to resign should someone else take over upon Chicherin's resignation.[13] As late as July 2, Ambassador Vittorio Cerruti was reporting to Rome that it was unlikely that Litvinov would succeed Chicherin.[14] And two weeks later, the Italian embassy reported that the Soviet ambassador in Berlin, N.N. Krestinskii, was most insistently seeking the post that Litvinov coveted.[15]

As one historian of Soviet diplomacy has pointed out, Litvinov's hold on power and policy from the beginning was weak. His influence came not from political muscle, but from informed recommendation. That Stalin frequently left specific tactics to Litvinov's discretion, however, "undoubtedly" presented the commissar with opportunities to create *faits accomplis*, which the leadership could not easily reverse.[16]

Meanwhile, Litvinov and the NKID actively sought support for Soviet policies. On September 3, 1930, for example, a "high official" pressed the Italian chargé for joint action against French intrigues in Turkey and added hopefully, "Italy and the USSR are unique amongst the nations of Europe in that not only are they not divided by any dispute, but on the contrary, they have interests in common."[17] That same day, a French official expressed his grave concern over a Soviet naval visit to Italy and its political significance as foreboding "a far-reaching rapprochement" between the USSR and Italy.[18] This certainly must have reminded the Kremlin that ties with Rome could prove valuable as a way of pressuring Paris.

Litvinov was eager to formalize any rapprochement with Italy by signing a nonaggression pact. The Kremlin regarded such formalities as the ultimate

litmus test in power politics. Although the new commissar himself doubted
that a capitalist war against the Soviet Union was imminent, he confided to
Dino Grandi, the Italian foreign minister,[19] that "public opinion in his country and many of his colleagues" were "preoccupied that any day the capitalist
states would attack militarily."[20]

Litvinov and Grandi at Milan, November 24, 1930. This fear prompted
Litvinov to seek a meeting with Grandi, a meeting held in Milan on November 24. According to Grandi, Litvinov underscored their two states as
part of a "grand European revisionist bloc," and he "confirmed . . . his desire
that *'something be done'* formally between the two countries to show publicly" their cordiality. France and its allies posed "the true danger to peace
in Europe." Grandi skewered the new commissar:

[He] . . . gives the impression of being a cultivated man, quick and nimble-witted.
He shows a remarkable knowledge and feeling for international problems, not limited
to those directly affecting the interests his country. . . . [But] his logic is simplistic,
crude, and without finesse. He gives the impression of being a politician of a certain
stature, endowed with shrewdness, but who lacks the resources for the art of
diplomacy.[21]

Unfortunately, both Grandi and Litvinov had raised their expectations for
the Milan meeting too high. The commissar found Grandi more reticent on
a neutrality and nonaggression pact than he had hoped. Rome proved most
reluctant to sanction too promiscuous a flirtation with bolshevist Russia,
which might merely alienate the other powers rather than provoke them
into recognizing Italy's importance. The foreign ministry in Rome was content to hold "the Russian card in reserve"; but it was not to be used "as a
bogey against the other players."[22]

Undeterred, Litvinov continued to explore every avenue. Upon returning
to Moscow at the end of November, he immediately contacted the Italian
embassy, which reported:

[Litvinov] put to me his ideas about the general situation, in his view dominated by
France, whose privileges derive from treaties, the power of its armaments and
financial prosperity, and the net of its political-military alliances with a series of vassal
states. All assure growing and threatening hegemony. . . .
    Hence the necessity for an entente between our countries, not in the form of an
alliance, which the Soviets opposed in principle, but a natural cohesion manifested
in a tighter collaboration and in coordinated and concrete action.[23]

This "natural cohesion," well beyond a nonaggression pact, put Rome off.
Grandi too was offered less than he had expected at Milan. Rome had
hoped to secure a definite commitment from the Kremlin to accept a place
on the League commission set up to deal with the Briand Plan.[24] Litvinov,

however, had confessed that his government had not yet made up its mind. Grandi therefore refused to commit Italy on the question.[25]

But in attacking French policy and scorning "the infallibility of the Pontiff Briand" at Geneva, Grandi had been reminded of the USSR's value. The League and the issue of Soviet participation in the European Commission was "the best field" for Italy's "necessary anti-French action." With so many opposed to Soviet participation, it was no surprise that Grandi, with less than full support from the more cautious German delegation, was only partly successful in gaining Soviet admission. They could participate only in discussions on economic issues—a "semi-victory," as Krestinskii termed it to the Italian ambassador in Moscow, Bernardo Attolico.[26]

After the Litvinov-Grandi meeting, the rumor mill ground out stories of an Italo-Soviet-German bloc to be joined by Turkey, Hungary, Greece, Albania, Bulgaria, and Austria to seek treaty revision. Rome supposedly was to use this bloc to pressure France to see things the Italian way, especially on naval parity. Litvinov denied these "fantastic" reports:

The relations existing for seven years between Russia and Italy, always more intense, have convinced the foreign policy heads of the two nations of the appropriateness of an exchange of ideas [at Milan] on mutual relations and on international questions of common interest.

Remembering that the foreign ministers of the various European states meet annually and at minor intervals, it is not exceptional that the foreign affairs commissar of the Soviet Union meet with the foreign ministers of those states with which Russia maintains relations not only formally correct, but effectively normal.[27]

Mussolini also denied the existence of an alliance project in his radio message to America on January 1, 1931. It was only logical, he said, that beneficial commercial relations would spill over into the political field. Together, these statements squelched the rumors of a secret, more-or-less offensive agreement between the two states.[28]

The Geneva Forum. The Kremlin received its invitation to Geneva on January 23, 1931, but delayed replying for a fortnight, presumably because of disagreements within the leadership.[29] Despite "the ambiguous invitation," the Kremlin decided to participate in the special conference of the European Commission, in order to be able to "ascertain on the spot" its plans.[30]

But perhaps not too much should be read into Italy's sponsorship of USSR at Geneva; it was merely a tactic temporarily useful in maneuvers against France. A month and a half before his meeting with Litvinov, Grandi already had explained publicly the pragmatic spirit governing Rome's contacts with the USSR:

The ideology of a political party is in reality one thing, the action of a government is another. . . .

Fascist Italy was the first European nation to enter into normal relations with Russia, and this was done even whilst the smoke was still rising from the ruins of the Communist organisation which Fascism destroyed. The latter was an act of courage and supreme wisdom which showed that Italy did not then intend, as it does not intend today, to subordinate the permanent interests of the Nation to the interests of a political ideology.[31]

While Grandi recommended continued friendship, Italy must not "venture so far as to offer excessive help in consolidating the Soviet Government by facilitating its ability to overcome difficulties and uncertainties in its foreign policy, the very continuation of which might be turned to our advantage."[32]

The Italo-Soviet rapprochement that Grandi so ably defended found its forum at Geneva and the Preparatory Commission for the World Disarmament Conference (November 6-December 9, 1930).[33] On controversial issues, the two states, together with the Germans, normally formed a solid bloc, sometimes supported by Turkey, Bulgaria, the United States, and some of the small ex-neutrals. This bloc opposed France, its associates, and usually Great Britain as well.

Armaments parity would have been a cheap way for economically strapped Italy to achieve equality with France—an equality impossible in an uninhibited arms race.[34] During the seven years between the first meeting of the Preparatory Commission in May 1926 and Hitler's investiture as chancellor on January 30, 1933, Italian statesmen thought to counter French dominance in postwar Europe by working with Berlin.[35] Relatively increasing Germany's strength to recreate the European balance of power, which in the past Italians had so successfully manipulated, would allow them an active and independent foreign policy. If Germany paid no reparations, France would be weaker financially; if Germany were allowed equality of arms, French power would be balanced. Italy's revisionist tendencies made it the logical leader of the defeated countries—Germany, Austria, Hungary, Bulgaria and even the USSR—all of which had revision as their chief policy. But where Germany's imperialist ambitions were concerned, Italy found common ground with France and the Soviet Union, neither of which wished to see Europe dominated by Germany or its necessary first step, Austrian *Anschluss*.

Likewise, the Soviets could not compete economically in a full-blown arms race, and their ideology assured them that hostile capitalists would eventually attack. The preferred solution was to reduce capitalist arms to the Soviet level. Because this was unlikely, the next best alternative was to reestablish the balance of power between France and Germany, an attractive idea given the Rapallo-based friendship between Berlin and Moscow. Mutual interest in building up Germany's strength vis-à-vis France justified the tripartite cooperation on the disarmament question, and Moscow believed that it had gained from its appearance in the League.[36]

Italy's decision, however, to participate in a treaty limiting naval armaments, the bases for which were agreed upon with Paris and London on March 1, 1931, came as a bitter blow to the Kremlin.[37] Ever-anxious to keep the Western powers at each other's throats and ever-optimistic at the prospects for Italo-Soviet cooperation against France, *Izvestia* despondently referred to the naval agreement as "a victory for French imperialism."[38]

ITALO BALBO'S FLIGHT TO THE SOVIET UNION, JUNE 1929

Overt acts illuminated the incipient Italo-Soviet rapprochement revealed at the League of Nations in 1929 and 1930. In September 1929, for example, two Soviet destroyers visited Naples while on an instructional cruise in the Mediterranean.[39] The Litvinov-Grandi meeting at Milan in November 1930 and the Soviet naval mission's visit to Italy the next month also marked the change in political weather. The dramatic visit of an Italian air-wing to the Soviet Union anticipated these contacts and showed most clearly that something was happening of political importance. It portended the extensive political-military contacts between the two nations over the next few years.

Italo Balbo, the Italian air minister in this golden age of flight records, wanted to mold the heroic efforts of individual *dive* into aerial armadas manned by regular military personnel.[40] Between 1928 and 1933, he participated in or led six such mass aerial cruises. Like traditional naval cruises, these served many purposes. Beyond acting as training missions, they showed the Italian flag, publicized fascism, and displayed Italy's technical prowess to prospective customers. In an age before airfields were common, Balbo found the small flying boat to be incredibly durable and versatile, as well as capable of turning most any body of water into a safe haven.[41]

After a successful cruise of sixty-one seaplanes in the western Mediterranean, Balbo next proposed a flight to Smyrna, Alexandretta, and Beirut. The Turkish government, however, rejected the idea but did offer Istanbul as an anchorage.

Meanwhile, a new and daring possibility developed. Through two Soviet officers from the *Krasin* and then the Soviet plenipotentiary, Balbo received permission to take his expedition to Odessa. This would be a courtesy call after the dramatic rescue of Umberto Nobile and the other survivors of the *Italia* airship crash.[42] The final plan had the planes flying from Orbetello to Taranto, Athens, Istanbul, Varna (Bulgaria), and on to Odessa. The return flight reversed the order, with Costanza (Romania) replacing Varna. The Italians planned to make the outgoing flight as quickly as possible and to return leisurely, to milk the international propaganda value of the trip and do some hard selling. Greece, Turkey, Bulgaria, and the Soviet Union, after all, were clients of the Italian aircraft industry.

The Italians took care with their logistical support. Officers were sent out a month early to make arrangements, stock fuel and oil, and prepare moorings for the planes. They also saw to the crews' lodgings and secured transportation from the moorings to town. Four destroyers and an explorer followed the air armada to provide weather forecasts and spare parts. Each aircraft had a transmitter-receiver radio, but only one of them could communicate by radio with these ships. Technically, the Italians did their job well, as accidents and mechanical failures were few. The only major incident occurred when, anchored at Costanza during a storm, three aircraft tore loose from their moorings. The damage, however, delayed departure by only one day.

The five-country cruise left Taranto at dawn on June 5, 1929. Balbo himself led the thirty-five seaplanes of Italy's Royal Air Force manned by fascist leaders, military personnel, and 11 reporters for a total of 136. Air attachés from various embassies followed the cruise in a special aircraft only to Athens, because Turkey and the Soviet Union refused their entry. On the eighth, the planes flew to Odessa. At Soviet request, the aircraft kept 20 km from the coast, and reduced that distance by half when 5 km from Odessa, whereupon the Red Navy and three airplanes from Sevastopol greeted the wing. Passing in front of the city at the prescribed distance, the flying boats aimed landward and touched down on Hadgibeiskii Lake. The 452 km of this leg had been flown in a little more than three hours.

Contradictions marked the Soviet welcome. On the one hand, many Soviet civil and military authorities, accompanied by Ambassador Cerruti, met the Italian aviators. The hosts hailed them as heroes and built a triumphal arch and a new wharf. They also had repaired the roads, refurbished two old hotels, and even baked white bread! At the same time, however, the Soviets kept the arrival as secret as possible. In addition to the distance restrictions placed on the planes upon their arrival, guards patrolled the hills above the anchorage to keep away the curious. Even so, the young, French-speaking officer who acted as guide made no effort to limit his charges' movements, and for a day and a half the Italians roamed about as they pleased. Balbo happily noted that when children in the streets called out "Mussolini" to the aviators, this was the same as if they were calling them "Italians."

On the morning of June 10, Soviet squadrons flew over the lake to cheer the Italian wing's takeoff, and the Soviets lifted the ban on flying over the city. The Italian formation circled Odessa three times before turning homeward. The 326 km to Costanza were flown in less than two hours. The whole cruise, totalling 5,300 km, was an impressive demonstration of Italian air prowess, not only to the Soviets, but to the whole world.[43]

Both the Soviets and the Italians had used the visit to enhance their diplomatic status and to minimize their ideological differences. No easy task, this last. As Balbo put it, Moscow was both the master and slave of the Comintern. The reactions of the antifascist press and the Comintern, particularly galled by a widely published photograph of Balbo and Soviet officers

·saluting the Red flag, complicated matters for the Kremlin. Balbo, for his part, showed no ideological qualms; he was merely fulfilling his obligations as an official guest. He did, however, once slyly comment that as a Blackshirt he was no stranger to the "Internationale," for he had heard the "subversive" peasants of Emilia and Romagna lustily sing it at their tumultuous rallies after the Great War. He also now claimed to hear something quite different— a "mystical" spirit rising above parties and street brawls and expressing Russia's national will to power. The air minister so eagerly sought common ground with his hosts that the once-hated bolsheviks now became fellow soldiers and revolutionaries: "They are good-looking soldiers. . . . Whoever professes a political faith strongly respects that of others, most of all when he opposes it." He even pointed up a certain convergence between fascism and bolshevism, remarking on their common antipathy toward the Western democracies, "rotten to the bone, lying and false, with all the wiles of a superior civilization."[44]

But this should not be taken too far. Balbo did not minimize the abyss cleaving Italy from Soviet Russia. He saw the country through his own nationalist, patriotic, and middle-class eyes, offended by totalitarian bolsheviks and quizzical at "oriental" Russians. At an official lunch, an Italian dignitary praised the limited bloodletting of the fascist revolution. When challenged about the bloodthirsty Bolshevik Revolution, a Soviet general laconically replied, "We are not vegetarians." Balbo commented, "The reply makes our blood run cold." And what a relief it was for him when he caught glimpses of prerevolutionary Russia, which lifted him beyond the "oppressive atmosphere of bolshevik uniformity" of the barracks-like city. He wondered at the "perverse mania" that the revolution had for rendering life "uncomfortable, ugly, squalid."[45]

ITALO-SOVIET COMMERCE, 1930-1931

Reflecting the overt political and implicit military cooperation, the trade turnover between the bolshevik and fascist ideocracies peaked in the first years of the new decade.

The Soviet Commercial Situation

The Soviet Five Year Plan (FYP), begun in 1928, sought to construct rapidly the heavy industries necessary to provide a foundation for more wide-ranging manufacturing capabilities. Although the First FYP tended toward autarchy, its immediate result was to strengthen, rather than to weaken, economic ties with the capitalist world. Moscow especially needed foreign technical assistance. For example, in 1932 in the Donets, Italian and German engineers erected the first plant for the large-scale production of ammonia for fertilizers. Exports of foodstuffs and raw materials, often through barter arrangements, financed much of the FYP program. But without long term credits, Moscow made most of its purchases in cash or on such short-term commercial credits as could be obtained.[46]

Commercial necessities altered the relationship between economics and politics in Moscow's foreign policy. Earlier Soviet commerce often had been a weapon in the NKID's hands: prospects of trade baited the hook for recognition and discouraged the hostility of rabid capitalists. But with economic development and the increased need of machines and technical experts, the range of choices narrowed. Foreign policy could not but be determined by the tasks imposed by the plan. Moscow sought not only to avoid war but to foster genuinely good economic relations, and Soviet nonaggression proposals of the time envisaged, above all, economic nonaggression.[47]

The Soviets often had to trade in the face of political hostility. The dumping charges that so bedeviled their relations were false, at least in that dumping was not Moscow's purpose. Dumping is a method of getting rid of surpluses, which the internal market cannot absorb, at below-market prices, even below the cost of production. Desperate for foreign currency to pay for indispensable imports, Moscow sold goods at tempting prices bearing no relation to production costs. Soviet exports, therefore, tended to disturb international markets, because their nature and quantity were not predictable by ordinary commercial standards. Hence, Soviet Russia's reappearance in international markets upset foreign businessmen, even though it now ranked only eleventh among the world's trading nations, its share of world trade languishing well below that of prerevolutionary Russia.[48]

The Pulitzer Prize-winning journalist H. R. Knickerbocker eagerly execrated Soviet dumping, and he frequently used Italy to demonstrate Moscow's perfidy: "For Italy . . . the Five-Year Planners have reserved their most audacious bit of specialty salesmanship and here today in the Milan Fair, in the home of spaghetti, one may see displayed fourteen varieties of Soviet Russian macaroni—fresh, toothsome, unashamed!"[49] Knickerbocker continued his alarmist description of Soviet goods offered at the fair at below cost and in short supply back home: "Last year Italy bought more than $1,000,000 worth of cocoons and about $200,000 worth of raw silk from the Soviet Union, where a pair of silk stockings is rarer than white bread."[50] He explained Italy's fascination with Soviet trade as growing out of resentment at America's tariff policies, reluctance during the depression to reject any trading opportunity, and inability to supply for itself what the Soviets had to offer.

Alexander Barmine, a member of the Soviet commercial delegation in Italy headed by Mikhail Levinson, explained the situation on a more personal level. The Soviets needed gold to purchase the machinery necessary to complete the First FYP, and they exported everything possible: "Nothing was spared," including comestibles, despite the Soviet famine of 1931 and after: "Even we Soviet employees abroad did not know the real gravity of the situation, and so carried on our export work with a free conscience."

Barmine denied that the Soviets were dumping: "The truth was much simpler. Foreign importers knew how desperately the Soviet Union needed gold, and offered prices for our exports so low that they were often less than the cost of production." He boasted that his government never defaulted on any debts: "What superhuman efforts were needed to save us from the catastrophes constantly over our heads. Every time heavy payments fell due, we officials of the foreign trade and our colleagues of the bank lived through a period of nightmare."[51]

The best year for the Soviets as a percentage of world trade was 1932. The initial increase in Soviet exports with the First FYP peaked in 1930 and then fell off. Imports increased in value until 1931 and then dropped sharply. Both declines reflected depressed world markets. As prices fell, especially for raw materials and agricultural products, the Soviets had to force up the volume of goods sold—at the expense of their own consumers--to secure foreign currency to pay for imports of industrial equipment, the prices of which declined less sharply. Thus not even the USSR could insulate itself from international market conditions. By 1933 idle and unfinished plants in the country betrayed the unbalancing of production.[52]

Italo-Soviet Economic Cooperation

Italo-Soviet efforts at economic cooperation were played out against this backdrop of initial success and subsequent distress in the carrying out of the First FYP. Political and economic collaboration intertwined into a tight knot.

Trade to 1930. Facing mounting financial difficulties, by 1930 the Soviets tended to direct their purchases toward Germany, Britain, and Italy, where businessmen extended credits, usually in cooperation with their respective governments. The common method, including Italy's, was to establish a fund through which an exporter could secure a government guarantee for payment for 60 to 70 percent of the total order. This virtually covered the manufacturer's risk, for the remainder of the bill usually was profit. The Italians and Germans granted the longest credits to the Soviets—up to fifty-four months—while the average ran from twenty-four to thirty months and some only to fourteen. In many cases, sellers demanded no cash until a year after delivery. The Soviet trade delegation in the country where the orders were placed ordinarily gave notes payable every three months until maturity. Although the Soviets always met their payments, these notes ordinarily were discounted anywhere from 12 to 30 percent.[53]

By the end of the 1920s, Soviet raw materials exports to Italy were growing rapidly and gave Rome no occasion to complain about dumping. Rejecting the idea that Soviet exports were a disturbance, Mussolini in 1930 "ironically" remarked that "Russian dumping is quite a serious matter" and that consequently Italy had bought 20 percent of its imported grain from the USSR during the latter part of the previous year.[54] For several years the Soviet

Figure 1
Soviet-Italian Trade

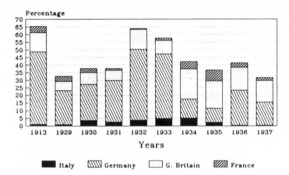

SOVIET IMPORTS
By Principal Countries

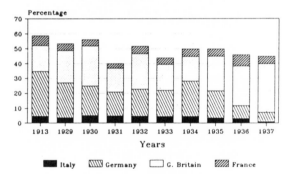

SOVIET EXPORTS
By Principal Countries

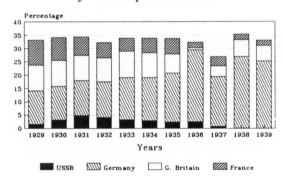

ITALIAN IMPORTS
By Principal Countries

For 1939, Jan.-June only

Figure 1 (continued)

ITALIAN EXPORTS
By Principal Countries

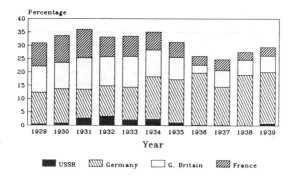

For 1939, Jan.–June only

SOVIET TRADE WITH ITALY
Turnover Balance in Rubles

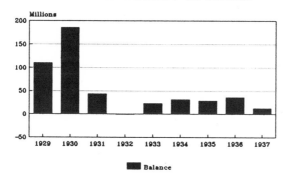

SOVIET TRADE TURNOVER
With Italy in Rubles

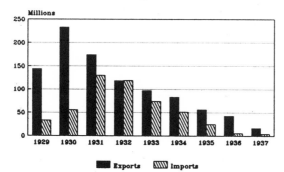

Figure 1 (continued)

SOVIET EXPORTS TO ITALY
All Wood Products in Rubles

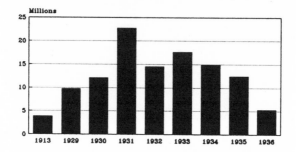

Petroleum Products in Rubles

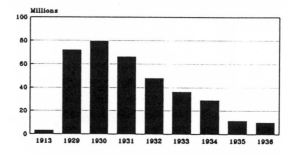

Coal in Rubles

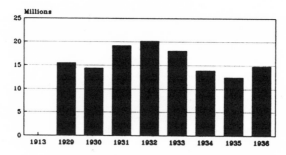

Figure 1 (continued)

SOVIET EXPORTS TO ITALY
Furs, Undressed, in Rubles

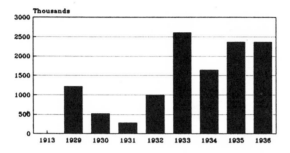

Silk in Rubles

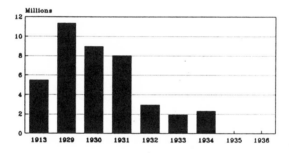

Chemicals and Drugs in Rubles

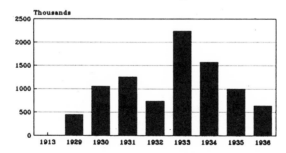

Figure 1 (continued)

SOVIET EXPORTS TO ITALY
All Grain in Rubles

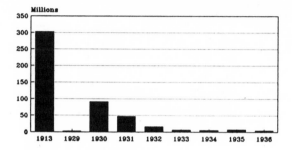

Butter in Rubles

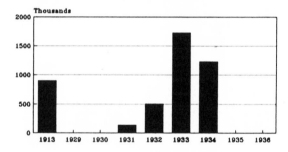

Beans and Lentiles in Rubles

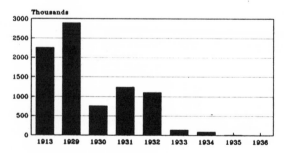

Figure 1 (continued)

SOVIET EXPORTS TO ITALY
Manganese in Rubles

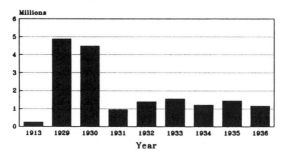

Cast Iron and Steel in Rubles

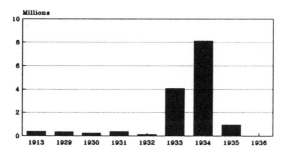

Ferrous Metals in Rubles

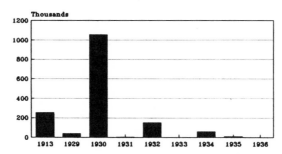

Figure 1 (continued)

SOVIET IMPORTS FROM ITALY
Machines and Apparatuses in Rubles

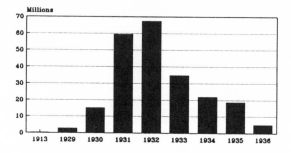

Motor Cars and Parts in Rubles

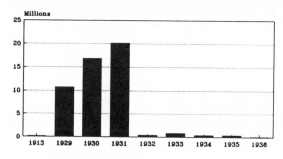

Electrical Machines in Rubles

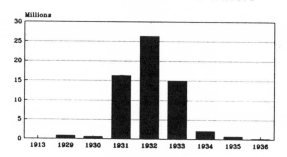

Figure 1 (continued)

SOVIET IMPORTS FROM ITALY
Chemicals and Drugs in Rubles

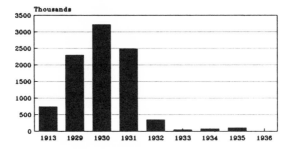

Sulphur in Rubles

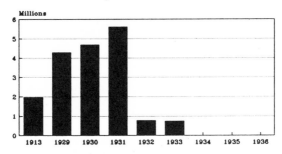

Light Metals in Rubles

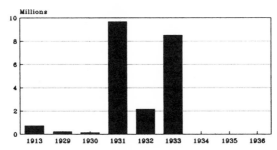

Copper, Aluminum and Others

Figure 1 (continued)

SOVIET IMPORTS FROM ITALY
Fresh Fruit in Rubles

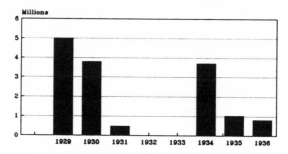

1929-31 includes dried fruit

Source: The figures depicted in these and the following graphs have been culled from a number of sources. Most important is Sergei Nikolayevich Bakulin and Dmitrii Dmitriyevich Mishustin, *Vneshniaia torgovlia SSSR za 20 let 1918-1937 g.g.* (Moscow, 1939), pp. 26, 84-87, 238-39.

Union dominated Italy's silk cocoon imports, reaching 85 percent of its total. Later, as the Soviet silk industry developed, the exports of cocoons declined.[55] In 1929 the Soviets exported 77,000 tons of iron ore to Italy and in 1930, almost 63,000 tons of manganese ore—the peak points for each.

As illustrated by Figure 1, the Soviets were aggressively displacing their rivals in the Italian market. For example, they conquered their competitors—the Baltic states, Yugoslavia, and Romania—and captured almost 100 percent of the Italian wood market through vigorous price cutting and better quality products. Less dramatically, in 1928 the Soviet Union delivered 0.6 percent of Italy's total imports of anthracite; by 1930 the figure had jumped to about 2.5 percent, enough to frighten competing businessmen.[56]

The Azienda Generale Italiana Petrolio (AGIP) dealt with Russian oil and was soon disposing of 25 percent of the petroleum consumed in Italy at the expense of the market shares of Shell and Standard Oil. Because of price breaks and low transportation costs, AGIP could sell Soviet gasoline at about 18 to 20 percent lower than world market prices. Soviet benzine, kerosene, and crude and fuel oil shipments to Italy rose dramatically between 1928 and 1930. After the 1930 commercial accord, the Soviets constructed at Savona, near Genoa, a depot for Soviet petroleum with a capacity of 50,000 tons, or about 10 percent of Italy's total petroleum imports in a year. This seemed to presage direct marketing by the Soviets of these products.[57]

Meanwhile, the Soviet FYPs demanded machines and equipment for heavy industrialization, and at the turn of the decade the Soviet trade delegation in Italy substantially increased such purchases both in absolute terms and as a percentage of total Soviet machine purchases. Large firms such as Ansaldo of Genoa, in fact, delivered 35 percent of Soviet imports of machines and apparatuses.

Montecatini, among others, sent a substantial proportion of the USSR's chemical imports, and FIAT and Lancia produced a major portion of Soviet imports of automobiles and trucks. The naval yards at Venice, Genoa, and Trieste executed a number of Soviet orders; for example, three fishing vessels, ordered on favorable credit terms, cost the Kremlin 1.18 million rubles. The Italians also offered rolled steel, ball bearings, compressors, electrical equipment, electric locomotives, airplane engines, and dockyard plants. Italian fruits, metals, textiles, and other exports played a smaller role in Soviet imports.[58]

The Commercial Agreements of 1930 and 1931. Moscow and Rome concluded a new credit agreement on August 2, 1930, by which the Italian government guaranteed up to 75 percent of Italy's export sales to the USSR and granted the Soviets credits for 200 million lire ($10.47 million) for orders placed in Italy between July 1, 1930, and June 30, 1931.[59] The Soviets, in turn, promised to take 200 million lire worth of goods. With this arrangement the two governments hoped to increase their mutual trade and to extend the sale in Italy of Soviet oil and other materials. Rome hoped to come closer to balancing its trade turnover, which in 1930 was 446 million lire in Moscow's favor. The foreign press credited the agreement with a political significance that did not exist, although in truth the accord did signify that relations already were fine.[60]

The commercial possibilities were quickly realized. For example, Moscow concluded an agreement with the Italian firm of Villar-Peroza for technical assistance in the construction of a factory for the manufacture of ball and roller bearings. Its foundations were laid in the latter part of August.[61] Villar-Peroza also sent to Moscow a group of specialists headed by its director, De Vendetti, and provided for the apprenticeship of a large number of Soviet workers and technicians in its factory in Italy. The Soviets also extensively used Italian merchantmen. From 1930 it was agreed that the USSR would employ only Italian ships from the Black Sea to Bari, where a great depot and a post for the transshipment of goods was to be constructed.

Because of the huge success of this arrangement, the two states on April 28, 1931, concluded a new credit agreement, which increased the sum of the guarantees from 200 million to 350 million lire, lowered the insurance coverage, and raised the term for repayment to 25 months from the moment of consignment.[62]

This agreement did not raise quite the same political fuss as had the one eight months earlier, but still some rumors of secret arrangements circulated. To combat them, Grandi put the accord in perspective by noting that it merely attempted to balance Soviet and Italian trade. The minister of corporations argued that Soviet Russia was destined to play an increasingly important part in the world economy, and therefore it was necessary to prepare to convert the expansion of its traffic from a source of danger for Italian exports to a powerful spur to a more intense and fruitful exchange.[63]

Underscoring the mutual hopes for increased trade engendered by these agreements, a semiofficial delegation of thirty-two leading Italian industrialists arrived in Moscow on June 18. Organized by the National Fascist Federation of Industry, the delegation represented the most important export concerns, such as Montecatini, Isotta Fraschini, Pirelli, Ernesto Breda, FIAT, Villar-Perosa, Banco di Roma, Credito Italiano, and Banca Commerciale, along with the shipbuilding and hydroelectric industries. A. P. Rosengolts, the foreign trade commissar, in the obligatory welcoming speech, cogently and optimistically stated the case for closer trade ties:

With the growth of our economy the possibilities for the utilization of foreign products and technique become greater. . . . The high technical achievements of Italian industry, especially in shipbuilding, high grade steels, automobile manufacture, aviation, chemistry, etc., assure the growth of our purchases in Italy. . . . the Soviet Union is a source of supply for Italy of agricultural products, raw materials and of semi-manufactured articles. . . . The geographic proximity of the two countries and

the convenience of communication will further encourage the development of economic relations. . . . Soviet-Italian economic interests . . . do not conflict at any
point.[64]

Rosengolts went on to tout that the recent credit agreements evidenced
the steady strengthening of economic ties. Since 1924, exports to Italy had
grown sevenfold and imports had doubled.[65] Beyond this, the USSR in the
previous year had spent 80 million lire ($4.2 million) for the use of Italian
shipping, and technical assistance contracts had been concluded with important Italian firms for the construction of ball-bearing factories and for
general construction work, among others.[66]

Two days later Professor Guarneri, who headed the Italian delegation,
told a Soviet trade group that the economic growth of the Soviet Union need
not arouse fears in other countries, because it spurred a greater trade
turnover.[67]

The Soviets were much interested in Italian aviation. In March 1931, they
ordered seventy-five Savoia-Marchetti seaplanes of the same type that Balbo
had flown to Odessa and across the Atlantic.[68] Italian manufacturers almost
closed the sale to the USSR of 150 Savoia Pomillo planes to be delivered at
fifty per year, Italy to take wheat in exchange. For reasons not entirely clear,
that deal fell through.[69]

The most casual examination of the graphs on the preceding pages describing the Italo-Soviet trade turnover reveals a dramatic drop in value in
most goods exchanged beginning around 1932 and 1933. This reflects, in
part, declining values of goods with the depression. Further, with the completion of the First FYP, the Soviets became less dependent on foreign
imports of many of the kinds of goods that the Italians had to offer. In the
face of declining sales, Rome, for the sake of its economically and politically
embarrassing trade deficits, decreased its purchases in the USSR. This decline in trade turnover, however, was part of a larger trend. Witness that,
as a percentage of its world totals, Soviet trade with Italy held up rather
well until after 1935, when political problems began to intrude upon the
commercial scene.

Alexander Barmine in the Royal Kingdom. Alexander Barmine gives an
all-too-brief firsthand account of Soviet economic dealings with Italy in this
general period. For his first assignment as director of imports on Levinson's
staff in Milan, he purchased 5 million lemons in Sicily. His presence in
Palermo and Messina boosted citrus prices by 20 percent, but, at least by
his own testimony, he got a good price "by dint of a fair amount of picturesque
haggling."[70] He believed that fascist Italy was well disposed toward the Soviet
experiment.

In the course of the First FYP Barmine secured a number of important
orders.[71] Backed by state-guaranteed credits, Italian firms quoted him prices
much lower than those offered by their British and French competitors.

Soviet technicians concluded that Italy, boasting the most up-to-date equipment in several areas, had taken enormous strides since the war—which
surprised them, because they had considered Italy to be industrially backward. Barmine traveled all over the country, meeting a number of industrial
leaders and negotiating, for example, for the purchase of a number of ships.
The Italians offered credits for three years, while the Soviets wanted five.
Even so, Barmine felt that the deal could have been struck, but an emissary
arrived from Moscow with even stricter instructions. He dealt with Giovanni
Agnelli and Antonio Benni of the electro-technical industry. Having hoped
for more extensive trade with Italy, he lamented that the Germans dominated
the market.[72]

Despite Barmine's lamentations, this extensive and symbiotic economic
cooperation reinforced, at least for the moment, the Italo-Soviet political
cooperation of the 1920s to form a foundation upon which to forge further
political bonds if the need should arise. And with Hitler reinvigorating
Germany, that need did quickly raise its hoary head.

NOTES

1. Maxwell Henry Hayes Macartney and Paul Cremona, *Italy's Foreign and
Colonial Policy, 1914-1937* (New York, 1938), pp. 1-3.

2. Ibid., pp. 6-9. Soviet commentators on Rome's foreign policy in the second
half of the 1920s noted that little remained for Italy in the western half of the
Mediterranean, where Rome acted merely to create bargaining chips, e.g., in its
squabble with France over Tunis. Consequently, Italy had to concentrate on the
eastern Mediterranean. But even there, the pickings were slim. Italy tried to turn
the Red Sea into its zone of influence, but failed on its own to cause sufficient trouble
in Yemen for the British. Thinking to gain from communist destabilization in the
Arab world, Rome thereupon welcomed Soviet intervention in the Arabian Peninsula.
See, e.g., *DDI* 7th, 4: nos. 245, 397, 414, 442, 444, 462, 466, 485, 591; 7: nos. 48,
59, 78, 86, 87, 104, 114, 165, 166, 224, 241, 290, 299, 309, 315, 245, 406, 500, 504,
526, 530, 583, 588, 595; 9: no. 334; Benito Mussolini, *Opera omnia di Benito Mussolini*, ed. Edoardo and Duilio Susmel, 36 vols. (Florence, 1951-63), 23: pp. 10-11,
161-62, 165; Francesco Bertonelli, *Il nostro mare: Studio della situazione politica
militare dell'Italia nel Mediterraneo* (Florence, 1930), pp. 18-94, 113-15. The Soviets
pictured the struggle on the Arabian Peninsula as being between Italian and British
imperialisms for the conquest of markets and about Italy's desire to prevent hostile
cannons from taking aim at Eritrea. *Izvestia*, May 8, 22, 1934; Attolico to Rome, 5/
17/34: AP URSS b15 f2.

3. Federico Curato, "Italia e Russia," *Rassegna di politica internazionale* (May
1934): 179.

4. *DVP* 16: n.130. NKID is the acronym for Narodnyi komissariat inostrannykh
del SSSR, also abbreviated as Narkomindel. Insabato was interested in Soviet nationality questions. See, e.g., his article on Tadzhikistan, "Il travaglio delle nazionalità
nell'U.R.S.S.," *Corriere diplomatico e consolare* (Apr. 4, 1930): 5 in AP URSS b8
f2.

5. Maksim Maksimovich Litvinov was foreign commissar from 1930 until his dismissal in 1939. A Westernized Jewish intellectual, on the strength of his ardent personality and oratory he came to personify "collective security" in the 1930s.

6. Max Beloff, *The Foreign Policy of Soviet Russia*, 2 vols. (London, 1947-49), 1: 42-45. "Tending" is the proper word. In the summer of 1931 Litvinov twice advanced to the German ambassador in Moscow the idea of a Soviet-Franco-German pact. Attolico to Mussolini, 12/27/33: AP URSS b12 f1.

7. Mussolini, *Opera*, 24: p. 235.

8. *The Times* (London), July 26, 1930.

9. Beloff, *Foreign Policy*, 1: 60–63; Vera Micheles Dean, "The Soviet Union as a European Power," *Foreign Policy Reports* (Aug. 2, 1933): 127.

10. Since the 1922 Rapallo Agreement bonding Berlin and Moscow, the Kremlin had followed a dual policy toward Germany. While the Comintern was trying to tear down the Weimar Republic by cooperating with the Nazis, the government prolonged the 1926 Treaty of Berlin and the 1929 Conciliation Convention by a protocol signed in June 1931.

11. Xenia Joukoff Eudin and Robert M. Slusser, *Soviet Foreign Policy, 1928-1934: Documents and Materials*, 2 vols. (University Park, PA, 1967), 2: 496.

12. Paolo Spriano, *Storia del Partito comunista italiano*, vol. 2: *Gli anni della clandstinitá* (Turin, 1969), pp. 350-53; Luidzhi Gallo, "O mestnoi i fabrichno-zavod-skoi pechati KP Italii," *Kommunisticheskii Internatsional* (Dec. 10, 1933): 104-06; Attolico to Rome, 3/29/34: AP URSS b13 f8.

13. Jonathan Haslam, *Soviet Foreign Policy, 1930-33: The Impact of the Depression* (New York, 1983), pp. 14-15. Haslam's fine work has guided me in much of the discussion in this section.

14. Cerruti represented Italy in Moscow from 1927 to 1930. Stationed in Berlin from October 1932, as early as March 1933 he was warning Rome about the Nazi threat, especially in Austria, to Italian interests. Hitler demanded his removal in July 1935.

15. Haslam, *Soviet Foreign Policy*, pp. 26, 126 n.30. From 1922 to 1930, Nikolai Nikolaevich Krestinskii (1883–1938) represented the Kremlin in Berlin, whereupon he rose to become deputy foreign commissar. He was sentenced to death during the Great Purges. Litvinov's bureaucratic struggle was not over, even after assuming the titular head of the NKID. Cerruti obtained information on his inability to remove Lev Mikhailovich Karakhan as deputy foreign commissar by sending him to China; see ibid., p. 17. Purged in 1937, Karakhan now has been rehabilitated.

16. These points have been made in ibid., e.g., p. 19. Surely, however, given Stalin's capriciousness, Litvinov had to have been careful in straying too far from the appointed path. In any case, even into mid-decade, Italy's representatives continued to debate Litvinov's ability to hold onto power. Cerruti to Mussolini, 11/19/34; Quaroni circular, 11/26/34; Attolico to Mussolini, 12/6/34: AP URSS b12 f4.

17. Haslam, *Soviet Foreign Policy*, p. 49.

18. *DVP* 13: no. 306.

19. Appointed foreign minister in September 1929, Grandi worked to end French hegemony on the continent and to create a colonial empire in Africa—but without a European war, which Italy could not survive and which would benefit only communism. The natural forum for this policy was the League of Nations, through which Italy could pursue peace and disarmament and extend membership to others, e.g.,

the USSR, to weaken French dominance. With growing Nazi successes, Mussolini decided that Italy needed a more dynamic foreign policy, and he reassumed personal control of the foreign ministry in July 1932. Grandi was named ambassador to London, where he often followed an independent foreign policy of inestimable value to Italy. Opposed to the German alliance, he was removed from his post in July 1939.

20. *DDI* 7th, 9: no. 398. Earlier in the year Ambassador Cerruti had been surprised by the "high level of anxiety" in the NKID "about the 'grave' international situation facing the USSR." One official insisted that "once again there was an attempt to build a united anti-Soviet front with the aim of attacking the Moscow Government militarily and of smashing Communism." Haslam, *Soviet Foreign Policy*, p. 24.

21. *DDI*, 7th, 9: no. 411.

22. Ibid., no. 115.

23. Ibid., no. 431.

24. Disturbed, Rome in early July 1930 sought Soviet participation at the forthcoming talks on the Briand Plan, the French idea that called for European cooperation through a "United States" of Europe. *DVP*, 13: no. 244.

25. *DDI* 7th, 9: no. 411; Haslam, *Soviet Foreign Policy*, pp. 47-48, 128 n.47. In early June Soviet missions stressed Moscow's concern over Briand's scheme for a European federation and its harm to those states excluded from it. *DVP*, 13: no. 208.

26. *DVP* 14: no. 27. In any struggle with France, Italy was a natural ally. Ibid., no. 37. Attolico, 1880–1942, served as ambassador to Moscow (1930–35) and Berlin (1935–40). He strove to prevent his country's total subservience to Nazi Germany, and he contributed significantly to Italy's decision for *nonbelligeranza* in 1939.

27. Curato, "Italia e Russia," pp. 179-80.

28. Ibid., p. 180.

29. *DVP*, 14: no. 39.

30. Ibid., no. 73.

31. Haslam, *Soviet Foreign Policy*, pp. 48-49.

32. Ibid., p. 53.

33. Kathryn Wesserman Davis, *The Soviets at Geneva: The U.S.S.R. and the League of Nations, 1919–1933* (Geneva, 1934), pp. 131-93; Wilbur Lee Mahaney, Jr., *The Soviet Union, the League of Nations and Disarmament, 1917–1935* (Philadelphia, 1940), pp. 49-109; Evgenii Aleksandrovich Korovin, "The U.S.S.R. and Disarmament," *International Conciliation* 292 (Sept. 1933): 293-354.

34. Charles Gates Dawes, *Journal as Ambassador to Great Britain*, foreword by Herbert Hoover (New York, 1939; reprint, Westport, CT, 1970), Oct. 18, 1930; Jan. 25, Feb 19, Apr. 15, 1931.

35. Arnold Joseph Toynbee, *Survey of International Affairs, 1933*, assisted by V. M. Boulter (London, 1934), pp. 198-99. Convinced of his own intellectual superiority, Mussolini believed he would be senior in any alliance with Weimar or Hitler. Italy was to play first fiddle—the axiomatic condition for the duet. See, e.g., Sergei Danilovich Skazkin, K. F. Miziano, and S. I. Dorofeev, eds., *Istoriia Italii*, 3 vols. (Moscow, 1970–1971), 3: 112-16.

36. Mahaney, *The Soviet Union*, pp. 7-48; B. Z. Goldberg, "The Seeds of Europe's Next War. I—Franco-Italian Rivalry," *Current History* 38 (June 1933): 265–69; B. Sh. (according to Haslam, *Soviet Foreign Policy*, p. 52, probably Boris Shtein), "Evropeiskaia komissiia," *Mirovoe khoziaistvo i mirovaia politika* (1931): 3-8.

37. *DDI* 7th, 10: nos. 96, 99.

38. *Izvestia*, Mar. 5, 1931. See L. Ivanov, "Franko-ital'ianskoe soglashenie," *Mirovoe khoziaistvo i mirovaia politika* (1931): 72-87.

39. *Brassey's Naval and Shipping Annual, 1930*, ed. Charles N. Robinson and N. M. Ross (London, 1930), p. 48. Italian naval units had visited Odessa in 1925. Vasilii Ivanovich Achkasov, et al., eds., *Voevoi put' sovetskogo voenno-morskogo flota* (Moscow, 1974), p. 135; Eric Morris, *The Russian Navy: Myth and Reality* (New York, 1977), p. 27 n.12.

40. Aviation pioneer and popular fascist leader, from 1929 to 1933 Balbo was minister of aviation. For the following story of the flight by the Società Italiana Aeroplani Idrovolanti to Odessa, see *S.I.A.I. ali nella storia* (Florence, 1979), pp. 17-18, 21-24 and Claudio G. Segrè, *Italo Balbo: A Fascist Life* (Berkeley, 1987), pp. 197-14.

41. Ibid., pp. 193-94. Although once in the air these squadrons moved quickly, limited by weather conditions and necessary logistical preparations, such flights were vulnerable to attack. Ibid., p. 213.

42. A designer and builder of dirigibles, General Nobile was best known for his airship explorations of the North Pole. In May 1928 he undertook extensive Polar explorations in the *Italia* airship, which crashed. Over the next month and a half, a series of rescue attempts splashed across international headlines. After he was saved by the *Krasin*, an official inquiry found against him—he had never supported fascism. William Barr, "The Soviet Contribution to the *Italia* Search and Rescue, 1928," *Polar Record* 18 (Sept. 1977): 561–74; Rudolf Lazarevich Samoilovich, *Na spasenie ekspeditsii Nobile: Pokhod "Krasina" letom 1928 goda* (Leningrad, 1967).

43. *Izvestia*, July 27, 1933; Attolico to Rome, 7/31/33: AP URSS b11 f1.

44. Sergè, *Italo Balbo*, p. 207.

45. Ibid., pp. 207-08.

46. Iakov Davidovich Ianson, *Foreign Trade in the U.S.S.R.* (London, 1934), pp. 91-137; Aron Iugov, *Economic Trends in Soviet Russia*, trans. Eden and Cedar Paul (New York, 1930); League of Nations. Economic Intelligence Service, *World Economic Survey, 1932–33* (Geneva, 1933), pp. 72-73; Henry Vincent Hodson, *Slump and Recovery, 1929–1937: A Survey of World Economic Affairs* (London, 1938; reprint, New York, 1983), pp. 108-09.

47. Calvin B. Hoover, *The Economic Life of Soviet Russia* (New York, 1931), pp. 153-70, esp. 165-67.

48. Beloff, *Foreign Policy*, 1: 29-32, 39.

49. Hubert Renfro Knickerbocker, *Fighting the Red Trade Menace* (New York, 1931), p. 5.

50. Ibid., pp. 11, 14-21.

51. Barmine, *One Who Survived*, pp. 174-75. In late 1937 Barmine made international headlines when he defected from his post in Greece rather than return to his homeland, perhaps to be murdered in the purges then striking the Soviet diplomatic corps.

52. William Henry Chamberlin, *Russia's Iron Age* (Boston, 1935), pp. 208-16; Alan Monkhouse, *Moscow, 1911–33* (Boston, 1934), pp. 225-35; Paul Winterton, "Soviet Economic Development since 1928," *Economic Journal* 43 (1933): 442-52; Ianson, *Foreign Trade*, pp. 125-27, 160-69.

53. "Soviet Trade Terms," *Business Week*, Nov. 23, 1933, 22; "Soviet Foreign Trade for Nine Months," *Economic Review of the Soviet Union* 9 (Dec. 1934): 275.

54. *Izvestia*, Dec. 29, 1930; "Premier Mussolini on Soviet 'Dumping'," *Economic Review of the Soviet Union* 6 (Feb. 1, 1931): 71.

55. Dmitrii Dmitriyevich Mishustin, ed. *Torgovye otnosheniia SSSR s kapitalisticheskimi stranami* (Moscow, 1938), p. 314; Vera Micheles Dean, "The Soviet Union as a European Power," *Foreign Policy Reports* 9 (Aug. 2, 1933): 127.

56. Knickerbocker, *Fighting*, pp. 32-40.

57. Ibid., pp. 24-31.

58. "Recent Soviet Purchases in Europe," *Economic Review of the Soviet Union* 5 (Aug. 1, 1930): 306; "Italy," ibid. 6 (Jan. 1, 1931): 7. Skazkin, Miziano, and Dorofeev, eds., *Istoriia Italii*, 3: 88-89 describes the peaking of the Italian economy in 1929 followed by its rapid decline with the world economic crisis and concomitant shrinking of international trade.

59. *DVP* 13: no. 279; Mishustin, ed. *Torgovye otnosheniia*, p. 316; Mishustin, ed., *Vneshniaia torgovlia SSSR*, 3rd., rev.(Moscow: 1941), p. 27; "Soviet Trade with European Countries," *Economic Review of the Soviet Union* 5 (Nov. 1, 1930): 435. The credits, which varied with the type of equipment ordered, matured in nine to fifty-two months. This agreement was automatically renewable for an additional year, unless notice of cancellation was given three months before its expiration. "Government Guaranteed Credits for Export to the U.S.S.R.: An Analysis of Methods in Force in European Countries," ibid. 6 (Jan. 15, 1931): 35.

60. Curato, "Italia," p. 179.

61. "Italian Technical Assistance Contract for New Ball and Roller Bearing Factory," *Economic Review of the Soviet Union* 5 (Oct. 1, 1930): 386.

62. For different categories of goods, again different terms were established. The accord was to be automatically extended for one year if it were not denounced three months before its expiration. "New Soviet Trade Agreements with Germany and Italy," ibid. 6 (May 15, 1931): 219-20; "Italo-Soviet Credit Agreement," ibid. 6 (June 1, 1931): 247-49.

63. Curato, "Italia," p. 180.

64. "Development of Soviet Trade with Europe," *Economic Review of the Soviet Union* 6 (July 15, 1931): 327; see "Italian Delegation to Visit Soviet Union," ibid. 6 (May 1, 1931): 211; "Foreign Trade: Italian Business Delegation Visiting U.S.S.R.," ibid. 6 (July 1, 1931): 305. The Italian notables included Giovanni Agnelli, Gino Olivetti, Eduardo Agnelli, Luigi Emanuelli, and Giovanni Malvezzi. Arkady Pavlovich Rosengolts, as a supporter of L. B. Trotsky, had been removed from his posts in 1925. After transferring his allegiance to Stalin, he was foreign trade commissar from 1930 until his expulsion from the party in 1937.

65. Rosengolts' figures for the purchases and sales of the Soviet trade delegation in Italy during the fiscal year ending September 30, 1930, totaled 74 million rubles ($37 million), a gain of 124 percent over the 34 million rubles for 1927–1928 and 32 million rubles over those for 1928-1929.

66. Mussolini bragged that Angelo Omodeo, the famous hydraulic engineer, was working in Soviet Russia to dam the Dnieper. Emil Ludwig, *Talks with Mussolini*, trans. Eden and Cedar Paul (London, 1932), pp. 151-52. This formed part of Mussolini's sanguine comments on the similarities between bolshevist Russia and fascist Italy, pp. 148-53.

67. Guarneri thanked Rosengolts for courtesies extended and expressed his belief that the visit had strengthened trade relations. "Foreign Trade: Italian Delegation Leaves U.S.S.R.," *Economic Review of the Soviet Union* 6 (Aug. 15, 1931): 377.

68. They were equipped with 750-horsepower Fraschini, single motors, and 150 additional motors were sent as reserves. Lozzi, *Mussolini-Stalin*, p. 126.

69. Hubert Renfro Knickerbocker, *The Red Trade Menace: Progress of the Soviet Five-Year Plan* (New York, 1931) pp. 22-23. FIAT took up the barter feature and agreed to deliver two-thousand trucks for grain. The Italian treasury gave two-year notes for 75 percent of the sum to FIAT, which discounted them. The government took up the notes within a year, the Soviet Union delivered wheat to the amount of the sales price, and the Italian government sold the wheat and with the proceeds redeemed the FIAT notes.

70. Barmine, *One Who Survived*, p. 189.

71. Ibid., pp. 189-90.

72. Antonio Stefano Benni was a member of the Fascist Grand Council, among other posts. Even so, he opposed the Corporate State. Beyond his economic duties, Barmine made many trips to art centers, museums, and the countryside. The 1931 air maneuvers in Milan particularly excited him. A small force of three-hundred "enemy" planes attacked in pitch-black darkness and broke through to bomb the city with flares. Despite the splendid spectacle, Barmine mourned that the air attacker was dangerously superior: "Under a real attack, in spite of an admirably organized defense, the city would suffer terribly." Barmine, *One Who Survived*, p. 253.

2

The USSR and Italy
Respond to Hitler

The tradition of Italo-Soviet economic and political cooperation was soon put to the test in radically changing international circumstances. Nazi dynamism threatened to overturn all the rules of the diplomatic game, and Europe's leaders scrambled to find their places in new order promising new opportunities and threatening new dangers.

THE ITALIAN REACTION TO THE RISE OF NAZI GERMANY

Recognizing the danger in Hitler's entry to power, Italy cooled its pro-German position, which had been given expression in the World Disarmament Conference a couple of years earlier. Nazi anti-Catholicism did not sit well with Mussolini, and not only did anti-Semitism shock him, but he thought it stupid. His counsel to the Nazis to restrain their persecutions was given greater insistence by Vittorio Cerruti, Italy's ambassador to Germany, whose outspoken wife was Jewish. Contrasting his government with Hitler's bloody expansionist dictatorship, Mussolini frequently painted Italian fascism as a peacemaker.[1]

The first concrete problem lying in the path of any Italo-German rapprochement concerned the Italian administration of the German-speaking minority in the Alto Adige (South Tyrol). Italy rejected the Reich's claims on the area, and according to Mussolini, its German speakers were not a national minority, but an "ethnographical relic."[2]

The Italianization program in the Alto Adige spurred on pro-Nazi feelings in Austria, where many felt that Hitler was their only remedy. His ideology, however, was flexible, and as early as 1923 Hitler had renounced the Alto

Adige in exchange for fascist support. The recovery of a mere 250 thousand Germans would not jeopardize his Italian alliance so essential to deliver the entire German nation. Recognition of the Brenner frontier became firm Nazi policy in the 1930s, but given the ups and downs of Italo-German relations, the Nazis used the issue tactically, especially after Italy's firm anti-*Anschluss* stance in 1934. Whatever the state of Italo-German relations, the Altoatesini were the victims, and the tensions between Rome and Berlin in 1934 and 1935 brought on a new wave of Italianization.[3]

The big question, however, the most difficult, was *Anschluss*, or Austria's union with a Greater German Reich. By making Germany the strongest power in Central Europe, it would jeopardize not only Italy's grip on the Alto Adige but also its plans for annexing Yugoslavia's Dalmatian coast and for dominating the Danubian valley.[4] Here, most clearly, lay the connections between fascist and prefascist foreign policy. Rome after the First World War had attempted to replace Austria-Hungary's preeminence in the region, and in 1925 Mussolini had declared that *Anschluss* would not be permitted. Italy would not allow its wartime sacrifices to have been in vain.

Rome worked hard to glue together the tripartite interests of itself, Vienna, and Budapest.[5] But while the Austrian and Hungarian governments were ready to fall in with Italian plans for establishing closer economic relations, their views on foreign policy diverged. Austria, for example, disassociated itself from treaty revision while Hungary wished to avoid Austria's dispute with Germany.

Hitler's arrival to power brought new threats and opportunities for all. Fearing that German expansion would not halt at the Brenner, Italians tried to deflect him from Austrian intrigues. Understanding Rome's concerns, the German ambassador to Rome, Ulrich von Hassell, worked tirelessly to bring Italy and Germany closer, and he especially wanted Rome's economic co-operation in Southeast Europe against France's "godlike position and her claims to hegemony."[6] Despite Berlin's wish to preempt any Italian attempt to erect a barrier against German advances in the region, Nazi machinations in Austria in 1933 continued.

Responding, Austrian Chancellor Engelbert Dollfuss visited with Mussolini at Rimini from August 19 to 20. On a languid Sunday morning the two met in the Grand Hotel at Riccione, and came to a commercial and political understanding of wide implications: Italy now could claim to have the right to intervene militarily to protect Austria's independence.[7] The Soviet press followed Dollfuss's trip to Italy with lively interest and hope: Italy was organizing an anti-German bloc with Hungary and Austria. *Izvestia* rejoiced that nothing could resolve capitalist contradictions in these threatened countries.[8]

Hassell, meanwhile, continued to nag Berlin about Italo-German relations, the deterioration of which he blamed on Berlin. He argued that Italy was the one large country friendly to Germany with a common interest in ending

French hegemony in Europe, and he urged that Berlin play up to Mussolini psychologically.[9] In November and December, Berlin tried to placate Rome over Austria and economic cooperation.[10]

THE SOVIET UNION AND GERMANY

Initial Indecision, January-June 1933

Despite Hitler's verbal tirades against Slavs and communism, the Soviets hoped that, once in power, he would work with Moscow to maintain the close relations established with the Weimar Republic.

Overview of Soviet-German Relations. Soviet foreign policy underwent major changes between 1932 and 1934.[11] Ironically, the bolsheviks had seen many of their long-standing hopes fulfilled—but these very successes had only endangered the proletarian state. The long-reviled Versailles settlement and League of Nations were crumbling, crushed under the boots of Germany and Japan, the two powers most threatening to the Soviet Union, and the world economic crisis was ripping apart the bourgeois, liberal-democratic, capitalist regimes; yet fascists, not communists, were picking up the pieces. In the next six years, Soviet diplomats, albeit reluctantly, were to probe whether those previously scorned institutions—the League, collective security, and the Western (French) alliance—could protect the bolshevik state by bringing Berlin back to its Rapallo senses or by keeping it out of war, or by providing it with allies if war should come.

As his first task, Foreign Commissar Litvinov had to prevent the German threat in the West from combining with the old Japanese threat in the East. As Soviet authors put it, Japan was the first "hot spot" of the coming world war. Moscow tried to neutralize Japan through agreements with the United States and Italy, covert encouragement of Chinese resistance, and appeasement.[12]

At the same time a more dangerous hot spot, the resurgent and fascist Germany, was stirring in Central Europe. Reacting to Franz von Papen's strongly pro-Western and anti-Russian government, the USSR in 1932 harvested a bumper crop of nonaggression treaties with Finland, Estonia, Latvia, Poland, and, most important, France. While these treaties did not yet mark a definite change of diplomatic course, they did reflect growing apprehensions, although many Soviets remained remarkably complacent about the Nazis.[13] For example, L. M. Khinchuk, the Soviet representative to Berlin, wrote Krestinskii in April 1932:

From 1928 we have seen a deafening growth of the "Nazis" . . . and in innumerable speeches Hitler clearly explains his task in his struggle with the USSR. Germany is not Italy, and Hitler is not Mussolini. I point this out, not to sow panic, but only to show the need to study and explore more deeply the actual movement, to have the possibility of correctly evaluating every factor in Germany.[14]

Although Moscow feared that Hitler might try to impose Alfred Rosenberg's philosophical ramblings on the Slavs,[15] until the spring of 1939, the Führer deferred his ambitions for the sake of domestic consolidation and rearmament. For domestic politics and personal preference, he did not want close relations, and, disparaging Soviet strength, he did not worry about Soviet animus. Hitler defied attempts by his diplomats, Rome, and the Kremlin to improve relations.[16]

Therefore, the inevitability of Nazism's philosophical anti-Soviet direction was not yet clear. Hitler's advent to power ironically first led to a slight diplomatic détente, as he seemed amenable to Moscow's desire for continued close ties. Many saw the possibility of a Russo-German friendship at the expense of Poland and the Western powers. Moscow also originally believed that German industrialists with orders in the USSR would keep the Nazis in line—this assumption seemed more reassuring than did the calming bleatings of German diplomats.[17]

The Italian View of Soviet-German Relations. This basic story of the Hitler-inspired wrecking of the Soviet-German harmony established by the 1922 Treaty of Rapallo and Stalin's reluctance to break with the security of those relations has been told many times in published documents and secondary sources.[18] More intriguing is the Italian response to the collapse of Soviet-German amity. Italy's ambassadors, especially in Moscow and Berlin, and the foreign ministry officials, including its head, Mussolini himself, closely followed the deterioration and vigorously counseled Hitler of the dangers of breaking with the Kremlin.[19] Rome insistently tried to position itself to mediate between Moscow and Berlin, between communism and Nazism.

Attolico, for example, reassured Litvinov in August 1932: "Even if Hitler comes to power, the fundamental lines of German policy vis-à-vis the USSR would not change." While Litvinov did not object to this, he confined himself to saying: "I don't know. However, I have no more faith in Hitler than in von Papen."[20]

Despite such mediation, Moscow feared fascist ties, and on April 15, 1932, Soviet intelligence asked its *rezident* in Rome to check whether the Italian government was subsidizing Hitler's movement. The reply was evidently positive, for on April 30 Moscow informed him that reprisals would be taken against the Italians: they would have to buy their grain elsewhere. This and other items, including the contents of the plenipotentiary representative's wastepaper basket, made their way into the archives of the Italian Interior Ministry. The Italian secret police had penetrated the Soviet embassy in Rome.[21]

As anticommunist oratory and incidents against Soviet nationals and institutions in Germany increased in the first half of 1933, the Soviet press retaliated in kind against Nazism.[22] Herbert von Dirksen, the German ambassador to the USSR, voiced his concern to Attolico that the February 15 ratification of the 1932 Franco-Soviet Nonaggression Pact signaled that the USSR was ready to join the Franco-Polish political system. He, nonetheless, believed that the Franco-Soviet pact would prove sterile despite Moscow's desire for French credits. Moscow, he explained to the Italian ambassador, remained keen to see ratified the 1926 Berlin treaty confirming the Rapallo relationship, and France feared the natural net of interests drawing Nazi Germany and fascist Italy together.[23] Pompeo Aloisi, the foreign ministry's head of cabinet, thought that France hoped to break its isolation by turning to the USSR, which wanted the French card to play at the German table.[24]

Rome, ill-at-ease at the implications of French flirtations with the USSR, strongly advised Berlin to improve relations with the Kremlin by strictly distinguishing between the Comintern and the Soviet government.[25] Thus prodded, Berlin tried to reassure Moscow that it would not change the directions established by previous German governments; likewise, the Kremlin, although fearing that Hitler was seeking a French rapprochement, assured Rome that it wished no change in relations with Germany. Litvinov, Attolico emphasized, was determined to prevent a Franco-German rapprochement.[26]

On February 27, Dirksen took up Rome's idea and told Moscow that "the struggle of the German government with Communism inside Germany can go completely together with the preservation of good foreign policy relations with the USSR, as has been the situation in relations between the USSR and Turkey, and the USSR and Italy."[27] Reassured, Soviet propagandist K. B. Radek promised his readers that despite Moscow's nervousness, "Versailles will pass, but Brest-Litovsk will live."[28]

In March through May 1933, just when the drafts of Mussolini's four-power pact scheme were being bandied about to the Kremlin's consternation, serious rifts between the USSR and Germany began to develop.[29] Convinced that a turning point had been reached, Dirksen predicted economic, political, and military consequences so dire that he wanted to return to Berlin to report personally.[30] Prodded, Berlin's ministerial mavins mulled over Germany's foreign policy situation.[31] They reassured themselves that "the fight against communism in Germany does not, as Italy's example shows, need in the long run to affect adversely our relations with Russia." And they agreed that Germany had to reestablish its prewar eastern borders but could not promote *Anschluss* because of Italian opposition. The Soviets were partially and temporarily mollified in the first week of April by the German proposal to ratify the 1931 protocol for extending the Berlin Treaty.[32]

Sparring continued, however, between Soviet and German diplomats over mutual allegations of mistreatment of nationals, unfair press accounts, and similar matters. The political implications of the visits to Rome of Hermann Göring and Papen were not lost on the Soviets, and Litvinov on April 8, 1933, once again thanked Attolico for Italy's friendly mediation in Berlin for improved Soviet-German relations. By later April, Hitler had decided to ease the contretemps, and Dirksen hoped that the German press might be instructed to be more conciliatory.[33]

On May 5, one day before Rome and Moscow signed their economic accord, the USSR and Germany ratified the diplomatic instruments implementing the 1931 protocol. The next day *Izvestia* publicly drove home the idea that "despite their attitude toward fascism, the people of the USSR wish to live in peace with Germany and believe that the development of German-Soviet relations is in the interests of both countries."[34] Ten days later Litvinov repeated to Dirksen the already familiar refrain that Moscow wanted "just as friendly relations with a National Socialist Germany as with a fascist Italy."[35]

Following his conversations with Krestinskii and K.E. Voroshilov, the military commissar and Stalin's crony, Dirksen came to fear the "profound" estrangement developing between Berlin and Moscow.[36] Voroshilov's remarks at that colloquy proved to be the opening salvo in Moscow's campaign to reestablish friendship with Germany. He had brought into action his big gun, the mutually advantageous military cooperation. Even after the last German officers involved in that cooperation had left the USSR, Moscow repeatedly approached Berlin with offers of friendly military collaboration— and warnings that the French were wooing them.[37]

The World Economic Conference, June 12-July 27, 1933, and the London Conventions Defining Aggression

The World Economic Conference, meeting from June 12 to July 27, gathered together sixty-four countries, including all those party to the Moscow Protocol of February 9, 1929, for the implementation of the Kellogg-Briand Pact.[38] Not content to await the problematic signing of a general disarmament convention, Litvinov proposed to those latter delegations that they should immediately sign an agreement defining an aggressor. By July 23, Afghanistan, Estonia, Turkey, Latvia, Persia, Poland, Romania, Czechoslovakia, Yugoslavia, Lithuania, and Finland were thus linked with Moscow.[39]

Amid the world economic crisis that had shattered normal foreign policy patterns,[40] the Soviets were seeking security for the states along their western borders and consequently for themselves as well. Offsetting the Four Power Pact and the German-Polish rapprochement, Litvinov's initiative placed the USSR among the leading diplomatic powers. The results were immediate and beneficial: a Soviet-Polish rapprochement of surprising warmth developed in the summer of 1933, and both Rome and Paris subsequently played court to Moscow.[41]

In a letter to Mussolini, Attolico predicted that Litvinov's London Conventions held "undeniable political value" and were "a clear success for the USSR."[42] They affirmed to the world that the USSR championed peace, and their signing had put into international law "positive principles" useful to it against potential enemies in the East and the West. Most importantly, the conventions raised the USSR's prestige as a great power. In a long discussion on the implications of the conventions for the countries of Eastern Europe, the Italian ambassador wrote that they would encourage a rapprochement between the Little Entente and the USSR; they might even permit the "insertion" of the Little Entente into the Moscow-Ankara system. A drawing together of the USSR and Little Entente, he continued, would encourage the position of the French diplomatic system in Moscow and spark a renewal of Russia's panslavic policies. For Attolico, the former, a "maneuver in the grand style," seemed likely, while the latter, for the moment, seemed less so. In either case, the conventions were of great importance to Italy, and because they represented Soviet opposition to the Four Power Pact, the London Conventions ironically strengthened Italy's position, especially in Turkey, and invited, the ambassador presciently added, a political pact between Rome and Moscow.

Fulvio Suvich, the Italian under secretary of state, also appreciated the significance of Litvinov's achievement.[43] On July 8, he congratulated the Soviet plenipotentiary, V.P. Potemkin, on the creation of this security/neutrality zone stretching along most of the Soviet border.[44] Concerned, however, that the conventions represented in Eastern Europe a counter-balance to the Four Power Pact in the West, he asked Potemkin if they amounted to a formal recognition of the new statute consolidating the Little Entente as a three-sided, intergovernmental formation. Potemkin answered negatively: Romania, Czechoslovakia, and Yugoslavia independently had signed the agreement defining aggression. Any government could join.

Despite these assurances, six days later Attolico told Krestinskii that he and his government, influenced by foreign sources, believed that the London Conventions represented a Soviet move against the Four Power Pact.[45] He assured Krestinskii that he had explained to a concerned and bewildered Duce that, although opposed to the pact, the Kremlin would take no action against its participants. Italy, Attolico said, wanted better relations with the Soviet Union.

This exchange between the Italian ambassador and the Soviet deputy foreign commissar conveyed more than mere diplomatic platitudes. Attolico was convinced that Italy had a place in the Soviet future, especially given the increasingly deep and permanent estrangement dividing Berlin and Moscow.[46] The ambassador acknowledged that Italo-Soviet relations proved that ideologically different regimes could get along, if this served their perceived interests. Far from one another, neither Rome nor Moscow threatened the other; further, Comintern hopes for communizing Italy, never too great in any case, had vanished with renewed relations in 1924. German fascism, on the other hand, grievously threatened the USSR.[47] Despite all the signs of a Franco-Soviet rapprochement, there were limits, set by Germany's economic influence in the USSR, Moscow's need to avoid making enemies, and France's desire to cooperate with Germany.

The Soviet expulsion of German journalists in September exacerbated declining relations between Moscow and Berlin. By early October, however, the Kremlin clearly wished to end the matter, but with dignity, and Berlin seemed to view mutual relations more calmly. Rome remained prepared to mediate. In midmonth Berardis, the Italian chargé in Moscow, reported that the Soviets would take a softer line toward Germany, because they were upset with the lack of results from the rapprochement with France. The anti-German press campaign, he added a week later, had ceased because of pressures in East Asia, the grave economic situation, and the desire to use the German threat in negotiations with Paris and Washington. The journalist affair was settled before the end of the month, and Soviet-German relations temporarily seemed on the upswing.[48]

Litvinov's and Stalin's Speeches, December 1933-January 1934

As Berlin worried at Moscow's flirtations with Paris, Litvinov's December 29 report on the year of 1933 examined the various pacts defining the aggressor, recognition by the United States, improved relations with France, and the Pact of Friendship, Neutrality, and Nonaggression with Italy.[49] On the other side of the coin, the commissar regretted the deterioration of relations with Germany. He fulminated against the ideas propagated by Hitler and Rosenberg, "a former Russian subject . . . [in] close contact with Russian—for the most part Ukrainian—counter-revolutionary organizations." Unconsciously revealing how the bolsheviks saw their own experience, he continued: "We well understand the difference between doctrines and policy. It sometimes happens that opposition parties, having come to power, try to forget those slogans which they proclaimed in their struggle with their political opponents. But this has not happened [in Germany]."[50]

At a New Year's Day reception ushering in 1934 at the Italian embassy, Radek responded to German criticisms of the speech by insisting that Moscow was not in the French tow. He uttered what was to become the *leitmotiv* of Soviet policy before the war: the USSR "did not intend to pull chestnuts out of the fire for other countries." Soviet policy, he admitted, was bent on preventing a German-Polish combination directed against the Soviet Union, and he complained that the new edition of Hitler's *Mein Kampf* still preached a crusade against the USSR.[51]

On January 9, 1934, Rudolf Nadolny, the newly arrived German ambassador to Moscow, comprehensively analyzed the situation for Berlin. For political, economic, and cultural reasons, friendship with Russia was advantageous for Germany. Berlin should assuage the foreign commissar. "If Paris was worth a mass," he wrote, "a decent treatment of M. Litvinov [even if he is Jewish] is in the end not too high a price to pay for Soviet Russia."[52]

Nadolny immediately objected to Berlin's negative response as meaning that Germany was giving up the effort to keep the Soviet Union out of the French camp. Attolico explained to Rome that Nadolny was doing all he could to salvage relations despite Berlin.[53]

Meanwhile, the Italians were pushing hard for improved Soviet-German relations as the key to disarmament. Seeing no possibility of reconciling the French and German positions, Rome feared that if the French induced Moscow to conclude a political agreement--whether an alliance, military convention, or mutual assistance pact—Paris would become even more un-yielding. On the other hand, if Moscow turned away from France, Paris would be profoundly affected, especially on disarmament. It was opportune to improve Soviet-German relations because Moscow had become more realistic since its failure to drag Poland into a joint guarantee of the Baltic States.[54] If Germany could allay Moscow's nervousness about its alleged expansionism to the northwest and south of Soviet Russia, Berlin could still mend the relationship. If nothing was done, Rome warned, then France would win the game. Berlin, the Italians added, was foolish to believe that a permanent estrangement from the USSR was impossible because of the Reich's importance as a Soviet market and the trust between the two military establishments.

The Soviets were not reticent to publicize their concerns. On January 29, Stalin delivered an important speech to the 17th Congress of the Communist Party of the Soviet Union, charging that Japanese military circles and some European leaders were planning a war against the USSR. He made it clear that Soviet diplomacy, which then favored France and Poland, was not ideologically committed against the fascist states, for the decisive question was not fascism but German hostility. "Of course, we are far from enthusiastic about the fascist regime in Germany. But the problem is not fascism, if only because fascism in Italy, for example, has not kept the USSR from estab-lishing the best of relations with that country."[55]

Then a dramatic event complicated matters for Moscow. Following the Kremlin's failed attempt to get Poland to assure the inviolability of the three Baltic States, at the end of January Warsaw signed a nonaggression pact with Berlin.[56] An anti-Soviet Poland, fearing for the security of its eastern prov-inces with their predominantly Ukrainian and Belorussian populations, and a Germany isolated since departing the World Disarmament Conference and the League, had found solace in one another's arms. Moscow considered the agreement as the first serious breach in the edifice of Europe's collective security and as a spearhead directed against itself.[57] Feeling betrayed by Berlin, the Soviets had believed that the Germans and themselves were united in hostility toward the Versailles system and the Poles. They painted this new German-Polish cordiality in particularly ominous hues as Hitler also refused their invitation to guarantee the Baltic States and would soon refuse to join the proposed Eastern Pact.[58]

The pact secured Poland some temporary security, and Hitler broke the ring of French alliances strangling Germany. Poland, however, also reinforced the very French weakness that had led to Warsaw's willingness to sign with Germany in the first place. Stalin now must have understood how completely Germany had cut loose from the old Rapallo ties. Perhaps, he must have reasoned, Hitler aimed at a deal with Poland whereby the Polish Corridor would be abolished and Poland compensated by Ukrainian territory. The new pact also potentially threatened Italy. Ambassador Cerruti feared that the agreement might be accompanied by more far-reaching German-Polish understandings. This could be followed by Austria's annexation and then moves against Czechoslovakia, which would produce a Germany most difficult, as he put it, "for any coalition, however powerful, to deal with without enormous sacrifice of life."[59]

Throughout the spring of 1934, Nadolny insistently told Berlin that the Kremlin wanted improved relations, and that realistic and proper relations such as Italy had were feasible. Nadolny's arguments did not sit well with Hitler; in the third week of June, the ambassador was forced to resign his post.[60]

Whatever illusions Moscow may have had about reversing the trend in its relations with Germany were killed along with the "radical" Nazi leaders on June 30, the "Night of the Long Knives." The liquidated included some of those who had wanted to return to the Rapallo tradition. At the same time, Warsaw attempted to allay Soviet suspicions and on May 5, 1934, renewed the Soviet-Polish Nonaggression Pact.[61]

On July 8, Attolico clearly explained Rome's opinions on Soviet-German relations to the German attaché in Moscow, who in turn told Berlin that the Italian ambassador had emphasized that in Moscow, Rapallo

had been completely written off. . . . [No] one . . . feels very happy at the thought of the Soviet Union . . . being compulsorily drawn into European affairs; what is desired . . . is . . . "the policy of the free hand." But, as they firmly believed here in the evil intentions of Germany, they wanted real security on their own western frontier in view of the situation in the Far East. If there were no other way out, they would swallow the bitter pill, join the League of Nations and make an alliance with France.[62]

Ernst Henri Views Fascism

One of the more imaginative analyses of Italian fascism, German national socialism, their interrelationship, and their relations with Soviet Russia, was offered by the long-lived publicist, Ernst Henri. A popular commentator in Western Europe, Henri claimed to have had no connection with either official or unofficial circles in any country; only in 1962 did the Soviet press reveal his true identity as a Soviet propagandist. Also employed as an agent of Soviet military intelligence, he almost certainly drew upon the Red Army's assessments.[63]

Henri's ideas are worth examining not only as a test of his analytical skills and perspicacity, but also because they exemplify relatively sophisticated, even if egocentric, Marxist thinking on international relations.[64] His analysis may fairly represent the kind of conceptualizing that took place in the Kremlin between 1933 and 1936. His conclusions were the sort upon which Soviet policymakers based their perceptions and actions toward Italy and fascism.

According to Henri, only Hitler and national socialism could carry out the plans of Fritz Thyssen, the Ruhr magnate; but without Thyssen, Hitler would not exist. Thyssen had instigated the Brown International and he, not Hitler, was the prime mover of German fascism. Because Thyssen's economic dynamic was no longer national, Hitler and Rosenberg wished to replace the national state system in Central Europe with a racial empire; that is, the Hitlerization of Europe with the exception of the western Latin and Anglo-Saxon zones, by federating, by force if necessary, all of the continent's "Germanic" nations. Hitler could then dictate to Europe and proceed to Russia's conquest along the road to Asia.[65]

Drawing historical parallels, Henri argued that Rosenberg provided Hitlerism with a concrete foreign policy, a multistaged program for imminent action. He planned to isolate the Soviet Union through an "international united front against the Bolshevik peril," to isolate France through an Italian alliance, and to separate England from the *Entente Cordiale*.[66] Germany could paralyze England by playing on traditional Anglo-Russian differences and by supporting Japan in Asia. Berlin, on the other hand, could return the favor for British support by moving against any new French Napoleonic continental hegemony, by rejecting the colonial independence movement by the colored races, and by opposing American competition with Britain.

Rosenberg, Henri argued, wished to establish a tight alliance with Japan based on anti-Sovietism and a free hand against China and Great Britain. He would paralyze Poland and the Little Entente by encouraging the insurgents' movement in the western Ukraine and by preparing under German protection a "Greater Ukraine" as a new ally against Moscow, Warsaw, and Prague. Rosenberg's plan then called for the neutralization of the United States by exploiting the fear of bolshevism and the Japanese threat, by kindling the flame of Latin American nationalism, and by inviting American investment in Germany.[67]

The Rosenberg plan would postpone military action until Germany's complete rearmament and would avoid simultaneous conflict against more than one power. To garner support from the other powers, Germany would attack the Soviet Union first. In the event of further Franco-Soviet rapprochement, Rosenberg would respond with a countercoalition of Germany, Italy, England, Japan, Hungary, Bulgaria, a separate Ukraine, and, if possible, the United States.

Hitler, predicted Henri, faced only two adversaries in his *Anschluss* plans, Italy and the Austrian working class.[68] If Mussolini could reach an understanding with Paris, he would close Hitler's road to Vienna. But so long as he rivaled France, the odds were even that the Duce would let Hitler get to the Austrian capital. Henri believed that Hitler would dupe Mussolini by playing up common fascist interests against France. Further, Germany could promise to divide up the Danubian and Balkan areas and help Rome against the Serbs. Finally, Italy needed German coal and iron. When Rome had become thoroughly ensnared in the web, Henri predicted, Germany would betray Italy and would seize the Alto Adige. Thus Hitler's only true adversary would be the Austrian working class.[69]

What would result from the meeting of the two fascist streams, the "left wing" under Mussolini and Oswald Mosely, the leader of English fascism, and the "right wing" under Hitler and Rosenberg? This would be one of the decisive international problems in the next few years. Central European fascism preached a pogromlike anti-Semitism and an unlimited racism. The western group, more elastic and cautious, concentrated on the Corporate State. More subtle, it devised its methods with an eye toward the western European liberal mentality. Its terrorism was more delicate, veiled, and psychological. Mussolini's master was not Oswald Spengler, but Niccolo Machiavelli for the initiated and Friedreich Nietzsche for the naïve.[70]

Mussolini could not use race for his expansion abroad, because the Italian race did not exist outside of the Adriatic, and he could not seriously proclaim any "Latin" race, because his French rivals would dominate it. Mussolini too had his Thyssen in Giuseppe Toplitz, the managing director of the Banca Commerciale and a Polish Jew. Thus western fascism had no need for anti-Semitism, which Mussolini rejected. Jewish competition presented no problem for the Italian middle class, which needed the homegrown Jewish finance capital. In racial policies and perhaps in this matter alone, asserted Henri, did the Italian and German fascisms strikingly differ.[71]

Central European and western fascisms represented different imperialist zones of energy, but would march together against the common social enemy—the working class. They were agreed on the Corporate State, but their foreign policies would not merge so long as the capitalist forces behind them did not fuse together. They could combine for tactical tasks, for example, in a common blockade of France; Mussolini could exploit German disarmament policies for his own Mediterranean aims; and Hitler could supply Mussolini with coal and iron for Italian arms. But neither would voluntarily submit to the other.[72]

Fascism's dynamic center, however, lay in Berlin. Overshadowing Mussolini, fascism's first prophet, the Brown International already had acquired a German shape and leadership. Mussolini, although more intelligent and innovative than Hitler, had fewer productive forces than had Thyssen. The Duce would remain as the theoretical head of world fascism, but the Brown International would dominate, and he for a time would remain outside of it and frightened by it.

Henri thought that Mussolini would never join Göring in a war of position or in a common struggle for the Danube Valley and against an offensive French army in the West. But the moment Göring applied a superior air strategy against France, thereby upsetting the balance of power and winning the initiative, Mussolini would jump ship. However Italo-French diplomatic relations stood at that moment, Mussolini would act for his ultimate purposes, which meant joining Germany against France.[73]

Assuming that his work fairly represented the Kremlin's thinking, several important points can be gleaned from Henri's propaganda. The first concerns the bolshevik penchant for using historical parallels to explain international circumstances. They were prepared to be enlightened, or blinded as the case may be, by their interpretation of the past. If, for example, they could find examples of Italo-tsarist cooperation in the Balkans against German encroachments, they might be more prone to seek such help in similar circumstances.

Henri also emphasized Nazi Germanic perfidy toward fascist Italy. Common ideology would not be enough to bind the two into a permanent symbiosis. Natural rivalries inevitably would flourish, especially in Southeast Europe.[74] The implication was that the alert, such as the Soviets, could use these rivalries and Italy's concern at being consumed by the stronger Germany. Soviet policy to shore up weak Italian will in the face of German strength, of course, should not be confused with Chamberlainesque, wimpish appeasement, or so say Soviet historians to the extent they discuss such embarrassing issues at all. From the Soviet point of view, the Italians could at least delay and complicate German plans for Southeast Europe, and could act as political, economic, and even military shock troops, expendable of course, against Germanic encroachments in the Danubian and Balkan areas. Every day that the Italians could be persuaded to perform thusly was a day of grace, saving Soviet expenditures on their vital southwestern front.[75]

Henri also raised the French connection in Italian foreign policy considerations. The Soviets, keenly aware of that connection in the mid–1930s, encouraged the new Italo-French rapprochement, which would "close the road to Vienna." That it foundered on the rocks of the Italo-Abyssinian War was not because of lack of effort by the would-be Soviet pilots.

NOTES

1. Elisabetta Cerruti, *Ambassador's Wife* (New York, 1953), pp. 112-92; Sergei Danilovich Skazkin, K.F. Miziano, and S.I. Dorofeev, eds., *Istoriia Italii*, 3 vols. (Moscow, 1970-71), 3: 115-16; Vladimir Petrovich Potemkin, ed., *Istoriia diplomatii*, 3 vols. (Moscow, 1941-45), 3: 476.

2. Conrad Franchot Latour, "Germany, Italy and South Tyrol, 1938-45," *Historical Journal* 8, no.1 (1965): 95.

3. Leopoldo Sofisti, *Male di frontiera (difesa del Brennero)* (Bolzano, 1950); Mario Toscano, *Storia diplomatica della questione dell'Alto Adige* (Bari, 1968).

4. Enzo Collotti [E. Kollotti], "Balkany vo vneshnei politike fashistskoi Italii (obzor issledovanni i dokumentov)," in V.N. Vinogradov, et al., *Mezhdunarodnye otnosheniia na Balkanakh* (Moscow, 1974), pp. 216-39; A.A. Iaz'kova, "Malaia Antanta i italo-fashistskaia v iugo-vostochnoi Evrope posle prikhoda k vlasti Mussolini," in ibid., pp. 147-59. See Filipo Filipovic [B. Boshkovich], *Balkany i mezhdunarodnyi imperializm* (Moscow, 1936), pp. 85-115.

5. Arnold Joseph Toynbee, *Survey of International Affairs, 1934* (London, 1935), pp. 488-91.

6. Germany. Auswartiges Amt. *Documents on German Foreign Policy, 1918-1945* (abbreviated as *DGFP*), from the archives of the German Foreign Ministry (Washington, DC, 1949-83), ser. C, vol. 1: nos. 35, 12, 14, 27, 51, 64, 78, 79, 112, 173, 191, 218, 232, 383, 385, 388, 390–93, 397–98, 401, 402; Gerhard L. Weinberg, *The Foreign Policy of Hitler's Germany: Diplomatic Revolution in Europe, 1933-36* (Chicago, 1970), pp. 47-50; *Pravda*, Apr. 29, May 12, 1933; Attolico to Rome, 5/16/33: AP URSS b11 f1; Paul R. Sweet, "Mussolini and Dollfuss: An Episode in Fascist Diplomacy," in Julius Braunthal, ed. *The Tragedy of Austria* (London, 1948), pp. 160-213; Oskar Grossman, "Fashizatsiia Avstrii i problema 'anshliussa,'" *Kommunisticheskii Internatsional* (May 20, 1933): 22–30; Great Britain, Foreign Office, *Documents on British Foreign Policy, 1919-1939* (abbreviated as *DBFP*) (London, 1946-85), 2nd ser., vol. 5: nos. 270, 271, 312.

7. *DGFP*, C, 1: nos. 407, 408, 411, 416, 443, 465; "Austria—Problem Child," *Business Week*, Sept. 9, 1933, 23.

8. *Izvestia*, Aug. 9, 21, 22, 23, 24, 1933; Attolico to Rome, 8/29/33: AP URSS b11 f1.

9. *DGFP* C, 1: no. 485; 2: no. 28.

10. *DGFP* C, 2: nos. 45, 50, 67, 78, 126, 144, 145.

11. Vernon Crafton Warren, Jr., "Russo-German Relations, 1933-1936: The Years of Uncertainty" (Ph.D. diss., University of Kentucky, 1965).

12. Max Beloff, *The Foreign Policy of Soviet Russia*, 2 vols. (London, 1947, 1949), 1: 24, 70, 89-90; Andrei Ianvar'evich Vyshinskii, *Diplomaticheskii slovar'*, 2 vols. (Moscow, 1948, 1950), 2: 40-41, 670-71. Vyshinskii was the chief prosecutor at the Great Purge Trials of 1936–1938, and during and after the Second World War, he was one of Stalin's highest ranking diplomats. One example of appeasement was the sale of the of the Chinese Eastern Railway and with it the liquidation of the Soviet stake in Manchuria.

13. Adam Bruno Ulam, *Expansion and Coexistence: Soviet Foreign Policy, 1917-73*, 2nd ed. (New York, 1974), pp. 203-10; Boris Nikolaevich Ponomarev, et al., *A Short History of the Communist Party of the Soviet Union*, trans. David Skvirsky (Moscow, 1974), p. 308; Weinberg, *Foreign Policy*, pp. 74-75.

14. *DVP* 15: no. 193.

15. Alfred Rosenberg, a member of the Baltic German diaspora and a descendant of the pioneers of the medieval German eastward expansion, aspired to lead a new Teutonic crusade to the East.

16. Weinberg, *Foreign Policy*, pp. 12-14, 75. On May 29, 1933, when Litvinov assured Foreign Minister Constantin von Neurath that a regime's internal complexion did not concern the Kremlin so long as it did not affect Soviet interests, Neurath

justified Rosenberg's extralegal role in German foreign policy with an Italian example. He recalled Moscow's protests in 1929 over Enrico Insabato's ties with Ukrainians. Litvinov rejected the comparison between Rosenberg's and Insabato's activities. The latter, although a member of parliament, had not played any role in either the government or the fascist party. *DVP* 16: no. 167.

17. Attolico to Rome, 1/2/33, 2/7/33; Cerruti to Rome, 3/16/33: AP URSS b9 f9; X.Y.Z., "Russo-German Relations since the War," *Slavonic Review* 15 (July 1936): 100–02; Ernst Fraenkel, "German-Russian Relations since 1918," *Review of Politics* 2 (Jan. 1940): 34-62; *DGFP* C, 1: nos. 6, 10.

18. Jonathan Haslam has produced two of the latest of such efforts. He is the only author I have found to use, however unsystematically, Italian archival materials to illuminate Soviet behavior in the period under discussison. See his *Soviet Foreign Policy, 1930-33: The Impact of the Depression* (New York, 1983) and *The Soviet Union and the Struggle for Collective Security in Europe, 1933-39* (New York, 1984), esp. pp. 8-26.

19. *DGFP* C, 1: no. 485.

20. Haslam, *Soviet Foreign Policy*, p. 116.

21. Ibid., p. 150 n.25. Published Soviet documents do not mention this incident, although Attolico, on December 1, 1932, complained that the Soviets were refusing Italy "hard grain for macaroni." *DVP* 15: no. 464.

22. *DGFP* C, 1: nos. 8, 41, 43, 55, 73; *DVP* 16: nos. 49, 53, 54, 57, 59, 62, 65; *Izvestia*, Mar. 4, 9, 11, 1933; Attolico to Rome 3/3/33, 3/7/33: AP URSS b9 f9. The Soviet minister to Prague expressed his doubts that a Franco-Soviet rapprochement was possible and his belief that a war with Japan was inevitable. Further, compared to Mussolini's anticommunist campaign when he had taken power, Hitler's efforts came off badly. He was wrong to antagonize the USSR, because there was "in the world no more implacable enemy of the Versailles Treaty than the USSR." Legation at Prague to Rome, 3/6/33: AP URSS b8 f1.

23. Attolico to Rome, 2/28/33: AP URSS b8 f1. The lead article in *Izvestia*, Feb. 18, 1933, to Dirksen's dismay, included Soviet-Polish relations within the ambit of the Franco-Soviet nonaggression pact. *DGFP* C, 1: nos. 29, 73.

24. Aloisi memorandum, 2/22/33: AP URSS b8 f1. For another evaluation of the Franco-Soviet Pact, see Paris embassy to Rome, 1/17/33: AP URSS b8 f1. Aloisi, active in blocking German expansion into Austria and the Balkans, brilliantly defended Italy at Geneva during the Italo-Abyssinian War. Mussolini dismissed him in July 1936, when Galeazzo Ciano's appointment to head the foreign ministry signaled accommodation with Germany.

25. Rome to Attolico, 3/9/33: AP URSS b8 f1; Attolico to Rome, 3/18/33: AP URSS b9 f9.

26. Attolico to Rome, 3/14/33: AP URSS b9 f9; *DGFP* C, 1: nos. 33, 43. See Ponomarev, *Short History*, pp. 308-09.

27. See *DGFP* C, 1: no. 41. Dirksen assured Krestinskii that he had told Cerruti the same thing. *DVP* 16: no. 51. On February 25, 1933, Berlin quietly extended a special credit, thereby deferring repayment of a portion of earlier Soviet debts. *DVP* 16: nos. 47, 48, n.35; *DGFP* C, 1: no. 43 n.7.

28. *Izvestia*, Mar. 24, 1933; Attolico to Rome, 3/28/33: AP URSS b9 f9. Immediately after the signing of the Italo-Soviet Pact in September 1933, Karl Bernardovich Radek again wrote that Moscow preferred Rapallo to Versailles. *Pravda*, Sept. 4,

1933; Attolico to Rome, 9/4/33: AP URSS b9 f9. Radek, who had supported Trotsky against Stalin, was arrested in 1937 and sentenced to ten years imprisonment. His fate thereafter has never been fully revealed.

29. Weinberg, *Foreign Policy*, pp. 25-86; United States, Department of State, *Foreign Relations of the United States* (abbreviated as *FRUS*) (Washington, DC, 1945-53), 1933, vol. 1: p. 120; Attolico to Rome, 3/14/33: AP URSS b8 f1; *DGFP* C, 1: nos. 104, 134 n.2. Through his four-power pact proposal, Mussolini sought to bind Italy, Great Britain, France, and Germany in a great-power directorate designed to reintegrate the latter into European family of nations and to enhance Italy's power within that family. It ostentatiously excluded the Soviet Union. For more, see Chapter 3.

30. *DGFP* C, 1: nos. 134, 137. For the Soviet complaints, see *DVP* 16: nos. 74, 81, 86, 95, 106, 111, n.45, n.46, n.70; *Pravda*, Apr. 2, 1933; and *Izvestia*, Mar. 28, 29, Apr. 3, 5, 8, 1933. For the Italian reports, see Rome to Attolico, 3/15/33: AP URSS b8 f1 and Attolico to Rome, 3/14/33, 3/21/33, 4/3/33, 4/4/33: AP URSS b9 f9.

31. *DGFP* C, 1: no. 142.

32. Ibid., nos. 140, 147; *DVP* 16: no. 112, n.90; *Izvestia*, Apr. 9, 1933; Attolico to Rome, 4/18/33: AP URSS b9 f9.

33. Attolico to Rome, 3/28/33, 4/4/33, 4/25/33, 5/3/33: AP URSS b9 f9; Cerruti to Rome, 4/10/33: AP URSS b8 f2; Attolico to Rome, 4/10/33: AP URSS b10 f1; *DGFP* C, 1: nos. 157, 166, 186, 194, 198, 204, 245; *DVP* 16: nos. 135, 138, 139, 142.

34. *Izvestia*, May 6, 1933; Vera Micheles Dean, "The Soviet Union as a European Power", *Foreign Policy Reports* (Aug. 2, 1933): 118-28; Attolico to Rome, 5/9/33: AP URSS b9 f9.

35. *DGFP* C, 1: no. 245.

36. Ibid., no. 232; Attolico to Rome, 5/16/33: AP URSS b9 f9. Klementii Efrimovich Voroshilov, after long tenure in diverse posts under Stalin, in 1961 was forced into obscurity for his opposition in 1957 to Nikita Khrushchev.

37. *DGFP* C, 1: nos. 252, 284, 339, 409, 439, 460, 470; 2: nos. 47, 176, 181, 191; Attolico to Rome, 6/6/33, 8/29/33; Cerruti to Rome, 6/12/33: AP URSS b9 f9.

38. *DVP* 16: nos. 213, 218, 220, 251, 253, 254.

39. The conference was not without problems. The Hugenberg Memorandum upset the Soviets, who believed that the German economics minister had unveiled Nazi plans to colonize the East and rip the Ukraine from the Soviet body politic. The Italian suggestion that it was no more than a plea for collaboration to develop the USSR's great resources upset Litvinov. Suvich memorandum, 6/17/33: AP URSS b10 f1. Berlin rejected Moscow's protests. *DVP* 16: nos. 189, 190, 209, n.166; *Izvestia*, June 20, 24, 29, 1933; *Pravda*, June 19, 23, 27, 1933; *DGFP* C, 1: nos. 325, 327, 331, 336, 338, 361. Attolico kept a close eye on the Soviet press campaign, responding to all of the sundry paranoias and real fears racking Moscow. Attolico to Rome, 2/27/33, 3/14/33: AP URSS b8 f1; Attolico to Rome, 3/20/33, 6/13/33, 6/21/33, 7/4/33, 7/5/33, 7/12/33: AP URSS b9 f9.

40. See *Pravda*, June 12, 1933, which for the conference's opening stressed the economic contradictions between the imperialists. Attolico to Rome, 6/13/33: AP URSS b11 f1.

41. Nina Dmitrievna Smirnova, *Politika Italii na Balkanakh: Ocherk diplomaticheskoi istorii, 1922-1935 gg.* (Moscow, 1979), pp. 187-88; Vilnis Sipols and Mikhail Kharlamov, *On the Eve of World War II, 1933–1939: A Foreign Policy Study* (Mos-

cow, 1974), p. 40; "The Soviet Union and Non-Aggression," *Bulletin of International News* 10 (Aug. 17, 1933): 97-107; Viktor Moiseevich Khaitsman, *S.S.S.R. i problema razoruzheniia (mezhdu pervoi i vtoroi mirovymi voinami)* (Moscow, 1959), pp. 341-43.

42. Attolico to Mussolini, 7/12/33: AP URSS b10 f1.

43. Suvich served as Mussolini's under secretary for foreign affairs after July 1932, when the Duce assumed the ministry's portfolio. He pushed for Italy's expansion in the Balkan and Danubian areas, and he was the principal architect of the Rome Protocols of March 1934 designed to block German penetration there. He laid the diplomatic groundwork for Italy's war with Abyssinia in 1935. But his firm opposition to *Anschluss* and rapprochement with Germany made him an embarrassment, and he was exiled to Washington as ambassador in June 1936. See Fulvio Suvich, *Memorie, 1932–1936*, ed. Gianfranco Bianchi (Milan, 1984).

44. *DVP* 16: no. 226. Vladimir Petrovich Potemkin (1878-1946) represented Moscow in Italy from 1932 to 1934 and thereafter held a number of high diplomatic posts. He also served as chief editor of the three-volume *Istoriia diplomatii*. Volume 3 covers 1919 through 1939, the very years of Potemkin's activity in some of that period's most important events. His polemical text, however, evidences no personal ruminations.

45. *DVP* 16: 270.

46. Attolico to Rome, 7/9/33: AP URSS b8 f3. For more Soviet-German contretemps, see *DVP* 16: no. 266; *DGFP* C, 1: nos. 379, 389, 404, 421, 462; and 2: no. 119.

47. The Soviets protested Berlin's "Brothers in Need" campaign to assist needy Germans in the Soviet Union. *DGFP* C, 1: no. 404 n.6. Centered in Dresden, the movement potentially could spread to other countries, or so feared Italy's representatives. They also worried that bolsheviks might infiltrate the group. At the end of the summer of 1934, "Brothers in Need" was liquidated. Consul General in Dresden to Rome, 5/21/33: AP URSS b8 f2; Attolico to Rome, 8/16/34: AP URSS b14 f3.

48. Attolico to Rome, 8/7/33, 8/15/33, 8/19/33, 9/4/33, 9/9/33, 9/22/33, 9/23/33; Berardis to Rome, 10/2/33, 10/17/33, 10/24/33, 10/31/33; Rome to Cerruti, 10/5/33: AP URSS b9 f9; Cerruti to Rome, 10/4/33: AP URSS b8 f4; *DGFP* C, 1: nos. 428, 438, 455-58, 461, 467, 476, 477, 487 n.3; and 2: 12, 14, 21, 24, 25, 30, 34. After five years as ambassador in Moscow, Dirksen left for good on November 3, bound for Naples, whence he departed for Tokyo on the twelfth. He had pushed for a close alliance with Russia, and the Soviets were sorry to see him leave. *DGFP* C, 2: nos. 44, 53; Attolico to Rome, 8/14/33; Cerruti to Rome, 11/3/33; Berardis to Rome, 11/7/33: AP URSS b9 f9.

49. *DGFP* C, 2: nos. 147, 148; *FRUS*, 1933, 2: pp. 830-32, 838-39. For this pact, see Chapter 7.

50. Litvinov went on:

We, of course, sympathize with the suffering of our German comrades, but we Marxists are the last who can be reproached with allowing our feelings to govern our policy. The whole world knows that we can and do maintain good relations with capitalist governments of any regime, including the fascist. We do not interfere in Germany's internal affairs or in the affairs of other countries, and not its internal but its external policy defines our relations. *DVP* 16: App. 2. See *Izvestia*, Dec. 29, 1933, and Jan. 1, 1934.

51. *DGFP* C, 2: nos. 161, 163.

52. Ibid., nos. 171, 173, 190, 210.

53. Attolico to Rome, 1/16/34: AP URSS b14 f3.

54. *DVP* 16: nos. 426, 431; *DGFP* C, 2: nos. 169, 187.

55. *DVP* 17: no. 28; Attolico to Rome, 2/13/34: AP URSS b13 f8. Viacheslav Mikhailovich Molotov on December 28, 1933, had sung the same song. *DVP* 16: App. 1; *Izvestia*, Dec. 29, 1933; *DGFP* C, 2: no. 277. An old crony of Stalin's, Molotov (1890-1941) from 1930 to 1941 was Chairman of the Council of People's Commissars, and from 1939 to 1949 he also headed the NKID.

56. For some of the negotiations, see *DGFP* C, 2: nos. 70, 75, 79, 118, 211, 219.

57. K. Liapter, "O pol'sko-germanskom soglashenii 1934 goda," *Voprosy istoriia* (Oct. 1962): 99-109.

58. For the negotiations and rejection of the guarantee, see *DGFP* C, 2: nos. 240, 251, 262, 364, 375, 376, 382, 390, 391, 396, 398, 401, 414–18, 421, 423, 425, 427, 430, 437.

59. Weinberg, *Foreign Policy*, p. 74, see pp. 57-74.

60. Cerruti to Rome, 7/6/34: AP URSS b14 f3; *DGFP* C, 2: nos. 424, 434, 447, 476, 488.

61. Sipols, *Sovetskii Soiuz*, pp. 62, 66-67; *DGFP* C, 2: no. 440.

62. Ibid., 3: no. 74.

63. Ernst Henri [Henri Rostovskii], *Hitler over Europe* (New York, 1934) and *Hitler over Russia? The Coming Fight Between the Fascist and Socialist Armies*, trans. Michael Davidson (London, 1936). See Walter Zeev Laqueur, *Russia and Germany: A Century of Conflict* (London, 1965), p. 228, and Haslam, *The Soviet Union*, p. 236.

64. Laqueur, *Russia*, p. 229, unimpressed, calls Henri's description of the June 1934 purge in Austria a "sensationalist farrago of unconnected facts and figures and sheer fantasy" and stresses his misunderstanding of Nazism's real nature. But Laqueur also acknowledges Henri's influence and quotes Bertrand Russell's description of *Hitler over Russia?* as "extraordinarily interesting and valuable."

65. Henri, *Hitler Over Europe*, pp. 3-27, 124-33.

66. Ibid., p. 199.

67. Ibid., p. 200.

68. Ibid., pp. 157, 199. See also Peter Grauman, "Fashistskaia diktatura Dol'fusa i kompartiia Avstrii", *Kommunisticheskii Internatsional* (Sept. 20, 1933): 49-55.

69. See D. A. Mironov, "Pozitsiia partii avstriiskogo rabochego klassa v period usileniia opasnosti anshliusa (iiul' 1936-noiab. 1937)," in I. N. Chempalov, ed. *Politika velikikh derzhav na Balkanakh i Blizhnem Vostoke, 1932-1945* (Sverdlovsk, 1984), pp. 47-55.

70. Henri, *Hitler over Europe*, pp. 60-61, 182-83. Göring represented a separate Bonapartist tendency. For more on Mosely, see *Pravda*, May 13, 1934. See also Karl Radek's article on Oswald Spengler and German fascism in *Izvestia*, Mar. 18, 1934.

71. Henri, *Hitler over Europe*, pp. 130-31, 183.

72. Ibid., pp. 175, 184.

73. Ibid., p. 241.

74. Soviet authors to this day harp on Italo-German antagonisms. See Smirnova, *Politika Italii*, pp. 188-91. Italy feared that Germany's *Drang nach Osten* would

swallow its interests in the Balkan and Danubian areas. Hitler sought Italy's friendship to liquidate German isolation and as a preliminary step to achieving Britain's friendship and the complete isolation of France. But German economic interests in Southeast Europe limited his ability to agree with Italy. From 1922 to 1938 Austrian *Anschluss* was the greatest threat to Italy.

75. See Filipo Filipovic [B. Boshkovich], *Pered novym vzryvom na balkanakh* (Moscow, 1934).

3

The Four Power Pact

Determined to rearm, the Germans had used the disarmament negotiations of the early 1930s to secure advantage without committing to agreements that they would have to break conspicuously and soon. Because neither London nor Paris appeared willing to take military action, Germany could rearm secretly while publicly making concessions. In 1933 there were two major efforts to break this cycle: Prime Minister Ramsay MacDonald's March 16 draft to the Disarmament Conference and Mussolini's proposed four-power pact.[1]

TREATY REVISION, THE LEAGUE OF NATIONS, AND MUSSOLINI'S PROPOSAL FOR A FOUR POWER PACT

One of the forces binding the Italo-Soviet-German cooperation before 1930 was their common attitude toward revising the Versailles treaty system.

Mussolini, often good as a statesman, was at his best when dealing with the idea of revising the peace treaties, which had drawn the curtain on the Great War. He told the Senate in 1928: "Peace treaties are not eternal. . . . It is not a question of doctrines . . . [but] a historical reality. . . . [P]eace treaties are not the result of divine justice but of human intelligence. . . . The work of men, I say, and therefore imperfect, but, I add, always open to being improved."[2] Mussolini and his cronies sang that the peace treaties "are chapters in, not epilogues to history," an eminently reasonable melody, throughout the 1920s and into the mid–1930s.

From the beginning, Mussolini was also unhappy with the League as an unjust obstacle to Italy's legitimate revisionist aspirations: "Either the

League of Nations must be reformed, or it is bound to perish." The problem
was the overweening power of the small states at Geneva:

A stable understanding among the big States . . . would guarantee the peaceful development of the smaller States. . . . [W]e must have agreement with the Powers
who are able to disturb the peace. The year 1934 must bring agreement between
these Powers or else, very probably, we shall lapse back into the old system of the
balance of Power.[3]

Purportedly designed to establish international justice and perpetual peace,
the League actually sought to maintain a status quo favorable to the satiated
powers—Great Britain, France, and their allies, leaving Italy, like Oliver,
always asking for "more" at the international banquet table.

The Duce especially feared that disarmament's failure would kill the
League: "That the Disarmament Conference will fail, at least regarding its
original grand objectives, is generally agreed. . . . The armed states will not
disarm. . . . To pretend to be able to keep eternally disarmed a people such
as the German, is a pure illusion."[4] Some might smugly dismiss the World
Disarmament Conference as naive utopianism or gross hypocrisy. But given
these statements, clearly Mussolini was not unduly optimistic about the
chances for a successful conference, and he drew distasteful conclusions
should it fail. In other words, as with the Soviets, it was a pivot around
which Italian policy turned.

Mussolini testified that the genesis of his proposal for a four-power pact
was his disappointment at the failure of the first phase of the Disarmament
Conference in the summer of 1932. His idea had grown more insistent with
"the lack of progress achieved in the second phase of the Disarmament
Conference" in March 1933. He asserted that Italy was following a true
peace policy, which "ought to restore equilibrium to Europe." And he eloquently predicted:

If tomorrow, based on justice, based on the recognition of our sacred rights consecrated by the blood of so many young generations of Italians, there were to be
realized the necessary and sufficient premises for a collaboration of the four great
western powers, Europe would be tranquil from the political point of view, and
perhaps the economic crisis, which has us in its grip, would come to an end.[5]

Italy blamed France for killing collective security. By spinning a web of
treaties to elaborate its own security to Italy's detriment, France and its
allies unwittingly had destroyed the League's prestige. Having reduced the
League to a juridical body concerned with treaty enforcement, they had
tainted international relations with all the faults and mistakes typical of
parliamentary governments, especially with the creation of special-interest
groups serving the commonweal only incidentally.[6]

Italy always seemed to be verging on withdrawal without actually doing so; at least not until December 11, 1937—all in all, a relatively late date.[7] Why so long to leave? Clearly Mussolini preferred to remain within its structure. Italy pointedly was present whenever international problems were discussed, even when its own interests were not at stake. In this way Italy demonstrated its great-power status and right to share in international life, even if, like Soviet Russia, Rome went about it defensively and self-consciously. League membership was a convenient forum where Italy could join discussions, state its case, defend its interests, and reject attacks. Italy's total estrangement from the League would place it in the same isolated diplomatic position as Germany's, but without the Reich's resources.[8]

Notwithstanding these advantages, the Duce hoped to forge a mechanism for handling international disputes that would supplement the League's institutions in truly important matters. He supposed that if the four great powers of Europe could establish an executive authority, they could short circuit hostile League machinery, augment their collective authority, and enhance Italy's influence vis-á-vis France. Mussolini's original plan implied that the four powers should coerce France by placing it in a minority of one on an executive committee of four. Mussolini hoped to use the four-power grouping to revise the territorial chapters of the four European peace treaties in favor of the ex-vanquished, one of which Italy felt itself to be, and to rearm Germany up to the levels of the victors in the event of a breakdown of the World Disarmament Conference. The revisions Mussolini had in mind were primarily those favoring Germany, but only in areas farthest removed from Italian interests.[9]

While the Soviets generally were prorevisionist, they could not countenance that any directory that excluded themselves should be its driving force.

NEGOTIATING THE PACT

Mussolini's Proposal

Mussolini tentatively had broached his ideas to the French by March 2, 1933, and on the tenth he told the Germans.[10] Four days later Ambassador Cerruti gave Mussolini's draft proposal to Foreign Minister Constantin von Neurath. By it the four powers would agree to reestablish a European concert and would use any necessary means, presumably and paradoxically including force, to ensure that the other European states acceded to their mutually agreed-upon policies promulgated in the spirit of peace, the Kellogg-Briand Pact's rejection of war, and the No-Force Pact's renunciation of force.[11]

According to the pact, the four powers would agree to work toward revision "within the framework of the League of Nations and in [the spirit of] mutual understanding and solidarity of reciprocal interests." Germany's recovery promised to upset the artificial and temporary European balance of power, which in turn threatened to end Italy's exceptional influence in international affairs since 1914. A renewed Franco-German conflict threatened to cast Italy back into the dark pit of secondary importance, in which case it might be compelled, contrary to its best interests, to join one of the two protagonists. As Mussolini made clear in his June 7 speech,

The rigid position maintained by some countries in the years since 1919 has created an atmosphere of tension; adaptations and revisions have taken place almost automatically, compelled by the force of circumstances, sometimes disturbing stability in Europe, but without resulting in the organic amelioration . . . that revision ought to produce.[12]

Certainly Mussolini was correct that the Versailles system was incapable of rectifying territorial claims, nor was he wrong in attributing international instability to this deficiency. His enlightened self-interest cannot be faulted for trying to move such revisionist questions out of the League and into a more favorable forum, where he could set in motion the process of territorial revision in directions favorable to Italy.

The next article demanded that if the Disarmament Conference failed, Germany would have the right to rearm to the levels of the other powers "by stages, which shall be the result of successive agreements to be concluded among the four powers through normal diplomatic channels." The inevitable German rearmament would be less awkward if carried out by international agreement through Italy's good offices and without the meddling interference of international bodies than if accomplished through unregulated Franco-German competition.

The last major article suggested that the four powers undertake a "common line of conduct in all political and nonpolitical, European and extra-European questions, as well as with regard to the sphere of colonies." To the extent that the four could agree on common action anywhere in the world, all things were possible for their mutual benefit. This article also implied that there ought to be colonial compensation for Italy and Germany at the expense of Great Britain and France. To be registered with the League, the pact was supposed to last for ten years and could be renewed for yet another ten if not denounced one year before its lapse.[13]

Hoping to maintain Italy as the balancing power in Europe, Mussolini attempted through his proposal to stabilize the European situation. This was his answer to the unreality of the Versailles system. Confiding the policing of Europe to a renewed great-power concert would limit their commitments. Flexible and realistic leadership would work Germany into a position where it would have to accept existing frontiers. It would isolate the Soviet Union and give Rome a free hand in Austria and Yugoslavia, and thus help establish Italy as a great power.[14]

Revising the Idea

Berlin quickly formed its opinion of the Duce's ideas. While considering the general proposal a good one, especially for espousing the right of equality, the Germans disliked the League's role in revision. Wanting stronger pro-revisionist wording, they resented the proposed realization of German equal-ity by stages. Although Mussolini's idea sharply attacked the French alliance system, Berlin also feared that it might lead to an Italo-French rap-prochement.[15]

Ambassador Hassell from Rome strenuously argued that Berlin could pre-vent this by attracting Italy through economic cooperation in the Danubian basin, despite its competition over Austria, which made such cooperation difficult. He also pleaded that the Soviets must be reassured about the pact's intent. The ambassador opined that the Italians were seeking to reduce international tensions and wanted to preserve Hitler's regime.[16]

Although Rome sniffed that Berlin's complaints about Mussolini's proposal were not entirely justified, it sought amendments from Berlin, and the two capitals agreed to tell the rest of the world that Germany had received a copy of the proposal only after the British had.[17]

Italy's first public move was to bid for Britain's sympathy.[18] Prime Minister MacDonald and Foreign Secretary Sir John Simon were in Geneva to present the British draft convention to the Disarmament Conference. Mussolini took advantage of their proximity to invite them to Rome, where they stayed from March 18 to the twentieth. On their arrival he presented them with his draft proposal, and on the same day he publicly announced the plan. MacDonald and Simon at once suggested changes, thereby publicly begin-ning the revision process.[19]

When Germany complained that these modifications diluted the principles of revision and equality of rights, Cerruti pressured them by passing on information that the French ambassador in Moscow was constantly talking about the danger of war. Given French rejection of either an extra-League pact or Soviet participation, the Kremlin's upset, and his own fears that Paris might launch a preventative war, Suvich was not hopeful for the pact's success.[20]

Its outlook, in fact, was not bright. The Little Entente opposed the project on the issue of treaty revision and, while welcoming the principle of collab-oration, it refused to admit that peace would be served by disposing of third-party rights. Czechoslovakia warned that it would resist any forcible frontier changes; Poland and Belgium also voiced concerns. As flurries of revised drafts filled the air at the end of March and into April, Edouard Daladier (the president of the French council of ministers and minister of war) prom-ised that Paris would not accede to any new "Holy Alliance." He insisted that the pact must build upon the Covenant, the Kellogg-Briand Pact, and the Locarno Pact.[21] A discouraged Mussolini complained to Hassell that "his proposal had been a boy at first, the English now wanted to make a her-maphrodite out of it and in the hands of the French it would become a girl. He would not play that game, for he wanted it to stay a boy."[22]

Soviet Opposition

On the thirty-first of March, when Attolico officially informed Litvinov of the proposed pact, he emphasized its "inoffensive" purpose—securing peace. The foreign commissar commented in his report, "Attolico therefore does not understand our objections to the pact."[23]

Ambassador Dirksen informed Litvinov on April 3 of the course of the conversations on the project.[24] Mussolini's proposal, he said, had surprised Berlin, which had made no diplomatic preparations for it. Explaining the Duce's concern at the inability of existing institutions to deal with change, he believed that Mussolini aimed his proposal against the French alliance system and European hegemony, and against the Little Entente. Pleased that Mussolini's idea had taken its position into account, Berlin contended that it could not stand alone against the other powers by sabotaging the proposal. But the French-inspired changes had made it less acceptable. Dirksen assured the foreign commissar that Germany would accept the pact only if it did not affect his government's relations with the Soviet Union. He doubted, however, that the pact would ever come to fruition. To reassure the Kremlin, Germany promised to keep Moscow informed on the negotiations and to take immediate steps to ratify the protocol extending the Berlin Treaty.

Repeating *Izvestia*'s earlier objections, Litvinov replied that, while the original purposes might have been limited, such political arrangements frequently take unknown directions. He worried that the pact existed outside of the League's structure, and that its signatories would discuss questions pertinent to the USSR without its participation. He pointed to his country's tense relations with Britain to show that such activities could never be accepted. As long as the four permanent members of the League Council confined themselves to questions within the League's competence, the Kremlin had less objection. After Dirksen rejected the notion that Germany and Italy would participate in anti-Soviet combinations, Litvinov replied that the USSR was interested in most West European questions and would consider an observer's role as best suited to its interests.

In his report to Berlin, Dirksen editorialized that this formula embodied Soviet policy regarding all international institutions, groupings, and conferences. The USSR craved "to be invited warmly to participate, but it wishes to confine itself only to the role of observer, which assumes no obligations, but reserves the right of unrestricted criticism." In what he called the "struggle to be present," Dirksen acknowledged that mistrust, hesitancy to commit, and prestige played a part. To demonstrate his point he quoted Karl Radek: "Soviet Power as a world power cannot remain indifferent at the sight of the conflicting currents on the world stage and the efforts to create a so-called concert of four Powers that arrogates to itself the right to direct the destinies of the nations."[25] Dirksen pointed to a long history of "luckless wars and disadvantageous conferences" in Russia's relations with the West. Litvinov's attitude toward the pact, Dirksen concluded, was mollified only by his skepticism regarding the positive outcome of the negotiations. Potemkin drove this last point home to Mussolini on May 22.[26]

The Soviet press, dramatizing these official positions, railed against the proposed pact, charging that the four-power plan was Italy's attempt to lead the movement for treaty revision.[27] Italy's revision, thankfully however, would not significantly annul Versailles; rather, it meant obtaining from France border rectifications between Tunisia and Libya, Italo-French naval parity in the Mediterranean, and French abandonment of Yugoslavia. Rome's differences with Germany over the Alto Adige and *Anschluss* limited Italy's revisionism. Although the USSR was upset at its exclusion from the negotiations, which it saw as anti-Soviet, the press promised that the socialist state could break any encircling ring of enemies.[28]

On April 10, the French government, while presenting a revised draft of Mussolini's proposal, repeated assurances that it would abide by its previous international commitments and that the four powers would not impose their will on others. To speak in general terms of revision was to risk raising anxieties and false hopes.[29]

The French ambassador to the USSR that same day asked Litvinov about the four-power pact project.[30] The foreign commissar explained that all he knew came from the newspapers and the Italian and German ambassadors. To the promise that French participation insured against the pact's becoming anti-Soviet, Litvinov replied that while this was true that day, it might not be the next, especially given the hostile nature of French politics. He observed that common Soviet and Little Entente opposition could form the basis of cooperation, but that moves for such joint action were not yet foreseen. The ambassador urged that the Soviet Union draw closer to the Little Entente.[31]

Litvinov averred that the USSR would seek to continue its previous relations with Germany, and that negotiations conducted between equals on revisionist questions concerned it less. Changes, for example, in the borders between the Little Entente and Hungary, or between Yugoslavia and Italy, would not affect Soviet interests as much as would changes in the Polish-German border. Moscow was determined to maintain the independence of the Baltic States, especially Lithuania.

The following day, the foreign commissariat instructed its representative in Paris to tell the French, "without us— consequently, against us."[32] Carrying out his instructions, on the twelfth he received French assurances concerning the four-power pact and hopes that the USSR and the Little Entente could come to agreement.[33]

International discussions continued to revise the proposed pact, and Italy pressed Germany for a quick decision.[34] In the third week of April, a German trade official explained to a Soviet official in Berlin that only Mussolini's original draft was acceptable to the German government, because only it permitted recognition of changing conditions without recourse to war.[35] He opined that, despite setbacks, Mussolini continued to work for the pact as a matter of prestige.

In the last ten days of April, discussions continued.[36] The Soviet ambassador in Paris relayed Litvinov's thanks for Daladier's ideas on the project, and he repeated that his government did not like the pact in any form, but the French variant was the "lesser evil."[37] Daladier replied that his government could not completely decline the pact.

As May arrived, the revision process did not slacken, with Germany, to Rome's consternation, now the main stumbling block.[38] Litvinov rejected Neurath's idea that the Kremlin's rapprochement with France was directed against Germany—the USSR would never do anything against German interests, and he pointedly remarked that Italy's internal policies did not concern him.[39] By month's end, Hitler was prepared to initial the pact, spurred in part by Italy's continued pressure to do so.[40]

The Permanent Council of the Little Entente, also on May 30, accepted the French amended text of the pact, believing that the League's competence had been preserved and that the French government had given formal guarantees against all attempts at revision. The Little Entente's opposition to the original scheme had led to the failure of Mussolini's project. The resulting pact thence was made acceptable, but the purged elements were precisely those that might have made it an effective instrument of revision for good or evil.[41]

Izvestia saw the four-power pact as Britain's bid for leadership in European affairs by averting an Italo-German alignment, which would conflict with France. It further thought that the pact revived former French Foreign Minister Aristide Briand's attempt to devise a general anti-Soviet coalition. Two days later Deputy Foreign Commissar Krestinskii explained to Attolico that because the USSR had not been invited to join the pact, it must be directed against the Soviets.[42]

THE PACT AND ITS CONSEQUENCES

The Pact Initialed and Signed

Despite last minute problems, Hitler, urged on by Rome, made his decision on June 7 and instructed Ambassador Hassell to initial and sign the latest text. Done in Rome that very day, the pact was a compromise between the original Italian idea and the French counterdraft plus those ideas on which the Little Entente had insisted.[43]

The Preamble marked the pact as superfluous. It did not go beyond international responsibilities, such as Locarno and the League Covenant, already incurred and would be no more effective than the desire already existing to fulfill them. The first two articles merely promised to consult, cooperate, and work toward peace within the ambit of the League of Nations. No vexing questions would be dealt with outside of its frame. In comparison, Article 3 boldly promised to work for a successful conclusion of the Disarmament Conference, but if it failed, the signatories reserved the right to reexamine those questions. Article 4 reserved the right of the parties to consult together on economic problems, once again limply "with a view to seeking a settlement within the framework of the League of Nations."[44]

Mussolini had been reserved during the negotiations, but in a speech before the Senate immediately after the pact's initialing, protesting too much, he proclaimed that the amendments had not affected the fundamental principles of the original draft proposal. While denying any intention of setting up an immutable hierarchy of powers, such a hierarchy, the Duce continued, did not necessarily connote a directorate, which would impose its will upon others. He denied that the original scheme or any subsequent draft imposed treaty revision by force, but merely attempted to deal reasonably with the inevitable revisions. The Duce rejected the idea that the pact was directed against anybody; rather it renounced any notion of rival groups or rigid political antagonisms, and it aimed at "safeguarding and harmonizing the interests of each individual state with the supreme interest of all, the consolidation of peace and the opportunity of revision."[45]

Simon's June 7 communication to the British ambassador in Rome nicely summarized Britain's attitude toward the emasculated pact. After denying that it opposed the League Covenant, he firmly promised that "adherence to the new Agreement does not imply an extension of the obligations of the United Kingdom in European affairs." The commitments of Locarno were enough: "We take our existing responsibilities too seriously to be willing in a lighthearted and speculative fashion to enlarge them."[46]

Beyond expressing its regret at the dilution of Italy's original idea, now that the pact was initialed, Berlin added its own reservation: "Germany's freedom of action toward all third powers . . . has been fully retained."[47] In other words, the pact would not restrain German revisionism. Berlin also wished to use the pact to improve Franco-German cooperation and deprive Paris of the opportunity of using it to improve its relations with Moscow and Rome.[48]

On June 9 Daladier declared to the French Chamber of Deputies that he wanted better relations with the Soviet Union and Italy.[49] At the same time Paris published notes exchanged with the Little Entente and Poland, that seemed to curtail the pact's utility for revision and prompted Berlin's complaint to Mussolini about France's commitment to third powers on interpreting the Four Power Pact. Italy worked diligently to soothe this latest German obstructionism.[50]

Overcoming these obstacles, the Four Power Pact was formally signed on July 15.[51] In effect, the very vindication of the Covenant and Locarno against the trespass of the Four Power Pact ironically had weakened them: well-regarded international agreements do not need to be reconfirmed prior to their expiration. The compromises had emasculated the pact and had demonstrated that territorial, armaments, and economic questions, legitimate or not, had run into a stone wall of vested interests, which could not be breached without resorting to war.[52]

European Consequences

Mussolini had proposed the Four Power Pact to advance Italy's interests by checking Germany's unrestrained revisionist adventurism and by defending Austria's independence. Surely, for the Soviets and many others, this was of much greater importance than was the Duce's own revisionism in the Danubian arena. He could be mistaken for a pillar of the status quo in Europe, at least until the beginning of 1936 when his revisionism again came to the fore. One does not have to agree with the hyperbole of that often offensive fascist apologist, Luigi Villari, to appreciate the high stakes he ascribed to Mussolini's initiative:

Independently of all other considerations, there is no doubt that the application of the Pact would have saved the world from the disaster of 1939–1945—and the members of the Little Entente themselves from the complete political annihilation they have since suffered, together with Poland and other countries as well. . . . Some time later Mussolini stated in an article written for the Universal Service Agency that, when the Pact failed, he had lost all hope for a peaceful solution of the problems tormenting Europe.[53]

Like Soviet Russia, Poland feared any diplomatic instrument, however innocuous, purporting to be the act of Europe's great powers, but negotiated without its participation. The Four Power Pact advertised offensively that Poland did not rank as a great power. Polish resentment focused on its erstwhile ally, France, and lubricated a Polish-German detente, which culminated in their Nonaggression Pact of January 26, 1934. This was one of Hitler's first significant diplomatic victories and one of the few concrete consequences of Mussolini's pact. Caught between the Charybdis of Germany and the Scylla of Soviet Russia, Poland thereby had cast its preference.[54]

Italy saw Germany's secession from the League as a natural consequence of the frustration of the Four Power Pact scheme. On December 6, 1933, one day after Litvinov had left Rome on an official state visit, the Fascist Grand Council passed a resolution stating that Italy's continued participation in the League was conditioned upon radical reforms.[55] Italy demanded that the League be remodeled to permit the entry or reentry of those great nations—Germany, Japan, the United States, and the Soviet Union—then outside, by freeing it from the Versailles Treaty. On the other hand, the collapse of the Disarmament Conference and Germany's withdrawal from the League and unilateral repudiation of the military clauses of the Versailles Treaty, all magnified by the Four Power Pact, intensified the stubborn hostility of those who refused to consider territorial revision.

Thus the Four Power Pact did not check the tendency toward forming rival blocs. While Poland had begun independent bargaining to counteract the pact's effect, Czechoslovakia, Yugoslavia, and Romania solidified their own regional bloc to offset the chance that France might come to terms with Germany. The Little Entente cemented its Pact of Organization by establishing an Economic Council.[56] Austria and Hungary signed the Rome Protocols with Italy in March 1934. One paradoxical result of the pact's failure, which redounded to Soviet advantage, was that it led Italy to closer ties with France, and Paris tried to effect an Italo-Yugoslav rapprochement.[57]

Mussolini implicitly had foresworn his policy of breaking up Yugoslavia, and the watered-down final draft reassured the Little Entente, but rumors that Rome desired the political union of Austria and Hungary under a Hapsburg monarch reawakened the Little Entente's suspicions.[58] The greater cooperation of the three fostered the formation of the Balkan Pact, a possibility that the Duce had not foreseen. He saw this latter collaboration as threatening panslavic unity, and no less a menace to Italy's influence in the region than was Germany.[59]

Old French hostilities toward Hungary and Austria were revived by the Mussolini-sponsored destruction of the Austrian Social Democratic Party. French Foreign Minister Louis Barthou went to Prague and Warsaw in April 1934 to refresh French friendship with those two capitals.[60]

Given these unforeseen effects, Mussolini's idea had been fashioned into something resembling Frankenstein's monster.

The Soviet Reaction to the Pact

The Soviets took the Four Power Pact seriously. In mid-June, Karl Radek pricked at Mussolini's pretensions, "Not all sweet dreams become reality." The pact, he forecast, would only temporarily limit the coming explosive conflicts, even though it expressed the *"tendency of the four West European capitalist powers to not permit a military solution to the conflicts dividing them."*[61] The failure of the Disarmament Conference had proved that the capitalists had not eliminated their contradictions, and Radek smugly noted that Paris and Berlin already were interpreting the pact differently. Mussolini had clearly said that with the pact Germany would gain equality in armaments. Isolated in the capitalist world only a couple of weeks before, Berlin had reentered the hierarchy of the powers. Clearly British imperialism wanted to use the pact against the Soviet Union. That the four would work through the League meant little to the USSR, a nonmember. In conclusion, Radek petulantly repeated that the USSR had the right to join European arrangements and warned that because of its political-economic-military might, it was ridiculous to exclude the Soviet Union.

Even so, the Soviet minister in Warsaw told his Italian colleague that the Soviet government was satisfied with Mussolini's assurances given after the conclusion of the Four Power Pact. Italy, he said, was more loyal than Germany, and Mussolini more loyal than Hitler.[62]

At the end of June, the Soviet plenipotentiary representative thanked Rome for an article in the *Giornale d'Italia* proclaiming fascist sincerity toward the USSR, yet Soviet unease over the Four Power Pact remained. Potemkin suggestively conceded that Mussolini was conducting a "realistic policy" and did not intend "to sacrifice the interests of Italy and the Church to the oil magnates and the lenders of millions to tsarist Russia." Further, he acknowledged that the fascist government did "not encourage the more-or-less clandestine movements against the Soviet state." Potemkin continued,

But it is no less true that our enemies propaganda finds help and agreement among certain intellectual fascists. In Rome itself, it is known, pamphlets significantly entitled, "We and the Ukraine" are being published. Who is "We"? They are certainly the fascists bound to Onatski, one of the heads of the Ukrainian mission to Rome. And who pays through Onatski for these numerous publications? And how did they escape the attention of the responsible officials?[63]

The representative concluded that although Mussolini did not want to turn the Four-Power Pact into an anti-Soviet instrument, he worried about the Vatican, Rosenberg, and the exiled Ukrainians. He feared that in the unsettled circumstances, it was difficult to predict how the Four Power Pact would be used.

In July 1933 *The Communist* semiofficially commented on a French article that had referred to the Four-Power Pact as part of an anti-Soviet crusade. Clearly showing the Kremlin's concerns, the journal charged that France's inclusion in the pact had to limit Paris's freedom of maneuver and would split France from Poland and the Little Entente. The latter would be isolated and forced to make territorial concessions to Germany, Hungary, and Italy. On the basis of these concessions, a temporary elimination of imperialist antagonisms and the formation of an anti-Soviet bloc would take place. To support this position the article referred to the official *Polish Gazette*, which claimed that the pact was based on four principles:

1) Intervention against other countries, because it is necessary to conclude a pact so as to make mutual concessions; 2) Compulsion, because if this were not the case the decisions of the. . . four governments would not be of any significance for the world which the pact wants to save; 3) The pact must further be based on the deprival of freedom of action of some of those participating in it; 4) It must be based on limiting of the rights of other states.[64]

The British position particularly galled the Kremlin, and Soviet historians have marked the pact as part of London's design to collude with Nazi Germany. British diplomacy, it is charged, seized upon Mussolini's draft suggesting the formation of a four-power directorate, because the pact would isolate the Soviet Union, exclude it from the solution of Europe's problems, undermine its international position, and improve cooperation between Great Britain and France on the one hand, and Britain and the fascist states on the other. *Pravda* promised that the proletariat recognized the pact's anti-Soviet purposes: "The die-hards will not be able to hide their interventionist cat in the diplomatic bag."[65] Litvinov on December 29 pointed out that the proposals for treaty revision involved the satisfaction of territorial claims at the expense of the Soviet Union and the Baltic States, which had not benefited from Versailles.[66]

The association of the four European powers always loomed in the nightmares of Soviet statesmen: it would be the prelude to a new war of intervention.[67] The Soviets had guarded against it until Hitler's arrival to power by encouraging German resentment against France and Poland and by promoting the economic and military cooperation with Germany begun at Rapallo. Unlike Western European statesmen, the Soviets took Hitler's diatribes seriously. The Soviet exclusion from the negotiating process probably was more threatening than was either the final pact or even the original Italian conception.

Mussolini's only mention of Soviet concerns in his June 7 speech before the Senate was in one sentence: "[The pact] is of equal interest to another great state, the Union of Soviet Socialist Republics, with which we have recently concluded a commercial treaty."[68] Coming at the end of a paragraph dealing with the concerns of Austria, Hungary, Turkey, and Greece, this hardly constituted a preoccupation, for good or bad, with Moscow.

Despite their egocentric worldview, most Soviet historians discuss the negotiations leading to the Four Power Pact without mentioning the USSR. That they can do so perhaps indicates an attempt at isolation by the other powers. It more strongly argues that the Soviets counted for so little in European affairs that a potentially major diplomatic accord, with repercussions for all of Europe, could be negotiated virtually without reference to them. Despite Soviet fuming, the pact was less a perfidious scheme directed primarily against the USSR than it was an overt sign of its lack of prestige. In fact, the Little Entente had greater input into the final product than did

Moscow. In other words, the three small states then counted for more in European politics than did the Soviet Union.[69] This explains why Moscow objected so vigorously to the pact.

NOTES

1. For details of the pact and its ramifications, see Konrad Hugo Jarausch, *The Four Power Pact, 1933* (Madison, WI, 1965); Fulvio D'Amoja, *Declino e prima crisi dell'Europa di Versailles: Studio sulla diplomazia italiana ed europea (1931-1933)* (Milan, 1969), pp. 259-354.

2. Benito Mussolini, *Opera omnia di Benito Mussolini*, ed. Edoardo and Duilio Susmel, 36 vols. (Florence, 1951-63), 21: 176-77. For Francesco Salata, *Il Patto Mussolini: Storia di un piano politico e di un negoziato diplomatico*, 2nd ed. (Milan, 1933), the Four Power Pact was a logical development of Mussolini's thought.

3. Maxwell Henry Hayes Macartney and Paul Cremona, *Italy's Foreign and Colonial Policy, 1914-1937* (New York, 1938), p. 245. Using this speech as evidence, the authors stress that Mussolini sought to limit the League's sphere of action and to establish a clear hierarchy among its members. For them this suggests an insidious and crass power grab. A more realistic judgment might be that Mussolini was noting the League's oft-demonstrated incapacity to act effectively without the concurrence of the major powers, and until the League's structure recognized that inevitable fact of international life, it could never be an effective organization. Mussolini was not demanding the unlimited self-gratification of the great powers, nor—ironically, given Italy's earlier successes at manipulating that form of international order—a return to the balance of power system. Rather, he remained willing to think in terms of the family of nations. He would not, however, allow its minors equal say in familial affairs. His mistake was to believe that Italy could assume parental responsibilities while still an adolescent.

4. Mussolini, *Opera*, 26: p. 189.

5. Ibid., 25: p. 143.

6. See Mussolini's June 7 speech following the initialing of the Four Power Pact in ibid., 25: pp. 239-49, and Salata, *Il Patto*, pp. 141-55.

7. Mussolini, *Opera*, 28: pp. 67-72.

8. Macartney and Cremona, *Italy's Policy*, pp. 240-57, passim.

9. Luigi Villari, *Italian Foreign Policy under Mussolini* (New York, 1956), pp. 94-109.

10. *DBFP* 2nd, 5: no. 37; *DGFP* C, 1: no. 68.

11. Salata, *Il Patto*, pp. 23-24. On Locarno and the Kellogg-Briand pact, see Carlo Schanzer, *Il mondo fra la pace e la guerra* (Milan, 1932), pp. 165-82, 202-28. On Anthony Eden's "No Force" idea, see *DGFP* C, 1: nos. 36 n.2, 37, 38.

12. Salata, *Il Patto*, p. 145.

13. Ibid., pp. 175-76, see also pp. 23-27; *DGFP* C, 1: no. 83.

14. Laurence Lafore, *The End of Glory: An Interpretation of the Origins of World War II* (Philadelphia, 1970), p. 116; Timothy Andre Taracouzio, *War and Peace in Soviet Diplomacy* (New York, 1940; reprint, Westport, CT, 1975), p. 166.

15. Salata, *Il Patto*, pp. 55-56; *DGFP* C, 1: nos. 84, 88, 95.

16. *DGFP* C, 1: nos. 87, 98, 101, 109.

17. Ibid., no. 100.

18. Ibid., no. 113. For an official British version of the events leading to the pact, see Salata, *Il Patto*, pp. 214-19.

19. Salata, *Il Patto* pp. 28-46, 178-79; *The Times* (London), Mar. 20, 1933; *DGFP* C, 1: no. 102.

20. Ibid., nos. 105, 108, 111, 115, 117, 120.

21. Salata, *Il Patto*, pp. 54-55, 60-62, 70-81, 150, 180-84, 195-96, 199. *DGFP* C, 1: nos. 115, 122, 126, 128, 135, 138, 146; *DBFP* 2nd, 5: nos. 61, 64-72, 79-82.

22. *DGFP* C, 1: no. 135.

23. *DVP* 16: n.92. See also ibid., no. 90 and Nina Dmitrievna Smirnova, *Politika Italii na Balkanakh: Ocherk diplomaticheskoi istorii, 1922-1935 gg.* (Moscow, 1979), p. 183.

24. *DGFP* C, 1: nos. 121, 136; *DVP* 16: no. 106.

25. See *Izvestia*, Mar. 30, 1933. The Soviets clearly regarded the proposal as a new move to isolate the USSR and to settle Europe's affairs without their participation, a point that Radek repeated in a series of articles from March to July. See ibid., May 12, 14, 18, June 10, 1933, and *Pravda*, May 10, 1933, the sum of which was that revision means war. See also Jarausch, *Four Power Pact*, pp. 105-08.

26. Vilnis Sipols, *Sovetskii Soiuz v bor'be za mir i bezopasnost', 1933-1939* (Moscow, 1974), p. 21; Igor Dmitrievich Ovsianyi, *Taina, v kotoroi voina rozhdalas' (Kak imperialisty podgotovili i razviazali vtoruiu mirovuiu voinu)*, 2nd ed. (Moscow, 1975), pp. 21-27.

27. Attolico to Rome, 4/10/33, 4/11/33: AP URSS b11 f1.

28. *Izvestia*, Apr. 11, 1933; see also Mar. 21, Apr. 3, 5, 1933.

29. Salata, *Il Patto*, pp. 88-95, 205-07.

30. *DVP* 16: no. 114.

31. See ibid., no. 77.

32. Ibid., no. 115.

33. Ibid., no. 116.

34. *DGFP* C, 1: no. 151, 153, 154, 159, 165, 170, 171, 172, 176, 181, 303.

35. *DVP* 16: no. 131.

36. *DGFP* C, 1: no. 178; Salata, *Il Patto*, pp. 207-09.

37. *DVP* 16: no. 136, n.111 p. 830.

38. *DGFP* C, 1: nos. 190, 208, 220, 230, 254, 271, 272, 274; Salata, *Il Patto*, pp. 99, 103, 184-90.

39. *DGFP* C, 1: nos. 258, 260, 284 n.1; *DVP* 16: no. 167.

40. *DGFP* C, 1: nos. 275, 276; *Izvestia*, June 2, 1934.

41. Salata, *Il Patto*, pp. 187-91, 212-14; Arnold Joseph Toynbee, *Survey of International Affairs, 1933*, assisted by V.M. Boulter (London, 1934), pp. 211-12. *Izvestia*, May 31, 1933, among its several articles on the proposed pact, stressed France's need to placate the Little Entente and Poland.

42. "Sipols, *Sovetskii Soiuz*, p. 23; *DVP* 16: n.202.

43. *DGFP* C, 1: nos. 282, 285, 286, 287, 290, 292; Toynbee, *Survey, 1933*, p. 217; M.P. Kim, ed., *Istoriia SSSR: Epokha sotsializma (1917-1957 gg.)* (Moscow, 1957), p. 442; Sipols, *Sovetskii Soiuz*, p. 222.

44. *DGFP* C, 1: no. 292; Andrei Ianvar'evich Vyshinskii, *Diplomaticheskii slovar'*, 2 vols. (Moscow, 1948, 1950), 2: 300-02, 671; Salata, *Il Patto*, pp. 159-74.

45. For the speech, see Mussolini, *Opera*, 25: 239-49. See *DGFP* C, 1: nos. 295, 394.

46. Salata, *Il Patto*, p. 218.

47. *DGFP* C, 1: no. 291; Salata, *Il Patto*, pp. 230-33.

48. *DGFP* C, 1: no. 320.

49. Ibid., no. 303.

50. Salata, *Il Patto*, pp. 224-29; *DGFP* C, 1: nos. 300-02, 304, 308, 311, 315, 317, 318, 321, 323, 332, 337, 340, 343, 358.

51. For a German report on the signing, emphasizing Mussolini's desire for a rapprochement between the USSR and Germany, see ibid., no. 368. See also *Izvestia*, July 2, 1934.

52. F. Jacomini Di San Savioni, "Il patto a quattro," *Rivista di studi politici internazionali* (Jan. 1951): 25-66; Pietro Quaroni, "Il Patto a Quattro," *Rivista di studi politici internazionali* (Jan.-June 1934): 49-67.

53. Villari, *Italian Foreign Policy*, p. 109.

54. Ibid., pp. 218-19.

55. *DGFP* C, 2: no. 104.

56. For more on these events, see Chapter 8.

57. Smirnova, *Politika Italii*, p. 187. See Chapter 9.

58. Cedric James Lowe and Frank Marzari, *Italian Foreign Policy, 1870-1940* (London, 1975), pp. 223-24; Arnold Joseph Toynbee, *Survey of International Affairs, 1934* (London, 1935), pp. 494-99.

59. Taracouzio, *War*, p. 167. See Chapter 8.

60. Macartney and Cremona, *Italy's Policy*, pp. 236-37, 247. See Chapter 9.

61. *Izvestia*, June 10, 1933; Attolico to Rome: AP URSS b11 f1. For Soviet concern, see Karl Radek, *Podgotovka bor'by za novyi peredel mira* (Moscow, 1934), pp. 79-84; Zinaida Sergeevna Belousova, *Frantsiia i evropeiskaia bezopasnost, 1929-1939 gg.* (Moscow, 1976), pp. 64-144; S.I. Riabokon', "Pozitsiia Maloi Antanty v period peregovorov o 'pakte chetyrekhy'," in I.N. Chempalov, ed. *Politika velikikh derzhav na Balkanakh i Blizhnem Vostoke (1933-1943)* (Sverdlovsk, 1977), pp. 3-28; Vladimir Konstantinovich Volkov, *Germano-iugoslavskie otnosheniia i rasval Maloi Antanty, 1933-1938* (Moscow, 1966), pp. 23-32; Jarausch, *Four Power Pact*, pp. 172-73; Sergei Danilovich Skazkin, K.F. Miziano, and S.I. Dorofeev, eds., *Istoriia Italii*, 3 vols. (Moscow, 1970-71), 3: 114-15; and *Pravda*, June 9, 1933.

62. Bastianini to Rome, 6/28/33: AP URSS, b8 f3.

63. Note, 6/30/33: AP URSS b10 f1.

64. N. Rudolph, "The Intensification of the Versailles Antagonisms and the Menace of the New Imperial War," *The Communist* 12 (July 1933): 678-79.

65. *Pravda*, June 10, 1933.

66. *DVP* 16: App. 2.

67. "The Four Power Pact," *Class Struggle* 3 (Aug. 1933): 9-10. On June 19, the Soviet ambassador in Berlin delivered a note complaining that the German press was saying that the Four Power Pact and the Italo-French reapprochement was the prelude to a Franco-German rapprochement. *DVP* 16: no. 249.

68. Salata, *Il Patto*, p. 153.

69. Smirnova, *Politika Italii*, p. 185.

II

The Italo-Soviet Rapprochement of 1933 and 1934

4

Ideological Rapprochement

Mussolini's Four Power Pact had paraded Moscow's isolation from Europe's great power councils. Despite Rome's continued assurances of its benign intent,[1] even this shaky association of the four European powers loomed in the nightmares of Soviet statesmen. It potentially could lead to a new war of intervention against the world's first socialist state.[2]

IDEOLOGICAL CONVERGENCE

One way for Moscow to break out of its embarrassing and threatening isolation was to draw closer to Italy, the creator of the Four Power Pact. This proved to be a surprisingly easy task despite the seemingly different philosophies governing the two societies. First, the economic accord of May 1933 and then the Pact of Friendship, Neutrality, and Nonaggression of September, both buttressed by intense military collaboration, eased the Kremlin's sense of isolation. This cooperation also provided Italy with room to maneuver once it had become clear that the Four Power Pact had been stillborn. Dictatorial cynicism and ideological hypocrisy, never easy to overestimate, did not alone explain the success of the process.

Politics does make for strange bedfellows. This truism, old but always new, is all the truer when ideology intrudes upon the stage of international diplomacy. Ideological leaders are forever succumbing to the charms of *Realpolitik* and then find themselves having to create intellectual justifications for their seduction. Often, what seems to be ideological walls blocking possibilities, with clever turns can become gates opening upon new vistas of cooperation.

So it was that the economic, political, and military rapprochement of the early 1930s between the Soviet Union and Italy, so fraught with possibilities for the future, was facilitated by the frequently expressed conviction, especially in Italy, that there were ideological, revolutionary, and practical affinities between the two. For many Italians, even astute diplomats solidly grounded in concrete realities, Stalinism seemed to be turning to fascism to ease the contradictions of failed bolshevism.[3] The airing of this "convergence" notion is difficult to pin down, full as it was with mushy definitions and soggy sentiments. But Mussolini, after all, had often boasted that fascism blended paradoxes; consistency and rationality were the false shibboleths of failed liberal, bourgeois dogmas that denied man's capacity for visceral greatness.

Italian fascism's political institutions derived in part, at least, from the Leninist model, and quite early Mussolini claimed that the fascist movement actually boasted more *bona fide* proletarian members than did the bolshevik party. The disciplined Fascist Party, Mussolini claimed with his usual hyperbole, had transformed Italy into the most totalitarian and efficient of all countries, including the USSR.[4] The philosophical and institutional similarities between his fascism and Leninist communism, both beyond the pale of liberalism, fascinated the Duce. Indeed, there eventually developed what one antifascist historian has called an "elective affinity" between the Roman and Muscovite dictatorships.[5]

Several Western writers have elaborated totalitarian theories, which stress the essential similarities underlying twentieth-century, one-party dictatorships.[6] The dictators themselves recognized some of their common professional imperatives. The Italian embassy in Moscow, for example, apparently operated on Mussolini's standing instructions to send him any material casting light on J. V. Stalin's methods.[7] Mussolini believed that the masses, not wanting debate, lacked the confidence to make their own judgments; they preferred to be commanded. He was training his people to mass collectivity, he admitted, just as was Stalin. Even Mussolini's preferences in art smacked of Soviet realism, and he thought that the bolsheviks were particularly adept at using film for propaganda: "The Russians set us a good example there."[8]

Given, then, that these similarities existed, what were their source?

PREWAR ITALIAN REVOLUTIONARY NATIONAL SYNDICALISM AND MODERNIZATION

In the *demi-monde* of Europe's revolutionary radicalism before the Great War, leftist intellectuals often seemed more interested in fighting one another than in fighting their common bourgeois class enemies. And despite facile assumptions, fascism and communism were not antipodes. Although their exact relationship remains difficult to define, there exist commonalities, as one author has pointed out:

Fascism was the heir of a long intellectual tradition that found its origins in the ambiguous legacy left to revolutionaries in the work of Karl Marx and Friedrich Engels. Fascism was, in a clear and significant sense, a Marxist heresy. It was a Marxism creatively developed to respond to the particular and specific needs of an economically retarded national community condemned, as a proletarian nation, to compete with the more advanced plutocracies of its time for space, resources, and international stature.[9]

Assuming that this point can be accepted today, the more important question for present purposes is: Was this kind of self-awareness present among the thinkers and politicians who struggled to define these two ideologies as they codeveloped earlier in this century? In fact, occasionally some did recognize that what they shared held much greater weight than did their Talmudic differences.

By 1903 Arturo Labriola's *Avanguardia Socialista* of Milan had become the forum for Italy's Sorelian syndicalist revolutionaries, who were struggling against reformist socialism.[10] Such luminaries as Vilfredo Pareto and Benedetto Croce graced its pages,[11] followed shortly by a second generation of Sorelian theoreticians, including Angelo Oliviero Olivetti, Roberto Michels, Sergio Panunzio, Ottavio Dinale, Paolo Orano, Enrico Leone, and Agostino Lanzillo, who came to dominate Italian radicalism for more than a generation. Together they built an alternative socialist orthodoxy, which they believed was the true heir to classical Marxism. Clearly, their ideas were no more heretical than were Lenin's. By 1904 Mussolini, then a socialist agitator in Switzerland, had begun his collaboration with *Avanguardia Socialista*, a relationship he maintained for the next five years. The syndicalist contributors to the journal substantially affected the future Duce's intellectual and political development.[12]

Radical syndicalists like Olivetti innovatively argued that under retarded economic conditions, socialists must appeal to national sentiment if their ideas are to penetrate the masses.[13] For him, both syndicalism and nationalism were dedicated to increasing production dramatically. As long as Italy remained underdeveloped, the bourgeoisie remained necessary to build the economic foundation requisite for a socialist revolution. Olivetti spoke of a national socialism, because in an underdeveloped economy, only the nation could pursue the economic development presupposed by classical Marxism.

When Mussolini took over as editor of the socialist paper *Avanti!* in December 1912, he attracted anarchists and even some rigid Marxists like Angelica Balabanoff, whom he took on as his assistant editor.[14] Paolo Orano, who served on the editorial staff, along with other syndicalists like Sergio Panunzio set the tone of the paper.[15] Mussolini also founded and edited *Utopia* from November 1913 until December of the following year. This bimonthly review attracted many of the most important young socialist and syndicalist theoreticians, who helped the future Duce to develop his own ideas.[16]

In the final years before the First World War, many independent national syndicalists, including Panunzio and Dinale, saw war as progressive. Helping to put together the rationale for fascism, they supported Italy's fight with the Ottomans over Libya in 1911, and with Mussolini they called for Italy's intervention in the First World War. Many socialists now passed into Mussolini's fascist ranks, and syndicalists such as Panunzio, Olivetti, and Orano became its principal ideologues.[17]

By October 1914, Olivetti in *Pagine Libere* was speaking of a socialism infused with national sentiment, a socialism destined to complete Italy's unification, thereby placing it among the world's advanced, productive nations. Over the next three years in *L'Italia Nostra*, Olivetti spoke of the nation as uniting men of all classes in a common pursuit of historical tasks; class membership did not align an individual against the nation but united him with it. Patriotism was fully compatible with the revolutionary tradition of Italian socialism.[18]

ITALIAN SYNDICALISM, FASCISM, AND LENIN'S BOLSHEVISM

By 1919 Mussolini was pointing out the absolute decline in economic productivity in Soviet Russia as proving the bolsheviks' failure to recognize their historical obligations and revolutionary necessities. He believed that they ultimately had to commit themselves to national reconstruction and defense, that is, to some form of developmental national socialism as defined by fascism's former syndicalists. Mussolini presciently predicted that Lenin had to appeal to bourgeois expertise to repair Russia's ravaged economy. Bolshevism, he said, must domesticate and mobilize labor to the task of intensive development, something which could have been anticipated, because Marxism had made it quite clear that socialism could be built only upon a mature economic base. Russia, not having yet completed the capitalist stage of economic development, met none of the material preconditions for a classic Marxist revolution. Russia was no more ripe than was Italy for socialism.[19]

In July 1920, Mussolini again denounced Lenin's regime. The irony was that he himself was to build his fascist state along the very lines he condemned in the bolshevik experiment. According to him they had built "a State in the most concrete meaning of this word . . . a Government, composed of men who exercise power, imposing an iron discipline upon individuals and groups and practicing "reaction" whenever necessary." In Lenin's Russia, Mussolini complained, "there is but one authority: his. There is but one liberty: his. There is but one opinion: his. There is but one law: his. One must either submit or perish." With no room for individuality, the Soviets had created a "super State" that swallows up and crushes the individual and governs his entire life. . . . The most powerfully armed State, for domestic and foreign purposes, that exists in the world is precisely Russia. . . . Whoever says State necessarily says the army, the police, the judiciary and the bureaucracy. The Russian State is the State *par excellence* . . . [whose] proletariat, as in the old bourgeois regimes, obeys, works, and eats little or allows itself to be massacred.

He praised the Communist Party, a minority, for its ability to govern "with absolute and unlimited power." Rejecting the notion that true socialism had come to power, he concluded, "Lenin is an artist who has worked men as other artists have worked marble or metals. But men are harder than stone and less malleable than iron. There is no masterpiece. The artist has failed. The task was superior to his capacities."[20]

Lenin, in the practical working out of his revolutionary government, did run headlong into many of these conundrums predicted by the syndicalists. In the months following his takeover, he had expected that the revolution in Germany would bail Soviet Russia out of its difficulties. Thus, while the first fascists were organizing for a national revolution, the bolsheviks were still dreaming of an international insurrection. Lenin, changing horses in 1921, proposed the New Economic Policy to replace the ideologically purer but failed War Communism. Like fascists, Lenin now spoke of holding the entire fabric of society together with "a single iron will," and he began to see the withering away of the state as a long way away: "We need the state, we need coercion."[21]

After Lenin's death in 1924, this logic culminated the next year with Stalin's "creative development" of Marxism: "Socialism in One Country," a national socialism by any other name. Mussolini tried to convince himself that Russian communism, which Stalin might be abandoning, was less revolutionary than was fascism. He and some of his followers even pondered the possibility that the two movements were drawing together close enough as to be no longer easily distinguishable. Stalin might be the true heir to the tsars and an imperialist with whom fascism could see eye-to-eye. In 1923 the Duce predicted, "Tomorrow there will not be an imperialism with a socialist mark, but it [Russia] will return to the path of its old imperialism with a panslavic mark."[22] This, it seemed, might provide economic advantages to Italy, and to Mussolini it made sense for his country to build ships and planes for the Soviets in exchange for one-third of Italy's oil supplies.[23]

Even dedicated fascist party workers such as Dino Grandi, Mussolini's foreign minister from 1928 to 1932, early recognized fascism's affinities with Lenin's bolshevism. He had taken at least part of his own intellectual inspiration from revolutionary syndicalism, and in 1914 he had talked of the First World War as a class struggle between nations. Six years later Grandi argued that socialists had failed to understand the simple reality of the Russian Revolution. It had been nothing less than the struggle of an underdeveloped and proletarian nation against the more advanced capitalist states.[24]

Not only fascists made this sort of analysis. Torquato Nanni, a revolutionary Marxist socialist and an early acquaintance of Mussolini, had anticipated these developments as early as 1922. He analyzed the common economic foundations of fascism and bolshevism, which produced the related strategic, tactical, and institutional features of these two mass-mobilizing, developmental revolutions. Both, he wrote, had assumed the bourgeois responsibilities of industrializing backward economies and defending the nation-state, the necessary vehicle for progress.[25]

Lev Trotsky, the organizer of the October Revolution, consistently, even mulishly, argued that fascism was a mass movement growing organically out of the collapse of capitalism. Although he rejected all notions of "national" communism, he too recognized a certain involution. "Stalinism and Fascism," he said, "in spite of a deep difference in social foundations, are symmetrical phenomena. In many of their features they show a deadly similarity. A victorious revolutionary movement in Europe would immediately shake not only fascism, but Soviet Bonapartism."[26]

He, however, refused to go as far as his sometime ally, Bruno Rizzi, who argued that the assumption of similar developmental and autarchic responsibilities could only generate social and ideological convergence. He lamented, "that which Fascism consciously sought, [the Soviet Union] involuntarily constructed."[27] For him, the governments of Stalin, Mussolini, Hitler, and even Roosevelt were lurching toward a global system of "bureaucratic collectivism," a new form of class domination.[28]

Fascist theoreticians agreed with such convergence notions. By 1925 Panunzio claimed that fascism and bolshevism shared critical similarities. Fascists noted that the Soviets had created an armed, authoritarian, antiliberal state that had mobilized and disciplined the masses to the service of intensive internal development. The supreme state generated and allocated resources, articulated and administered interests, and assumed and exercised primary pedagogical functions.[29]

Thus, while the first fascists were formulating the rationale for a mass-mobilizing, developmental, authoritarian, hierarchical, antiliberal, and statist program guided by a charismatic leader, events had forced the bolsheviks along the same course. Both intended to create a modern, autarchic, industrial system, which would insure political and economic independence for what had been an underdeveloped national community. With forced industrialization and "state capitalism," the Soviets hoped to bring Russia all the benefits of bourgeois modernization. In the face of required austerity, to mobilize their respective populations, the communists and fascists supplemented economic incentives with pageantry, ceremony, ritual, and parades. All this, plus territorial aggression, completed a compelling picture of systemic symmetry.[30]

THE CRITICA FASCISTA DEBATE OF THE 1930s

Beginning with the October Revolution, the literary flood on bolshevism that inundated Italy suggested a deep and abiding fascination with the Soviet experiment.[31] The freewheeling debate that emerged took new directions in 1922 and 1923 with Lenin's introduction of the NEP and again in 1928 with collectivization and the First FYP. At least until the mid–1930s, the fascist press, although frequently severely critical, as often expressed a surprising degree of sympathy toward Soviet Russia. The debate, in fact, was not finally laid to rest until June 22, 1941, with the Nazi invasion of Soviet Russia.[32] Although many leftists in the West then considered fascist criticisms of Stalinist Russia to be strident, in retrospect they appear mild. On the other hand, these criticisms were often defensive in tone, as if trying to prove to Italy's laboring masses that things truly were better under fascism.

While Russia's moral and intellectual "spiritual" life concerned several Italian authors,[33] others, probably with economic-political cooperation in mind, surveyed the political geography of the Soviet Union and its component parts.[34] Italians were keenly aware of the centrifugal forces threatening to fracture the fraternal unity of the socialist republics. Some, on the other hand, worried at the "expansionist," "primitive," "Asiatic" nature of Russia and bolshevism, which culturally and politically threatened Europe, the bulwark of which was Italy.[35] Nor did Italian authors ignore the political and philosophical nature of the power struggle that eventually enthroned Stalin on the seat of dictatorial power.[36]

One of the chief venues of this debate was the pages of *Critica Fascista*, the respected polemical journal of the "corporativist left." The journal's editor, Giuseppe Bottai, the *"Crusader of the regime,"*[37] by the mid–1920s was arguing the frequently heard refrain that fascism and bolshevism were as one against the spirit of the bourgeoisie and plutocracy.[38]

In 1930 and 1931, *Critica Fascista* ran a series of articles, which the journal eventually dubbed "Roma o Mosca?." In midspring of the former year Bruno Spampanato explained Leninist violence as a consequence of the "primitiveness of the Russian spirit"; the Russians remained political "children."[39] Bolshevik thought, he said, merely reflected this immaturity. The government's antireligious drive, for example, had resulted from the "childish ignorance of the first revolutionary phase." He predicted that just as Robespierre's antireligious policies had passed on to Napoleon's regard for religion, so too the bolsheviks would change their antireligious violence.

Spampanato added that Stalin, to continue Lenin's work, could not ignore "necessity." New socioeconomic groups were joining the proletariat's ranks, and the antikulak campaign in the rural areas was weakening. In fact, the war, revolution, and civil war had amounted to Russia's Nietzschean rebirth out of chaos and death. But because tsarist development had been retarded, the bolshevik experience had been more violent than had been revolutions elsewhere in Europe. Tsarist Russia had been slow to develop the national idea, and while Leninism was trying to create the idea of a nation, ideological baggage was encumbering the bolsheviks.[40]

Reminding his readers that fascism was the highest stage of political development, Spampanato concluded that Russia's situation in 1930 pitted the Soviet state against fascist democracy. Even so, he saw a thread that might conceivably tie the two together. "Not fearing any example because they are solidly attached to the vitality of their historical experience, Fascists can fasten on to some fundamental points of esteem for the bolshevik experience. . . . We dare to say that bolshevism in Russia is the prelude to fascism."[41]

The *Critica Fascista* debate began in earnest a year and one-half later. Sergio Panunzio, fortifying his argument with the Duce's recent statement that Italy's commercial relations with the USSR were better than those with anyone else, denied that any *economic* antithesis existed between Rome and Moscow:

Therefore, if we put ourselves exclusively on an economic ground, we arrive not only to the "absurdity" that fascism opposes communism, we also come to the *point* of not being able any more to discern a difference, and on the contrary to glimpse a balancing synthesis—the diagonal of the historical contact of two great forces and of two great modern revolutions: Communism and Fascism—Rome and Moscow.

But not all was compatible. Fascism was a "religion of the spirit," of the "will" and the "nation." Bolshevism, on the other hand, was a "religion of matter" and the "giant factory." Here the antithesis was "absolute, raw, and irreducible between Moscow and Rome, and in the field of the spirit and of moral and religious values . . . the duel between bolshevism and fascism is and *ought* to be absolute and eternal."[42]

For neither the first time nor the last, Italians, despite seemingly different ideological regimes, could contemplate collaboration in practical, pragmatic ways, while preserving their fundamental spiritual differences with the bolsheviks. This article by the former syndicalist became the focal point of the subsequent debate in *Critica Fascista*.

Riccardo Fiorini maintained that the economic differences existing between communism and fascism did not lie in the contrast between private and state production.[43] More important was that fascist production was quintessentially nationalistic, whereas communist production was not. Communism, he predicted, eventually would lead to an internationalization of production; fascism would lead to a confederation of productive states. Yet even he predicted that communism's economic practices, different as they were at the moment, would grow ever closer to fascism.

On spiritual matters, Fiorini rejected Panunzio's distinction between fascism and communism. He doubted, despite the Kremlin's verbiage, that the Soviets truly were practicing a religion of materialism. Besides, there had been features of tsarist Russia's family and religious life that deserved destruction. Unlike Panunzio he found reason to emphasize the possibilities of spiritual cooperation between the two regimes. Both their ideologies opposed liberalism and democracy: "Russia and Italy are united in the effort to create a new order." He predicted that communism would move closer to fascism.[44]

Within a month and a half, Mario Rivoire supported Panunzio's idea that the antithesis between Rome and Moscow was not to be found in their economic natures, because fascism was in physical matters "relativistic" and "polytheistic." Rejecting Fiorini's argument, he claimed that a real difference existed, and that it lay in the metaphysical, with communism worshiping the material and fascism the spiritual. Rivoire justly pointed out that the earlier discussion in *Critica Fascista* had been poorly defined, and that with the Soviets there was always the problem of whether to focus on their words or deeds. He found the resolution to his problem in a 1921 speech by Mussolini:

I recognize that between us and the communists there are no political affinities, but there are intellectual affinities. We, as you (the communists) think that it is necessary to have a centralized and unitary State which imposes on all the unity of an iron discipline: with this difference, that you arrive at this conclusion through the concept of classes, and we come to it through the concept of the nation.[45]

For Rivoire, this was the heart of the matter: class or nation? For Rome the state functioned for the nation; for Moscow it functioned for the class. "In other words," Rivoire concluded aphoristically, "for Moscow, all the State is of the party, while for Rome, all, including the party, is of the State." He doubted that these two ideas would soon merge.[46]

Meanwhile, other fascist publicists aired other matters and attitudes, such as the historical Russian threat to Europe.[47] Alberto Luchini, for example, objected to what he called the emerging *moscofilia*. Rejecting the notion of convergence, he declared that those who focused on the last ten years of good relations and who claimed that there was some empathy between the two regimes were ignoring the anti-Italian tsarist tradition. From the end of the eighteenth century through 1915, Russia had opposed Italy's interests, especially during the Risorgimento and in Africa and the Adriatic.[48] The Racconigi Accord of 1909, St. Petersburg's Italophile attitude during the Italo-Turkish War of 1911 and 1912, and Brusilov's Galician offensive of 1916 that had eased Italy's situation on its Austrian front had but briefly interrupted the larger trend. Fascism was anti-Slav and antibolshevik, and the revolutions that had brought the two ideologies to power had nothing in common.

Taking another tack, in that same issue Bruno Spampanato rejoined the fray. A year and a half earlier he had suggested that any convergence between

fascism and communism was something only for the future. Now warming
to the immediacy of the idea, he rejected its normal framing, "Rome or
Moscow?" The proper way to put that question was, instead, "Rome and
Moscow, or the old Europe?"—that decrepit Europe with its liberal-democratic, bourgeois regimes. France, he noted, hated both Rome and Moscow,
and he suggestively added that Germany geographically lay between Rome
and Moscow.[49]

Two weeks later Luciano Ingianni entered the literary tumult to critique
both Panunzio and Fiorini. He maintained that even the idea and practice
of materialism did not distinguish bolshevism from fascism, because Soviet
Russia was striving after the "ideal" of materialism. To be sure, many foreigners equated Moscow and Rome, and these two meccas were, in fact,
two solutions to Europe's problems. They seemingly differed mainly in that
in one, authority came from the state, and in the other, from the class. In
Italy, he rejoiced, the dictatorship was personal and unambiguous; in Russia
it was of the class and a matter of faith.[50]

In addition, Ingianni maintained that there were substantial differences
between the two economies, although he also agreed with Rivoire that the
economic differences were insufficient to give an "acute" sense of antithesis.
He doubted, however, that the ultimate difference lay in the contrast between legitimization by class or nation. Rather, class and corporate conceptions vied with one another, as did the national and international conceptions.
Ingianni added that perhaps the ultimate difference was racial. He contrasted
Mediterranean-Latin spirituality against Marxist-Leninist materialistic cer-
ebralness. Here the antithesis, he argued, was profound, a conclusion with
which Armando Tosti, in the same issue of *Critica Fascista* agreed.[51]

In what proved to be the final salvo in this round of the debate, Bruno
Spampanato in two articles at the beginning of 1932 again discussed the
nature of the bolshevik and fascist states. He had fired the opening shots in
the fascist journal nearly two years before, and he now cleverly, even starkly,
sought to resolve the genuine and important relationships. He denied the
existence of a fascist international.

There is, instead, a universality of fascism in the sense that the modern revolution
is developed and is destined to be realized according to a few political and economic
postulates, according to the few governing ideas characteristic of the new Italy....
Fascism is Italian and universal: two conditions of the same reality.... Fascism is
born in Italy, but it is born for the world.[52]

Nationalistic fascism thus would expand through imperialism, and consequently share an international dimension with Marxism. As for the bolshevik
state, although it was totalitarian, it was not in reality a class dictatorship.
As he had earlier, Spampanato waxed confident that Stalinism would merge
into fascism.

Throughout the 1930s, the *Critica Fascista* debate continued to echo in the tones originally sounded by the pre-World War I Italian syndicalists. In 1937, for example, Agostino Nasti saw Stalinism as a non-Marxist "political formula" that "galvanizes the Russian people in the service of a nationalistic industrial-economic development." This formula also "serves to bewitch the masses of other countries, exploiting the people's aspirations for better social justice, and to mask an actual expansionist and imperialist policy."[53] Rejecting the "reactionary anti-bolshevism" of the threatened bourgeoisie who wished to return to the laissez-faire liberalism of the past,[54] fascist antibolshevism grew out of the recognition that the Soviets had misunderstood the challenge of the modern world. They mistakenly continued to mouth internationalist, antistatist, and proletarian slogans.

Gone was the frenetic, antireligious, antimilitarist, antinationalist bias of the "revolutionary socialism" that had been fascism's mortal enemy.[55] But even here fascists such as Tomaso Napolitano concentrated their gaze on what such internal developments meant for international relations. Clearly, they generally agreed that Stalin's reforms of the mid–1930s had "dialectically thrown overboard the principles in whose name" the Russian revolution had been conducted—and that anarcho-syndicalist "Marxist-Leninist principles" had been transformed into their "'contraries', that is to say, the ideas that provided body and substance to Mussolini's fascism."[56]

Full of vague, unsupported assumptions and generalizations, this wide-ranging and unsettled debate often lacked substance and concrete detail. Even so, it did accurately reflect the thoughts and sentiments of a wide range of fascists, many of whom, to a greater or lesser degree and for varying reasons, proved surprisingly sympathetic to the notion of ideological convergence. And if not that, they at least saw no philosophical problem to political and economic cooperation. Despite the bitter words screamed at one another during the Italo-Abyssinian War (1935-1936) and the Spanish Civil War (1936-1939), in fact, Italian attitudes were not finally fixed in anticommunist cement until the German invasion of Soviet Russia in the summer of 1941. This suggests that, for all of their supposed ideological differences, not only was any potential Italo-Soviet rapprochement not *a priori* out of the question, there was even a philosophical imperative toward cooperation.

THE WIDER IDEOLOGICAL DEBATE

On a wider scale than the *Critica Fascista* debate, Italian authors investigated the quality of Soviet social, economic, and political life during the early 1930s. They provided sufficient concrete information so that any decision to work with the USSR in whatever sphere—economic, diplomatic, or military—could be based on an accurate appraisal of what the Soviet regime was, or was not.

One author, Tomaso Napolitano, was particularly tireless in dissecting the harsh conditions for labor, families, artists, writers, and those who had run afoul of the Stalinist legality: "[These documents] . . . are chiefly extracts from Soviet newspapers which contain facts of incredible misery, abjection, and an appalling lack of humanity. . . . [These facts] are the most sure expression of a decayed world, of a civilization which is walking centuries backward."[57] Despite these harsh judgments, Napolitano's articles were always well informed and solidly grounded in Soviet public sources. As for ideology, Napolitano felt that Stalinist Marxism had followed the path traced by revolutionary syndicalism before the First World War. He and other fascists insisted that because Soviet Russia faced developmental tasks, Marxists would have to assume fascist institutions and political organizations.[58]

The FYPs particularly intrigued Italians, who wondered whether Stalinism was moving toward corporativism and state capitalism. For example, Gaetano Ciocca, one of the Italian engineers who worked to build the Kaganovich ball-bearing plant, illuminated the economic and political successes of the First FYP in his book, *Giudizio sul Bolsevismo*. Even more, he shone his harsh, searching light on its cruel failures and the differences between Soviet communism and Italian corporativism.[59]

What Mussolini praised in Ciocca's book as "objective reality,"[60] Moscow castigated as an anti-Soviet provocation. On October 30, 1933, the eve of the plant's opening, *Pravda* published an article, allegedly written by a worker, that claimed that Russians had nothing to learn on technical organization from foreigners, especially Italians.[61] Berardis, the chargé d'affaires in Moscow, protested to the foreign commissariat and haughtily pointed out that Russians had been receiving Italian technical assistance from at least the time of Ivan III. Meanwhile, in his report to Rome, Berardis conceded that despite the accuracy of Ciocca's book, the Soviet response was understandable.[62]

Equally understandable was the reaction of Secondo Marocco, the leader of the Italian engineers in Moscow. He protested to the plant's director, who apologized profusely. The next day, *Izvestia* published an article by the chastened director praising foreign—in context, Italian—assistance in the ball bearing industry.[63] At the ceremony inaugurating the opening of the new factory, and in the presence of party bigwigs such as L. M. Kaganovich, the factory's namesake, and G. K. Ordzhonikidze, the director again praised the Italian contribution to the industry and his factory.[64] A plaque on the factory wall confirmed that contribution, and a banquet that night revelled in Italo-Soviet cooperation. A mollified Marocco concluded that the *Pravda* article had not represented Kremlin policy.[65] Ultimately, the government gave an award to him.

But the matter was not yet finished. In November, as Italy and the USSR were preparing for Foreign Commissar Litvinov's state visit to Rome the next month, an impolitic and unrepentant Ciocca gave a press interview.[66]

Rome's official rejection of Ciocca's conclusions was not sufficiently strong to assuage a miffed Moscow. The Soviet plenipotentiary, Potemkin, explained to Under Secretary of State Suvich that when Ciocca had been fired from his position for incompetence, he then had asked to remain in the USSR to work on other projects. He was refused, and Potemkin believed that Ciocca's behavior reflected his private resentments. To ease the situation for Litvinov's trip, he asked that the Italian government disassociate itself from the engineer's criticisms. In the contretemps's final gasp and sputter, after Litvinov's return to Moscow from Rome, *Pravda* again derided Ciocca's book and praised the technical development of the Soviet ball-bearing industry.[67]

In 1933 Mussolini also favorably reviewed Renzo Bertoni's *Il trionfo del fascismo nell'U.R.S.S.*[68] Like Ciocca, Bertoni stressed the harsh conditions of the Second FYP: family life had been destroyed; cold and hunger lurked everywhere; the government had failed hopelessly in everything it had tried; all the peasants wanted to emigrate to Italy; and Mussolini thrilled the Soviet population. On the FYPs, Bertoni argued that fascism and communism had adopted different tactics to reach the same goal. The Soviets, however, had failed, and only fascism could save Russia, economically, spiritually, and socially—especially if it wished to win the next war.[69] Mussolini heartily agreed that the only viable course Russia could follow was to abandon Marx: Russia's salvation lay in fascism.[70]

For Rodolfo Mosca it was unclear whether Russia belonged to the East or West; he was certain, however, that Italy was well placed to mediate and therefore could bridge that country to the rest of the world.[71] Ottavio Dinale, the old syndicalist, agreed. While calling bolshevism and fascism antithetical, one coming from the East and the other from the West, he also admitted that in their origins and methods they had "formidable" elements in common.[72] Writing emotionally four years later during the Spanish Civil War, Eurgeio Coselschi viciously rejected these notions: "Bolshevism is not *European* and neither is it *Asiatic*. It is outside of humanity, it is beneath the thought of man, of human civilization, of all the eternal and immutable laws of our life."[73] At about the same time, *Il Piccolo* warned that "the world all Red is all Russian."[74]

SOURCES OF INFORMATION: OFFICIAL, SEMI-OFFICIAL, AND PRIVATE CONTACTS

In the early 1930s many Italians—engineers, technicians, businessmen, merchant sailors, cultural exchange scholars and artists, and tourists—traveled surprisingly widely in the USSR, especially given the disrupted conditions of the early plan period and Soviet secretiveness. Clearly, the Kremlin was willing to suffer embarrassment at exposure of the harshness of Soviet life in order to appease a hoped-for ally against Germany and Japan.

These "civilian" travellers were an important source of information, and their publications helped to ground in some sort of reality Italian polemics about the nature of the bolshevik state.[75]

More importantly, Italian diplomats flooded the foreign ministry with detailed, graphic reports on the purges and trials, religious persecutions, economic inefficiencies, famines, troop disorders, catastrophic living standards, and, in fact, all aspects of Russian and nationality life in the Soviet Union.[76] Although they did not fail to praise Soviet successes, overall the picture they painted was appalling.[77]

Not only appalling, the picture also called into question the very security of the Soviet state. With collectivization, for example, the morale of the Red Army plummeted. As always, Italy's representatives were on top of the situation, or at least they were to the degree that any foreign observer could be. They rejected the notion that Marshal Voroshilov was behind the widespread unrest in the army. One Italian report described a party meeting at the end of February 1931:

[The] head of political education in the Red Army [supported by his predecessor], delivered a powerful speech declaring that the situation created as a consequence of the policy of "liquidating the kulaks" and of agricultural collectivisation to the bitter end, demanded by Stalin, had given rise to an incurable discontent amongst the soldiers—in large part the sons of peasants—who did not conceal their resentment of the Soviet Government. Thus either the system changed or they would no longer be able to count on the Red Army.[78]

Although Stalin had remained silent at that session, immediately afterward, he asked the Politburo to pronounce on these criticisms. Seven members voted against the dictator's policy, leaving only him and Molotov in favor. Apparently Stalin then asked for twenty-four hours in which to reach a decision, and during that time, without consulting his colleagues, he wrote his famous "Dizzy with Success" speech, which called a halt to forced collectivization.[79]

CONCLUSION

Despite acrimonious international differences erupting between Italy and the Soviet Union in the second half of the decade, for a long while many fascists did not change their deeply felt notion that the two states were not necessarily ideological enemies. In 1938, for example, at the height of the bitter Spanish Civil War that had split Europe into two contentious ideological camps, Mussolini had no problem in calling Stalin "a crypto-fascist."[80] Sergio Panunzio, in his important study of fascism published in a revised edition as late as 1939, argued once again that, although prewar socialism had been antinational, distributionistic, "proletarian," and anarchistic, the state system that had evolved under Stalin had taken on more and more fascist features: "Moscow bows before the light radiating from Rome. The Communist International no longer speaks to the spirit; it is dead."[81]

Clearly, many fascists, even to the eve of the Second World War, continued to stress the shared similarities between bolshevism and fascism, equally Marxist heresies. They saw both as developmental regimes bent on the modernization and industrialization of their respective national communities through analogous strategies and institutions. Nor were the fascists alone in their perceptions; these systemic similarities also impressed some communists as well as bourgeois commentators.

The quality of these fascist works on the USSR varied—often it was quite good, and these authors expressed a wide range of opinions. Italians understood quite well the purposes, methods, and consequences, both successful and brutal, of Soviet economic development under the first FYPs. With all this information available, Rome, when entering into any political-economic relationship with the Kremlin, had no excuse not to know the nature of the Soviet regime with all its faults as well as its virtues. And, again, its virtues, particularly the presumed convergence toward fascism, were substantial enough to have justified close cooperation for mutual advantage.

Nonetheless, despite all of the philosophical talk about convergence, the travails associated with the FYPs must have given Rome pause. Aside from the moral outrage that many in the more benign Italian authoritarianism felt, the working out of the Stalinist dictatorship seemed to indicate weakness, not strength and self-assurance. In its own struggle against Germany's advance in Austria and Southeast Europe in the 1930s, did Rome want—could it risk—close association and dependence on a self-flagellating power that might not be able to stand by its international obligations?

Until September 1935 and the beginning of the Italo-Abyssinian War, as will be shown, Mussolini seriously toyed with the idea. As it turned out, however, he decided in the end not to stand with the Soviet Union and collective security, but for practical rather than ideological reasons. First, Moscow supported the League-imposed sanctions directed against Italy during the Italo-Abyssinian War, and then Rome and the Kremlin turned the indigenously caused Spanish Civil War to their own international political purposes, using ideology as their cover.

The point is that the competing ideologies did not cause the breakdown in the good relations that had existed between Rome and Moscow from 1924 to the fall of 1935. Rather, ideology was the handmaiden to *Realpolitik*. It served to justify the political decisions already made for other reasons. In the early 1930s there was no clearly dominant view of the Soviets in Italy or within fascism. For Rome, no less than for Moscow, ideology after 1935 justified enmity; before then it had been equally adept at justifying amity.[82]

92 RUSSIA AND ITALY AGAINST HITLER

NOTES

1. Bastianini to Mussolini, 6/28/33: AP URSS b8 f3; Note, 6/30/33: AP URSS b10 f1.

2. See, e.g., Karl Radek's article in *Pravda*, June 10, 1933. See also ibid., June 9, 10, 1933; *Izvestia*, Mar. 21, Apr. 3, 5, May 31, June 6, 10, July 2, 1933.

3. See, e.g., Attolico to Rome, 3/29/34: AP URSS b13 f1, wherein the Italian ambassador to Moscow passed on rumors of the rise of fascist currents among the Soviet urban population.

4. Benito Mussolini, *Opera omnia di Benito Mussolini*, ed. Edoardo and Duilio Susmel, 36 vols. (Florence, 1951-63), 15: 178-81; 19: 195-96, 310; 20: 110, 127, 205; 26: 399-401.

5. Gaetano Carlo Salvemini, *Prelude to World War II* (Garden City, NJ, 1954), p. 62.

6. In 1936 Elie Halevy defined bolshevism as one form of "fascism." *The Era of Tyrannies*, trans. R.K. Webb, note by Fritz Stern (New York, 1966), pp. 282-84. Peter Ferdinand Drucker commented, "Russia has . . . been forced to adopt one purely totalitarian and fascist principle after the other." *The End of Economic Man: A Study of the New Totalitarianism*, introduction by H.N. Brailsford (New York, 1939), p. 246.

7. Louis Fischer, *The Life and Death of Stalin* (New York, 1952), p. 142.

8. Mussolini, *Opera*, 22: 83; Emil Ludwig, *Three Portraits: Hitler, Mussolini, Stalin* (New York, 1940), pp. 76-77; Clare Consuelo Sheridan, *My Crowded Sanctuary*, 2nd ed. (London, 1946), pp. 209-12; I. Phayre [W. V. Fitz-Gerald], "Mussolini," *Current History* (Jan. 1937): 81.

9. Anthony James Gregor, *Italian Fascism and Developmental Dictatorship* (Princeton, NJ, 1979), p. 123; see also his *Young Mussolini and the Intellectual Origins of Fascism* (Berkeley, 1979), p. xi. For much of the following discussion, I am indebted to Gregor's convincing analysis. Likewise, Renzo De Felice, *Fascism: An Informal Introduction to Its Theory and Practice* (New Brunswick, NJ, 1976), pp. 67-68, maintains that Mussolini's fascism shared considerable affinities with the traditional and revolutionary left. In a similar way Domenico Settembrini, "Mussolini and the Legacy of Revolutionary Socialism," *Journal of Contemporary History* 11 (1976): 239-68, persuasively outlines some of the similarities shared by Lenin and the young Mussolini—both products of the revolutionary socialist tradition.

10. Labriola, 1873-1959, sought solutions for the problems rising from industrialization. Rejecting the revisions that led many syndicalists to corporativism, he went into exile in France in 1927. Favoring Mussolini's aggressive foreign policy, he returned to Italy in 1935 during the war with Abyssinia, but he stayed out of fascist politics.

11. Croce, 1866–1952, was the most influential Italian philosopher of the twentieth century. After 1925 he took an antifascist stance. Pareto, 1848-1923, was an economist, sociologist, and political theorist. Much influenced by Maffeo Pantaleoni, his polemics against the liberal state influenced both the nationalists and the fascists.

12. Gregor, *Young Mussolini*, pp. 22, 44-45.

13. Olivetti, 1874-1931, was particularly influential as editor of *Pagine Libere* from 1906 to 1911 and from 1920 to 1922. Central to the revision of revolutionary synd-

icalism and originally skeptical about fascism, Olivetti became an active fascist only in 1924 in the hope of forcing fascism toward corporativism. Gregor, *Young Mussolini*, pp. 114-17, 222.

14. Balabanoff, 1869-1965, was born near Kiev but left Russia and her wealthy, Jewish, landowning family in 1898. In Italy she was by 1912 a member of the Socialist Party's executive committee, and in 1917 she joined the Bolshevik Party. An outspoken critic of both Mussolini and Stalin, she was exiled from Russia as well as Italy from 1921 to 1945.

15. Paolo Orano, *Il fascismo*, 2 vols. (Rome, 1939-40), 1: 26, 37. Orano, 1875-1945, also codirected *Pagine Libere* in 1907 and 1908. By 1938 he was leading the anti-Semitic campaign, and in 1943 he rallied to the Italian Social Republic. Panunzio, 1886-1944, after 1910, when it had become clear that revolutionary syndicalism was making little headway in Italy, spearheaded the revisionism that led many syndicalists through interventionism to corporativism. His mature vision was totalitarian and populist, and he gave Mussolini's dictatorship a veneer of revolutionary legitimacy. Panunzio actually saw his position as an extension of the Marxism to which he was dedicated. See Gregor, *Young Mussolini*, pp. 28, 50, 66, 73, 135, 138.

16. The socialist contributors included Angelo Tasca, Amadeo Bordiga, and Mario Missiroli; the syndicalists Labriola, Lanzillo, Panunzio, Georges Yvetot, and Enrico Leone also graced its pages.

17. Dinale, 1871-1958, wrote widely for socialist and syndicalist newspapers before the First World War. He worked with Mussolini before and after the war as a close friend and confidant. See Sergio Panunzio's articles in *Utopia*, "Il socialismo e la guerra," 2 (Aug.-Sept. 1914): 323-25 and "Il lato teorico e il lato pratico del socialismo," 2 (May 1914): 200-05. See also Ottavio Dinale, *Quarant'anni di colloqui con lui* (Milan, 1953), pp. 59-66, and Gregor, *Young Mussolini*, pp. 85, 118, 154-55, 162, 166-67, 176-77, 194, 197, 233.

18. Edmondo Rossoni, 1884–1965, was a leading exponent of fascist syndicalism. In 1913 he went to New York, where he published the interventionist paper *L'Italia Nostra*. He returned to Italy in 1916. Ultimately his conception of syndicalist unions lost out to Mussolini's concessions to industrialists. Gregor, *Young Mussolini*, pp. 194, 222-23.

19. Mussolini, *Opera*, 9: 74-78, 82-84, 109-12; 10: 20-22; 11: 44-47, 341-44; 13: 6-11, 77-79, 346-49; 14: 67-69; 15: 97-99; Gregor, *Italian Fascism*, pp. 122-23, 213-14.

20. Mussolini, *Opera*, 15: 91-94.

21. Vladimir Il'ich Lenin, *Collected Works*, 45 vols. (Moscow, 1960-70), 27: 118, 217; see also 27: 94-109, 147, 187-90, 209-18, and Gregor, *Italian Fascism*, pp. 124-25.

22. Mussolini, *Opera*, 20: 110; 15: 123-25; 21: 317-19; 25: 134-36; 26: 84; Dinale, *Quarant'anni*, pp. 331-32; Nino d'Aroma, *Mussolini secreto* (Bologna, 1958), pp. 63-64.

23. Benito Mussolini, *Mussolini corrispondenza inedita*, ed. Duilio Susmel (Milan, 1972), p. 70; Denis Mack Smith, *Mussolini: A Biography* (New York, 1982), pp. 126, 135, 171.

24. Guido Nozzoli, *I ras del Regime: Gli uomini che disfecero gli italiani* (Milan, 1972), pp. 166-85, esp. p. 169; Dino Grandi, *Giovani* (Bologna, 1941), pp. 37-43, 85-86, 94-96, 219-20, 223-28; Gregor, *Italian Fascism*, pp. 121-23; Anthony James

Gregor, *The Fascist Persuasion in Radical Politics* (Princeton, NJ, 1974), pp. 177, 230-31, 237, 267.

25. Torquato Nanni, *Bolscevismo e fascismo al lume della critica marxista Benito Mussolini* (Bologna, 1924), esp. pp. 229-35, 277-78; Gregor, *Italian Fascism*, pp. 92, 94-95, 170. Other leftists by the mid-1920s were remarking on the shared attributes characterizing the two revolutionary regimes. See Giuseppe Prezzolini, "Ideologia e sentimento," and Rodolfo Mondolfo, "Il fascismo in Italia," in Renzo De Felice, *Il fascismo e i partiti politici Italiani: Testimonianze del 1921–1923* (Rocca San Casciano, 1966), pp. 522-23, 527-50, and esp. pp. 545-50. See also Roberto Michels, *Lavoro e razza* (Milan, 1924). Michels, 1876-1936, foresaw the unavoidable domination by party organization over membership. Increasingly pessimistic over the possibilities for genuine democracy, he eventually settled for fascism as both authoritarian and based on broad appeal.

26. Leon Trotsky, *The Revolution Betrayed: What Is the Soviet Union and Where Is It Going?* (New York, 1937, 1965), pp. 278-79. See Robert S. Wistrich, "Leon Trotsky's Theory of Fascism," *Journal of Contemporary History* 11 (1976): 157-84.

27. Bruno Rizzi, *La lezione dello Stalinismo* (Rome, 1962), p. 38. Stalinism and fascism expressed the "same historical forces" (pp. 46, 95f). Rizzi had dropped out of the Italian Communist Party soon after its founding in 1921. Although long loyal to Stalin, by 1939 he was veering toward Trotskyism. For more Marxist interpretations of fascism, see John M. Cammett, "Communist Theories of Fascism, 1920–1935," *Science and Society* 31 (1967): 149-63. According to him, Marxists saw fascism in four major ways: a reactionary movement of the industrial bourgeoisie and the great landowners, an expression of twentieth-century imperialism, an essentially petty-bourgeois movement in its origins, and an irrational movement expressing a crisis in Western civilization.

28. Bruno Rizzi, *The Bureaucratization of the World*, trans. and with an introduction by Adam Westoby (New York, 1939). For a brief description of later Soviet opinions, plus "unorthodox" Marxist interpretations, which stress the developmental heart of fascism and hence its similarity to bolshevism, see Anthony James Gregor, "Fascism and Modernization: Some Addenda," *World Politics* (Apr. 1974): 379-83.

29. Sergio Panunzio, *Lo stato fascista* (Bologna, 1925), pp. 145-49. Giovanni Gentile, the idealist philosopher and an author of fascism's official ideology, acknowledged his intellectual debt to Marx. Anthony James Gregor, "Classical Marxism and the Totalitarian Ethic," *Journal of Value Inquiry* 2 (Spring 1968): 69-72.

30. Gregor, *The Fascist Persuasion*, pp. 183-86; Gregor, *Italian Fascism*, pp. 167-70.

31. See, in addition, Concetto Pettinato, *L'ora rossa* (Bologna, 1920), which covers the Red revolution in Hungary.

32. See Philip V. Cannistraro and Edward D. Wynot, Jr., "On the Dynamics of Anti-Communism as a Function of Fascist Foreign Policy, 1933–1943," *Il Politico* 38 (1973): 645-81.

33. Eugenio Anagnine, "I conflitti spirituali nella Russia moderna," *Critica Fascista* (Feb. 15, 1927): 70-71; (Mar. 15, 1927): 106-07; and (Apr. 1, 1927): 131-32; Angelo Oliviero Olivetti, "A proposito di neoplatonismo bolscevico," ibid. (Dec. 1, 1928): 452-53.

34. Aurelio Palmieri, *La geografia politica della Russia sovietista* (Rome, 1926);

Scytha, "L'Ucraina contro Mosca," *Nuova Antologia* (Feb. 1, 1933): 435-42; Umberto Nani, "Paneuropa," *Critica Fascista* (Sept. 15, 1929): 355-57.

35. Enrico Massis, "La verità sulla Russia dei sovieti," *Critica Fascista*, (Dec. 15, 1926): 462-64; Michele Pirone, "Nel decimo anno della rivoluzione russa," ibid. (Feb. 1, 1927): 48-50; H. Van Leisen, "La difesa dell'occidente," ibid., (Jan. 15, 1926): 30-31. See also Aurelio Palmieri, "La politica asiatica del bolscevismo russo," *Oriente Moderno* 2 (June 1922): 1-8.

36. Erminio Mariani, "La recente crisi del partito comunista russo," *Critica Fascista* (Oct. 1, 1925): 364–66; Ugo Barni, "Trotzki e il bolscevismo," ibid. (June 15, 1930): 228-29.

37. Giordano Bruno Guerri, *Giuseppe Bottai, un fascista critico: Ideologia e azione del gerarca che avrebbe voluto portare l'intelligenza nel fascismo e il fascismo alla liberalizzazione*, preface by Ugoberto Alfassio Grimaldi (Milan, 1976), p. 257. Bottai, 1895-1959, ultimately joined the plot that overthrew Mussolini in 1943.

38. Giuseppe Bottai, "L'essenza ideale del fascismo," *Critica Fascista* (June 1, 1925): 210-11.

39. Bruno Spampanato, "Equazioni rivoluzionarie: Dal bolscevismo al fascismo," ibid. (Apr. 15, 1930): 152.

40. Ibid. pp. 152-53.

41. Ibid. pp. 153-54.

42. Sergio Panunzio, "La fine di un regno," ibid. (Sept. 15, 1931): 342-44.

43. Riccardo Fiorini, "A proposito dell'antitesi Roma o Mosca," ibid. (Oct. 15, 1931): 383-85. Fiorini also was replying to Ernesto Brunetta's article described below in note 47. He denied the contention therein of communism as the direct transition to state capitalism. Luciano Ingianni, in "La rivoluzione fascista: Lo spirito e gli interessi," ibid. (Oct. 15, 1931): 381-83, also criticized Panunzio's article, although he discussed more the nature of fascist Italy than that of communist Russia.

44. Ibid p. 385.

45. Mario Rivoire, "Affinità ed antitesi fra Roma e Mosca," ibid. (Nov. 1, 1931): 413-14.

46. Ibid. p. 414. The French press picked up this sort of argument. One article claimed that the fascist revolution had been the product of ex-socialists, who now wished to end the struggle between classes through the establishment of the Corporate State. Stefani to MAE, 8/31/33: AP URSS b10 f1.

47. Ernesto Brunetta, "Influenze di Mosca," *Critica Fascista* (Sept. 15, 1931): 352-53. The level of his argument can be gauged easily: "The phenomenon of feminism and also of feminist Russian nihilism, found their origin in that the Russian woman never had a sense of family." (p. 252). For more on feminism and related issues, see Mario Parodi, *Il bolscevismo si confessa* (Milan, 1943), pp. 9-108, and Tomaso Napolitano, *Le metamorfosi del bolscevismo* (Milan, 1940), chapt. 1.

48. Alberto Luchini, "Una discussione: Roma o Mosca? Obiezioni al neo-moscovitismo (Lettera a Bottai sulla moscofilia)," *Critica Fascista* (Nov. 15, 1931): 432-34.

49. Bruno Spampanato, "Universalità di ottobre: Roma e Mosca o la vecchia Europa?," ibid. (Nov. 15, 1931): 434-36.

50. Luciano Ingianni, "Roma e Mosca: Nettissima antitesi," ibid. (Dec. 1, 1931): 455-57.

51. Ibid.; Armando Tosti, "L'abisso," ibid. (Dec. 1, 1931): 457–59. Tosti approached the problem from the direction of Sorelian myths. For a later echo of this

debate, see Giuseppe Lombrassa, "I giovani nella Russia sovietica," ibid. (Feb. 1, 1934): 59-60. To resolve the contradictions in Soviet life, Russia must give up its slavophile messianism for the "Nation," the only real existence. Giuseppe Lombrassa, "L'equivoco russo," ibid. (Oct. 1, 1932): 375-77.

52. Bruno Spampanato, "Universalità di ottobre: Ottobre, principio del secolo," ibid. (Feb. 1, 1932): 54; see pp. 54-56 and Bruno Spampanato, "Universalità di ottobre: Dove arriva lo Stato," ibid. (Jan. 1, 1932): 16-19.

53. Agostino Nasti, "L'Italia, il bolscevismo, la Russia," ibid. (Mar. 15, 1937): 162-63.

54. F.M. Pacces in "Antibolscevismo e antibolscevismi vari," ibid. (July 1, 1937): 289, used the phrase.

55. Tomaso Napolitano, "Il 'fascismo' di Stalin," ibid. (July 15, 1937): 317-19. See also Bruno Ricci, "Quelli che si meravigliano," ibid., p. 319.

56. Tomaso Napolitano, "Il 'fascismo' di Stalin ovvero l'U.R.S.S. e noi," ibid. (Oct. 1, 1937): 397.

57. Tomaso Napolitano, *Maternità e infanzia nell'U.R.S.S. (Saggio di politica sociale)* (Florence, 1938), from the foreword.

58. See Gregor, *Italian Fascism*, pp. 170-71. In the second half of the decade, Napolitano ran "Radio Moscow," a highly successful black propaganda operation, which posed as the radio voice of an opposition group inside the USSR sufficiently well to fool the Soviets into believing that the broadcasts came from within their territory. Cannistraro and Wynot, "Dynamics," pp. 665-68, 675. Mirko Ardemagni, "Deviazioni Russe verso il fascismo," *Gerarchia* 15 (July 1934): 571-72, rejoiced that the Soviets had foresworn their internationalism and "Trotskyist idealism" for "Stalinist realism"; they were "embracing the nationalist conception" and fascism. *Gerarchia*, which had been founded by Mussolini, was an authoritative journal of revolutionary fascist thought.

59. Gaetano Ciocca, *Giudizio sul Bolscevismo (Con il tavole fuori testo)* (Milan, 1933); see esp. pp. 265-70 on those differences. The plant's construction had begun in March 1931.

60. Mussolini, *Opera*, 26: 57-58.

61. *Pravda*, Oct. 30, 1933.

62. Berardis to Rome, 11/7/33: AP URSS b10 f1.

63. *Izvestia*, Nov. 1, 1933.

64. Ibid., Nov. 2, 1933. Lazar Moiseevich Kaganovich, an early Stalin supporter and active in the collectivization and industrialization drives, headed the fuel industry from 1934 to 1941. Grigorii Konstantinovich Ordzhonikidze, the people's commissar of heavy industry, committed suicide in 1937, evidently out of despair over Stalin's purges.

65. Berardis to Rome, 11/7/33; Marocco to Berardis, 11/3/33; Attolico to Rome, 1/3/34: AP URSS b10 f1. Berardis hypothesized that trade representative Mikhail Levenson had written the *Pravda* article.

66. Suvich memorandum, 11/6/33: AP URSS b8 f4; Quaroni to Suvich, 11/10/33: AP URSS b10 f1.

67. *Pravda*, Jan. 26, 1934; Attolico to Rome, 1/26/34: AP URSS b14 f1. As if to reassure its readers about Italian awe at the successes of the FYP, *Pravda* and *Izvestia* on Jan. 17, 1934 commented on articles from the Italian papers praising Soviet economic development. Attolico to Rome, 1/25/34: AP URSS b15 f2.

68. Mussolini, *Opera*, 26: 84; Renzo Bertoni, *Russia: Trionfo del Fascismo*, 2nd ed. (Milan, 1937). For more on the First FYP, the transition to the Second, and the chaos and repression involved, see Rodolfo Mosca, *Russia, 1932: Verso il secondo piano quinquennale* (Milan, 1932); Eugenio Anagnine, "Caos russo," *Critica Fascista* (July 15, 1930): 272-73; Mario Da Silva, "Il piano quinquennale," ibid. (July 1, 1931): 252-53; Luigi Chiarini, "L'economia agricola e industriale nell'U.R.S.S.," ibid., (May 1, 1930): 172-73; Enrico Emanuelli, "Una ragazza russa," *Nuova Antologia* (Apr. 1, 1934): 367-73; and Giuseppe Gregoraci, *Riuscirà la Russia?* preface by Virginio Gayda (Rome, 1932), which also includes a brief discussion of the chances of Moscow moving toward Fascism; see pp. 123ff.

69. "Bertoni, *Russia*, pp. 5, 6, 9, 184, 220, chapt. 10. While Bertoni portrayed the FYP experience accurately enough, he also copiously quoted the Duce to meet every contingency and often descended into childish, naïve propaganda to console the Italian working man who might be looking with interest toward the USSR. Also see Amor Bavaj, *Il principio rappresentativo nello stato sovietico*, preface by Sergio Panunzio (Rome, 1933). Bavaj was sure that the individual was irrelevant to the despotic Soviet state; he was but "a molecule, morally, spiritually, juridically irrelevant," pp. 134, 217. Panunzio in his preface described the Soviet state as "dictatorship *over* the proletariat, and not *of* the proletariat," p. ix.

70. Mussolini, *Opera*, 26: 84.

71. Rodolfo Mosca, "La crisi in Estremo Oriente: Questioni preliminari," *Rassegna di Politica Internazionale* (Mar. 1934): 33-40.

72. Ottavio Dinale, *Tempo di Mussolini* (Milan, 1934), p. 164; see also pp. 164-70.

73. Eurgeio Coselschi, *Tre bandiere sul mondo* (Florence, 1938), p. 90. This strident polemic argued that Soviet barbarism hungered for war; see, e.g., p. 19.

74. *Il Piccolo*, Jan. 23-24, 1937. Once back in Rome, the former Consul General at Odessa, Barduzzi, wrote a series of personal letters in January 1937 to Foreign Minister Galeazzo Ciano describing his three-year stint in the USSR. A compelling mixture of acute observation and patent nonsense, the latter presumably encouraged by Italy's increasing cooperation with the Nazis in Spain, Barduzzi painted in broad strokes a picture of the political, cultural, and economic life in the Soviet Union. Barduzzi rejected *Il Piccolo*'s notion that bolshevism was panslavism. Rather, it equaled Judaism: "Rome and Moscow. . . . Romanism against Judaism. Europe against Africa." Barduzzi to Ciano, 1/26/37: AP URSS b21 f5. Barduzzi had long complained about Soviet efforts to propagandize the many Italians, such as merchant seamen, moving through Odessa and other Black Sea ports.

75. Adriano Lualdi, "Viaggio musicale nell'U.R.S.S.," *Nuova Antologia* (Oct. 1, 1933): 357-88; (Oct. 16, 1933): 541-651; (Nov. 1, 1933): 57-86. In the spring and summer of 1934 Corrado Alvaro visited European Russia and wrote a series of articles for *La Stampa* in 1935. Entitled "I maestri del diluvio," these articles were reprinted in *Viaggio in Russia* (Florence, 1943).

76. The reportage from the embassy and consulates was quite good despite the limitations placed on all foreign representatives residing in the USSR. This was especially true in the early 1930s, when the Kremlin was trying to find points of cooperation with the Royal Kingdom and allowed Italians a remarkable degree of access to large areas of the country and showed special favor to the Italian ambassador, Bernardo Attolico. For a translation of some of these reports, see *Investigation of*

the Ukrainian Famine, 1932-1933 (Washington, DC, 1988), pp. 395-506. Foreign representatives in the USSR, more than in other countries, had to rely on the state-controlled press for their sources. It was all but impossible to form personal relationships with Soviet officials. Thus the whole information- gathering system became quite incestuous in that the representatives from the various states accredited to the Soviet Union found in one another important sources of information. How much was reported back to the various capitals that was nothing more than wild, unsubstantiated gossip gleaned over drinks with other equally ignorant and drunken foreigners!

77. For those who wished to be reassured about the stability of the Soviet regime for the sake of Italy's diplomacy, occasionally this sad litany was broken. Attolico, e.g., characterized Stalin's speech of Feb. 1934 as foreswearing the "myth" of the world revolution and concentrating on normalization of relations with capitalist states. Although Attolico recognized that definitive answers were impossible, he believed that Soviet life was tending to normalize and stabilize, responding to the old Russian national spirit; the regime had closed its revolutionary phase of destruction. Attolico to Rome, 2/24/34: AP URSS b13 f8.

78. Jonathan Haslam, Soviet Foreign Policy, 1930-33: The Impact of the Depression (New York: 1983), p. 122.

79. Ibid.

80. Mussolini, Opera, 29: 63.

81. Sergio Panunzio, Teoria generale dello stato fascista, 2nd ed. (Padua, 1939), pp. 9-10; see pp. 4-10.

82. The Soviet-German alliance of August 23, 1939, encouraged some in Italy to continue their investigations of the Soviet state and society. See, e.g., Guido Manacorda, Il bolscevismo: Marxismo-mistica-meccanesimo-ateismo-morale-politica-economia-letteratura e arte-scuola e propaganda, 3rd ed., rev., enl., updated, (Florence, 1940).

5

Economic
Rapprochement

Beyond the morass of ideological nuance, the leaders in Rome and Moscow
had more concrete foundations on which to build their cooperation. Since
1921 Italy and the USSR had established a symbiotic commercial relationship. Basically, Italy exchanged finished industrial goods and machinery for
Russia's natural resources. Nor did their goods compete in foreign markets.
Moscow, appreciating this nexus, pushed the political dimension of economic
relations.

INSTITUTIONAL CONVERGENCE

During the depression, much of the world experienced increasingly large-
scale organizational and monopolistic control of national economies, consciously reinforced by government policy. Motives differed, but dissatisfaction with the workings of democratic institutions in critical emergencies grew
in many countries. Resentments against international financial commitments, widespread even before the Great Depression, crystallized into economic nationalism in the 1930s. These autarchic tendencies encouraged
attempts at balancing trade bilaterally rather than at finding an overall trade
balance. Multilateral international trade suffered.

The Soviet and Italian economic organizations similarly called for more
national regulation. Production controls, including those directed toward
capital costs, profits, and wages, inevitably were bound up with trade reg-
ulations and credit policy. Trade unions in both ideocracies became part of
the state machinery and acted only within the framework of new institutions
resting on the foundations of the corporative cooperation of workers, em-

ployers, and state in Italy, or on the socialist cooperation of party and state in the Soviet Union.[1]

The composition of international trade was changing by the end of 1933. Complications from regional and preferential agreements and the greatly increased tendency toward protection of national markets caused a decline in trade turnover for manufactured articles and foodstuffs for manufacture. Public officials everywhere desperately tried to improve their gold and foreign currency reserves. The Soviets, for example, sold gold bonds in the United States. Increased tariff protection and currency depreciation in many industrial countries, combined with the increasing restrictions on comestibles exports, checked increased imports from the industrial countries. Efforts to balance trade bilaterally hurt the exchange of manufactured goods between the industrial countries.[2]

The Soviet state monopoly in foreign trade paid little attention to prices but concerned itself with achieving a foreign payments balance.[3] With the onset of the Great Depression, the USSR had to export more, especially foodstuffs, to receive the same volume of imports, and by 1932 its total trade turnover had declined by over 50 percent. Continued low prices on the world market for raw materials and foodstuffs, the main classes of its exports, curtailed both export and import operations. Exports declined in quantity by less than 1 percent from 1932 to 1933; imports, on the other hand, dropped by 47 percent.[4] Principal Soviet exports included raw materials, foodstuffs, various consumption goods, lumber, oil, grain, silver, furs, cloth, hemp, and flax. Principal imports included machinery and equipment, ferrous and nonferrous metals and their products, crude rubber, sheep wool, and live animals.

By 1933 Moscow realized that it would be better to limit imports to the value of exports that could be spared. A more rapid decline in the volume of exports probably would have occurred, except that the government had to find foreign exchange to meet maturing liabilities due from previous imports.[5] The Soviets, nonetheless, had ambitious import pretensions. At the World Economic Conference in London in mid–1933, Litvinov declared that his government was prepared to place abroad one billion dollars in orders, about $400 million of which would be for machinery, $50 million for ships (mostly for fishing, seal hunting, and dredging), and $200 million for ferrous metals.[6]

Defense considerations began to impinge on Soviet economic policy to a greater extent than at any time since the end of the Allied Intervention in Russia following World War I. Trade questions seemed less decisive than political issues, especially because the Second FYP projected fewer imports and credits than had the First. Between 1933 and 1937 a favorable trade balance and increased gold production meant that the Soviets could purchase basic imports without undue difficulty.[7]

THE ITALO-SOVIET ECONOMIC AGREEMENT, MAY 6, 1933

Faced with a decidedly unfavorable trade balance, Italy's businessmen had not found the trading arrangements of 1930 and 1931 to their liking. While the Soviets obtained Italian goods on long-term credits, Italians had to pay cash for Soviet products. The Kremlin countered that its purchases in Italy had increased since 1930; further, it had chartered a number of Italian ships. Protecting their fourth largest export market (behind only Britain, Germany, and Mongolia), the Soviets had increased their purchases to retain their hold on the Italian import market for oil, coal, manganese, and iron ore.

The Economic Negotiations

In March 1932, a Soviet delegation began negotiations in Italy for a new economic accord. The discussions made little headway, largely because Moscow had requested that credits be extended beyond the established maximum of 54 months. In the semiofficial daily, *Giornale d'Italia*, Virginio Gayda demanded immediate payment and suggested that Moscow deposit gold to guarantee new commercial obligations.[8] Moscow, however, reiterated its inability to pay without credits: growing debts, which had reached 306 million rubles in 1931, meant that it had to restrict imports or be granted long-term credits.[9]

Professing a desire to negotiate new arrangements to increase economic exchanges, at the start of 1933 Italy denounced its commercial, navigation, and customs conventions with the USSR.[10] Referring to the Soviets' refusal to accept Italian proposals, Mussolini wrote the plenipotentiary, Potemkin, that the situation resembled that of March and April 1932, when an agreement also had seemed impossible; a solution had been found then, and he was sure that another could be found again, preferably as soon as possible.[11]

The Kremlin at first did not react publicly to the Duce's ploy. For example, Molotov did not mention it in his January 24 speech running down, country by country, Soviet relations with the outside world. The Kremlin's functionaries, however, complained privately that the denunciation was inadvisable.[12] The Italian move stirred little excitement elsewhere because Europe was preparing for the World Economic Conference, and the most practical way of putting one's delegates in a favorable bargaining position was to clear the decks of encumbering ties.[13]

Potemkin, at last, officially responded on January 28, writing Mussolini that his government regretted the denunciation prior to the conclusion of negotiations.[14] Moscow, too, wanted improved trade relations, and he proposed a new agreement based on most-favored-nation reciprocity.

In the unsettled international situation marked by increasing German animosity toward the USSR and the death of the Disarmament Conference, Moscow was ready to respond to any Italian move toward rapprochement—so Aloisi concluded from his February 22 colloquy with Litvinov.[15] In answer, Mussolini telegraphed Attolico that Italy had always distinguished between the struggle against the Comintern and friendly ties with the Soviet government.[16] He advised his ambassador not to show alarm at Franco-Soviet intimacy and not to be drawn into Soviet advances for a nonaggression pact, because the Soviets for the moment had a strong political position, and therefore a pact with Italy could have only a secondary importance for them. To agree to it would be seen as a naïve attempt to block the French blow; nor was the time yet ripe to conclude an economic accord.

On March 7, Aloisi spoke with Potemkin. Upset at Berlin's provocations, the Soviet plenipotentiary conceded that France was trying to isolate Moscow and to sow discord between the USSR and Germany, as well as between the USSR and Italy. Alarmed at Italian press attacks,[17] Potemkin asked if Italy was changing its policy. Following Mussolini's orders, Aloisi replied that Rome was not attacking the Soviet government but rather the Third International, the seat of the world communist revolution. That brazen Soviet policy of "dual diplomacy," conducted by the regular NKID establishment on the one hand and the unique Comintern establishment on the other, had given Soviet diplomacy enormous flexibility in the 1920s and 1930s. But it had an unpleasant reverse side. Throwing Soviet cleverness back into their faces, Aloisi unctuously maintained that the Kremlin ought not to be upset, because many times it had declared that it had nothing to do with the International. He smugly noted that Potemkin "had no retort."[18]

That same day Attolico spoke with Litvinov about the USSR's attitude toward the League.[19] The commissar explained that, although he did not want to change policy toward Germany, he remained skeptical about Hitler and his ability to master the difficult situation in Germany. Litvinov then laughed, "Hitler is not Mussolini." Attolico insisted to Rome that for the Soviets, successful economic negotiations depended upon improved political relations.[20] Although skeptical that commercial negotiations could find success, he advised that it was not the time to estrange Moscow.

In reply, Rome told Attolico that it was advising Berlin to "cure" its relations with Moscow by strictly distinguishing between the Kremlin and the Comintern, between the fight against domestic communism and friendship with Moscow.[21] Sanguine about the threat of a serious Franco-Soviet rapprochement, Rome again advised Attolico not to show alarm, but rather to be satisfied with Litvinov's assurances. For the moment Rome would remain cool toward Soviet advances for a nonaggression pact, particularly because it still would be of only secondary importance for Moscow. Finally, given Soviet hopes for the French market, it was still not a good time for

Italy to conclude a trade agreement with the USSR. Options must be kept open.

Italy's coolness disappointed the Kremlin. The deputy people's commissar for foreign affairs, Krestinskii, instructed Potemkin to express regret at the absence of progress in the commercial negotiations with the Italians and to emphasize the absence of Italian concessions as the cause:

Point out that we long ago met the Italian representative halfway on the three main questions of interest to him, to wit: on the questions of equality of [trade] balances, on shortening the term of credit, and on the deconsolidation of customs duties. The Italians have met us halfway on not one question. They are making entirely new demands and in general have not shown an inclination to come to agreement.[22]

Krestinskii also confirmed the Kremlin's earlier instructions to demand from the Italian government equality in trading arrangements.[23] Potemkin a week later informed the NKID that the Italians had made some concessions, although they continued to make unacceptable demands, such as giving Italy the same trade and customs preferences that the Soviets might grant to the Baltic states and their contiguous countries in Asia.[24]

In March and April, Moscow appeared especially upset at recent Anglo-Italian conversations in Rome. The Soviet press attacked British trade policies and the alleged spies lurking in British concerns in the USSR, and it unfavorably compared Britain with Italy, which had accepted the Soviet government's trade monopoly.[25]

In this context Potemkin challenged Suvich about Italy's policy.[26] The gallimaufry of topics covered typified Moscow's tendency to link political issues to economic negotiations. Potemkin first inquired if London had discussed Soviet admission into the League of Nations and asked what the Italian position was. Suvich replied that nothing specific had been said in the Rome conversations about Soviet Russia. Potemkin promised that if Germany's betrayal of Rapallo continued, the USSR would have to change radically its relations with Berlin, which would greatly affect international politics. Pressed to intercede for the USSR in Berlin, Suvich lamely drew the distinction between Berlin's internal struggle against communism and its external policies, and unctuously continued that as far as he knew, Soviet-German relations were in no danger. Potemkin finally expressed his fear that the current economic negotiations were dying. His government, he said, already had made many concessions in the face of Italy's intransigence and could make no more. Suvich replied that Rome also wanted amicable relations.[27]

On April 5, Potemkin told Suvich that the economic negotiations were far advanced because of Soviet concessions, to which Suvich replied that the concessions had been reciprocal.[28] The only major difficulty remaining concerned the exceptions to most-favored-nation status, which the USSR had received in its treaties with Germany and Britain and in the 1924 agreement with Italy. These included the countries that had been part of the Russian Empire (Estonia, Latvia, and Lithuania) and those lying along its Asiatic border (Persia and Turkey). Potemkin asked Suvich to remove this obstacle to an economic agreement, which, he said, would have political repercussions as well.

The problem was Turkey. Rome was not particularly concerned about the practical implications of the Soviet request; after all, Soviet and Italian exports to Turkey did not compete. To ease the other, the more serious question of principle, the Soviets recognized the need for reciprocity and offered to make similar exclusions in some Central European countries for Italy. Suvich promised that Italy would work to come to an agreement. Potemkin, turning up the pressure, added that Germany had made concessions on credits for a term of forty-five months.[29]

Moscow negotiated not only in secluded diplomatic chambers but in the public arena as well. *Izvestia* declared that Italy's financial situation had been hurt by the American dollar's devaluation.[30] The next day, Foreign Trade Commissar Rosengolts reminded *Izvestia*'s readers that Italy had a way out—commercial relations, after all, had developed to the symbiotic advantage of both Rome and Moscow.[31]

In the spring of 1933 Moscow was particularly eager to improve its relations with Rome, the source of the proposed four-power pact, especially to counterbalance its deteriorating relations with Britain and Germany. Tangible signs of those poor relations were the arrests of Soviet citizens in Germany and the Metro-Vicker's trial of British engineers in Moscow.

In this light, the Kremlin was especially concerned about the Borev case, which involved the arrests in Italy in March of a member of Petrolea (part of the Soviet commercial delegation in Milan), his wife, and several Italians for military espionage.[32] Although there was apparently sufficient proof against him and the Soviet legation, the Soviet embassy asked that the detentions be kept secret and that the Borevs be released to its care, just as Moscow had done for the arrested British engineers. Rome, hoping to confirm its friendship, suspended the prosecution and set the Borevs free, subject to their immediate departure from Italy. On May 6, Potemkin thanked Suvich for this solution to the case.[33]

The Economic Accords Concluded

Those thanks were in order. Capping the negotiations of the last several months, Mussolini and the foreign trade representative, Levenson, met in the Palazzo Venezia that same day to sign a customs convention, which substituted for the 1924 agreement.[34] It granted reciprocal most-favored-nation status to most imports. This status did not apply to: privileges granted to facilitate traffic in frontier districts to a depth of 15 km on either side of the border; obligations assumed under a customs union; preferential treatment Italy might grant its colonies, protectorates, and possessions; privileges the USSR might grant to Latvia, Estonia, Lithuania, Persia, Afghanistan, and Mongolia; or privileges granted to China and Turkey to facilitate frontier traffic. Internal taxes on products originating in the other state would not be any more burdensome than those on native products.

Italy was to export manufactures such as motor cars and electrical equipment and to import wheat, timber, metals, and other raw materials. Along the lines already laid down in the accords of 1930 and 1931, the Italian government guaranteed to Italian exporters 75 percent of the value, up to 200 million lire annually (down from 350 million), of Soviet orders placed in Italy. The Soviets pledged to shorten the maturity dates, and the term for most products became twenty-seven months.[35]

At the signing Potemkin thanked the Duce for his active support during the negotiations, and the two exchanged wishes for the successful conclusion of further talks.[36] The Ministry of Corporations gave the Soviet delegation a banquet, and Potemkin hopefully believed that friendly commercial relations could grow between the two nations.

The Soviet press quickly published news of the signing. For *Izvestia*, in the depressed world economy the pact signified "a great success for the realistic policies of two states."[37] Differences in social-political systems did not have to obstruct the development of economic relations between capitalist countries and the USSR. The paper rejoiced at the constant improvement and symbiosis of economic relations since 1924: "It is enough to point out that the share of the USSR in Italian imports has grown from 1.6 percent in 1929 to 4.2 percent in 1932. The share of the USSR in Italian exports has grown from 0.46 percent in 1929 to 4.8 percent in 1932." Italy for a long time had been the USSR's "most important and regular supplier" of electrical materials, ships, ball bearings, and so forth; the Italian merchant marine dominated the carrying trade of Soviet goods, with the Soviets chartering "a total tonnage of 1,500,000 in 1932"; and Italian technicians had created a bond between Soviet and Italian industry. *Izvestia* predicted that the accords would beneficially affect Soviet exports and increase Soviet orders in Italy. The pact, in general, demonstrated the stupidity of trying to organize an economic bloc or a military front against the USSR. The Soviet Union, the paper assured its readers, was becoming ever more important in international relations.[38]

Potemkin happily told Suvich at the end of the month that relations were good from all points of view, and he contrasted them with Moscow's perturbations with Germany. The Kremlin hoped that the friendship would be "continuous," not "episodic." Suvich replied that Italy, too, wanted such ties.[39]

Table 1
Flag Carriers at Novorossiisk in 1933

Country		Import Tonnage	Export Tonnage
Italy	127	1,145	330,581
Greece	106		
USSR	103		
Great Britain	48		
Norway	18		
France	14		
Germany	14		
Totals	447	45,706	1,439,385

Source: Barduzzi to Rome, 5/18/35: AP URSS b18 f8.

Table 2
The Italian Flag in the Port of Novorossiisk in 1934

Number of Ships Arriving, 89 with total of 205,263 tons		
Goods Loaded	**Total**	**Total Bound for Italy**
petroleum products	23,753 tons	23,753 tons
cereals	60,160 "	21,330 "
cement	4,830 "	4,230 "
asbestos	1,921 "	1,921 "
sulphur	1,730 "	1,730 "
flour	865 "	638 "
chrome	510 "	510 "
minerals	500 "	500 "
cast iron	493 "	493 "
turpentine	387 "	289 "
lentils	150 "	150 "
paraffin	177 "	101 "
soda	104 "	20 "
sunflower	31,607 "	0 "
metals	9,480 "	0 "
cotton seeds	4,948 "	0 "
oats	520 "	0 "
magnesia	149 "	0 "
various goods	338 "	78 "
wood	8,991 cm	8,991 cm
Totals	142,622 tons	55,740 tons
	8,991 cm	8,991 cm

Source: Moscow embassy, Uff. Commerciale to Rome, 5/23/34: AP URSS b14 fl.

FIGURES FOR SELECTED SOVIET PORTS

At the port of Novorossiisk, in 1933 the Italian flag carriers were in first place in trade. Compared with the 1932 figures for the port, total trade had contracted by 5.3 percent for goods and 1.9 ercent for ships. Of Soviet exports

Table 3
The Italian Flag in the Port of Odessa in 1934

Number of Ships Arriving and Departing
  number loading 233, of which 83 were bound for Italy
  number unloading 203, of which 144 were from Itality
  Italian flag vessels, 54		

Goods Loaded	Total	Total bound for Italy
wood	4,888.0 cm	3,224.0 cm
kaolin & clay	4,347.0 tons	4,347.0 tons
cereals	36,347.0 "	2,137.0 "
cast iron	1,666.0 "	0.0 "
chemical products	1,677.0 "	1,073.0 "
flour and fodder	333.0 "	333.0 "
cocoons	41.0 "	41.0 "
machinery and		
various goods	16,994.0 "	106.0 "
Totals	4,888.0 cm	3,224.0 cm
	62,071.0 tons	8,037.0 tons
Goods Unloaded	Total	Total from Italy
tobacco	514.0 tons	0.0
ball bearings	90.0 "	90.0 tons
figs	55.0 "	0.0 "
citrus fruits	37.0 "	0.0 "
general food	30.0 "	25.0 "
new sacks	47.0 "	47.0 "
machinery	26.0 "	26.0 "
black coal	25.0 "	25.0 "
diverse essences	8.0 "	8.0 "
various goods	26.0 "	14.0 "
Totals	858.0 "	235.0 "

Source: Moscow embassy, Uff. Commerciale to Rome, 5/23/34/: AP URSS b14 fl.

carried in Italian bottoms, 53.6 percent was grains, 23.4 percent was mineral oils, and the rest was wood and various other goods. In 1933 from Novorossiisk, 90,685 tons of goods left for Italy and 240,189 tons to non-Italian ports. For 1934 the comparable figures were 60,236 tons (wood) and 86,881 tons, declines respectively of 30,449 tons and 153,308 tons. In 1933, Italian ships unloaded 1,145 tons of goods. The following year, they unloaded nothing. The Italian flag for a long while had been in first place in Novorossiisk; by 1934 the Greeks were in first position, at least in numbers if not in tons carried.

The royal consul general, Barduzzi, lamented that in 1934, only 54 Italian-flag ships called on Odessa compared to 65 in 1933, a decline of 11. In 1934 Italian ships loaded about 81,266 tons fewer than in 1933. In 1934, those same ships unloaded 21,720 tons compared to 51,405 in 1933, a decline of 30,315 tons. In 1934, 41 ships of the Lloyd Triestino Co. arrived in Odessa, compared to 42 in 1933. Of these, 11 fewer nonsubsidized ships arrived in

1934: 22 in 1933 and 11 in 1934. In 1934 the company loaded about 14,500 tons of goods (wood) compared to 22,766 in 1933, a decline of 8,266 tons. Barduzzi was unable to provide figures for Black Sea ports other than Odessa and Novorossiisk, but he believed that similar declines had occurred elsewhere, because Soviet exportation of cereals, petroleum, and wood had notably contracted. Further, the USSR, thanks to its purchases abroad of ships, had become more independent in maritime transportation.[40]

NOTES

1. Vera Micheles Dean, "Risks of Trade with Russia," *Current History* 38 (May 1933): 158–60; League of Nations, Economic Intelligence Service, *World Economic Survey, 1933–34* (Geneva, 1934), pp. 74, 182, 201.

2. *World Economic Survey*, pp. 192, 194; "Soviet Bonds Popular," *Business Week*, May 17, 1933, 23.

3. Leonard Egerton Hubbard, *Soviet Money and Finance* (London, 1936), pp. 166-70. By 1933 the ruble had at least three values. The one used to buy goods on the open market was worth very little, 450 to the lira. At the closed shops the ruble was worth about 20 to the lira, and the official rate was about 6.50 to the lira, down from 9.50 when, with the Great Depression, Britain had gone off the gold standard and the Soviet Union for external purposes had remained on. This figure was not intended to be anything but a coefficient for use in conjunction with gold ruble prices. At par, in 1933 the lira was worth 5.26 cents. "Russia Revisited—II," *Economist* 116 (June 10, 1933): 1234.

4. Foreign Trade in 1933," *Economic Review of the Soviet Union* 9 (Apr. 1934): 86.

5. Hubbard, *Soviet Money*, pp. 289-90.

6. "The Russian Market," *Business Week*, Sept., 23, 1933, 26; Peter Bolm, "The World Economic Conference," *Communist* 12 (July 1933): 621. Ambassador Attolico termed the proposal "amazing" and opined that, given the immense needs of the Soviet population, it should be higher. He nonetheless felt it was a bluff and a trial balloon directed at the United States. Attolico to Rome, 6/19/33: AP URSS b10 fl. For Litvinov's desire for French credits, see Attolico to Rome, 4/11/33: AP URSS b11 fl. By early August, Franco-Soviet commercial negotiations had stumbled on the problem of credits. At the same time, the Soviets were also dissatisfied with the progress of negotiations by their military attaché in Paris for establishing terms of military cooperation.

7. Max Beloff, *The Foreign Policy of Soviet Russia*, 2 vols. (London, 1947, 1949), 1: 93.

8. The proudly caustic Genevieve R. Tabouis in *They Call Me Cassandra* (New York, 1942), p. 250, skewered Gayda:

At first sight, Virginio Gayda seemed inoffensive enough—even fairly agreeable. It was only after one had talked with him for a while that one felt his bitterness, and his constant need for praise and admiration. . . . [He was] a really spiteful person consumed with jealousy for all those who might be more famous, or more intelligent than himself. He was a real Fascist in the petty sense of the word. . . . In St. Petersburg, where Gayda was staying when the war broke out in 1914, the brilliant diplomatic set gathered about the Court of the Czar snubbed the insignificant employee at the Italian Embassy, and, as a result, Gayda developed the "inferiority complex" which has never left him.

Tabouis, p. 251, also punned that he was nicknamed "the much-married Virgin" for the changes in direction his articles in the *Giornale d'Italia* took for the foreign ministry.

9. "Russian Orders," *Business Week*, Oct. 28, 1933, 9; "Rome to Moscow," ibid., Feb. 1, 1933, 24.

10. Suvich memorandum, 1/2/33; see Attolico to Rome, 1/31/33: AP URSS b8 fl.

11. Mussolini to Potemkin, 1/16/33: AP URSS b8 fl; *DVP* 16: pp. 66-67.

12. Attolico to Rome, 1/24/33, 1/31/33, "Molotov's Report on the International Situation of the USSR." n.d. Ambassador Dirksen, originally pleased at the speech, later grew discontented. Attolico to Rome, 1/31/33. For earlier speeches by Stalin and Molotov on the FYPs, see Attolico to Rome, 1/17/33: AP URSS b8 fl.

13. "Rome to Moscow," *Business Week*, Feb. 1, 1933, 24. See "Notes," *Annalist* 41 Feb. 17, 1933, 260.

14. Potemkin to Mussolini, 1/28/33: AP URSS b8 fl; *DVP* 16: no. 26.

15. Aloisi memorandum, 2/22/33: AP URSS b8 fl; *DVP* 16: n.129.

16. Rome to Attolico, 3/9/33; Rome circular, 3/10/33: AP URSS b8 fl.

17. See, e.g., *Giornale d' Italia*, Mar. 5, 1933.

18. Rome to Attolico, 3/7/33: AP URSS b8 f5; Aloisi memorandum, 3/7/33. Three weeks later the Soviets insisted that Potemkin's pass had been on his personal initiative. Attolico to Rome, 3/27/33: AP URSS b8 fl.

19. Attolico to Rome, 3/7/33: AP URSS b8 f2.

20. Rome circular, 3/10/33; DGAE to the Cabinet, 3/15/33: AP URSS b8 fl.

21. Rome circular, 3/10/33: AP URSS b8 fl.

22. *DVP* 16: no. 68.

23. Ibid., n.58.

24. Ibid., no. 79 and n.66.

25. *The Times* (London), Apr. 21, 1933.

26. Suvich memorandum, 3/23/33: AP URSS b8 fl.

27. Other issues covered included Potemkin's concern over a pair of articles in the Italian press, MacDonald's disarmament plan, and Göring's plan for a Franco-German treaty to be directed against the USSR. For Papen's suggestion to Premier Herriot for a united front against the USSR, see Rome circular, 4/12/33: AP URSS b9 f9.

28. Suvich memorandum, 4/5/33; Quaroni circular, 4/22/33: AP URSS b8 f5.

29. Mussolini simplistically explained to Cerruti that the Soviets resented German success in the struggle against communism and the Comintern. He held out hope, however, that Italy could mediate between Berlin and Moscow, even though the latter would badly interpret Rome's economic cooperation with the former. Rome to Cerruti, 4/9/33: AP URSS b8 f2.

30. *Izvestia*, Apr. 29, 1933.

31. Ibid., Apr. 30, 1933; Attolico to Rome, 5/3/33: AP URSS b11 fl; Frederico Curato, "Italia e Russia," *Rassegna di Politica Internazionale* (May 1934): 180.

32. Puppini, promemorial, 3/28/33: AP URSS b10 f10; Note for Suvich, 4/15/33: AP URSS b8 f2; Suvich memorandum, 5/6/33: AP URSS b8 f5.

33. Italy's representatives closely watched the Metro-Vickers affair, see, e.g., AP

URSS b9 f2. There was more Soviet espionage in Italy. Ivan Markov of Petrolea, an agent of Soviet military intelligence, was put under surveillance. Rome to Attolico, 5/20/33; Servizio Corrispondenza, Uff. 3, to Buffarini Guidi, 6/7/34: AP URSS b10 f13. Viktor Suvorov [pseud.], *Aquarium: The Career and Defection of a Soviet Military Spy*, trans. David Floyd (London, 1985), p. 293, notes that Soviet military intelligence was interested in Italian aviation, submarines, and high-speed launches. He claimed that Col. Lev Efimovich Manevich shipped from Italy tons of technical documentation, for which he was arrested and given a long prison sentence. Turned over to the Germans in 1943, he contracted tuberculosis in the camps. He died in 1945 soon after his liberation by American troops.

34. Printed copies are in AP URSS b8 f2. See *DVP* 16: no. 144; *The Times* (London), May 8, 1933; Preliminary Note on Special Commerce for Imports and Exports for the Kingdom of Italy, May 1933: AP URSS b10 f1; and Suvich circular, 5/13/33: AP URSS b8 f2.

35. Vera Micheles Dean, "The Soviet Union as a European Power," *Foreign Policy Reports* 9 (Aug. 2, 1933): 128; "Soviet-Italian Trade," *Current History* 38 (July 1933): 492. See Cesare Ghezzi, "I rapporti politico-economici Italo-Russia," *Rassegna di politica internazionale* (May 1934): 187–204. Meanwhile, on May 10 Levenson signed a protocol on payments for Italian technical cooperation, and Rome negotiated on the living and working conditions of its technicians employed in the USSR. These included salaries and other payments, transportation, lodging, food, baggage, customs duties, medical attention, property ownership and its disposal, taxes, arbitration for workplace disputes, legal protections, and freedom of religion. MAE to DGAP, 5/14/33: AP URSS b14 f1. "Proposte di clausole di stabilimento per un testo unico delle condizioni di vita dei technici italiani nell'U.R.S.S.," 5/16/33; Ministro delle Corporazioni to MAE, 5/18/33; DGAE to Ministro delle Corporazioni, 6/13/33: AP URSS b10 f1.

36. *DVP*, 16: no. 145.

37. *Izvestia*, May 9, 1933; Attolico to Rome, 5/16/33: AP URSS b11 f1; Dean, "Soviet Union as a European Power," p. 128. The presence of renowned Soviet author, Maxim Gorky, in Italy in May before traveling to Istanbul added extra sentiment to the developing relations. *DVP* 16: n.120.

38. Curato, "Italia," pp. 180–81, agreed with these sentiments and added that the difference in systems also had not hindered the development of political relations, as evidenced by the September 2, 1933, accord. Alexandra Mikhailovna Kollontai in Stockholm praised the accord and the Royal Navy's recent visit to Batum. She too called for good relations. Embassy at Stockholm to Rome, 6/7/33: AP URSS b8 f2.

39. Suvich memorandum, 5/27/33: AP URSS b8 f2. For a long report on the history of Soviet foreign policy and its justifications, based on an article written by N. Rudolf, a pseudonym used for important party statements, see Attolico to Rome, 5/14/33: AP URSS b8 f2. There had been some minor altercations, e.g., the Italians had been upset at reports of anti-Fascist radio broadcasts in Italian emanating from the Soviet Union; on May 13, Litvinov assured Attolico that there had been no such broadcasts. Attolico to Rome, 5/16/33: AP URSS b11 f2.

40. Barduzzi to Rome, 5/18/35: AP URSS b18 f8.

6

Political
Rapprochement

As Suvich and Potemkin had implied in their conversation at the end of May, the next task was to build a political structure upon the economic foundations laid down on May 6.

THE MUSSOLINI-POTEMKIN COLLOQUY OF MAY 28, 1933

On May 28, 1933, at 10:00 A.M., Potemkin met with the Duce at the Palazzo Venezia and said that he would meet Litvinov in Geneva and then go to Moscow for two weeks.[1] He explained that he wanted to inform the NKID of the status of Italo-Soviet relations and map out their further development. He downplayed the differences between their two systems; Italy and the Soviet Union held many views in common: disarmament, equality between nations, and opposition to military and economic blocs. Potemkin underscored his pleasure with Italian efforts at establishing friendly cooperation, especially Rome's work to help reestablish good Soviet-German relations. He praised the signing of the recent economic accord and the cordiality extended to Soviet missions visiting Italian shipyards and naval bases.

But all was not well. "Against a clear general background of Italo-Soviet cooperation there are several transient shadows," he said. Anti-Soviet articles in the fascist press, using Soviet exclusion from the imminent Four Power Pact as proof, suggested that the Italian government had no interest in political cooperation with the USSR.[2] Equally offensive was the notion that Italy's more developed economy would import raw materials and export the "products of its intelligence and labor." His pride hurt, he insisted that the developing Soviet economy was capable of offering more than unfinished goods. These articles, Potemkin said, seemed contrary to the political and economic cooperation in which Mussolini and his ministers claimed an interest.

The plenipotentiary assured Mussolini of Moscow's desire for harmony with Italy and Germany, but opined that the Reich's government was not reassuring. He was concerned about Italo-German intimacy and was upset that his country had not been invited to participate in the Four Power Pact. The goal of any Franco-Soviet agreement, he explained, was to forestall a Franco-German rapprochement. No such agreement would affect Soviet attitudes toward Italy, and he wished to firm up political relations as had been attempted at the Milan meeting between Litvinov and Grandi in November 1930.[3]

Mussolini, having listened attentively, generally agreed with Potemkin's appraisal of their relations, but he played down the "shadows" by noting that the articles that had so exercised the Soviet representative in no way reflected his government's attitude. The Duce continued that Grandi earlier had explained the suspension of talks on furthering political relations by noting that the time was not yet ripe, and that until the Franco-Soviet agreement had been concluded, Rome preferred to temporize so as to avoid the impression of running ahead of the French. Mussolini now thought that the situation had changed, and that if Moscow were to decide that the time was ripe for a political agreement, it would consolidate international peace and friendly relations between Italy and the USSR.[4]

An agreement would also eliminate Soviet concerns about the Four Power Pact, which Mussolini emphasized was not a weapon directed against the USSR. After all, the Soviets already had treaty relations with Germany, France, and Poland, and the Little Entente was inclined toward concluding a pact with Moscow. As for an Anglo-Soviet clash, even if London wished to create an anti-Soviet coalition, it could not, because no one wanted to be the dupe of perfidious Albion. Besides, London was commercially interested in the USSR and would find a way out of the blind alley it had created.

The Duce stressed the Four Power Pact's composite nature, which reflected the specific desires of its participants. In addition to placating Italy's parliamentarians, it had three more parents: Britain had insisted on the first amendments; France had wished to emphasize the pact's ties with the Locarno Agreement, the League's charter, and the Kellogg-Briand Pact; and Germany had insisted on equality in armaments. The Little Entente had nothing to fear, Mussolini continued, because the draft pact underscored the principle of the inviolability of borders and unanimity for any reexamination of the agreement.[5]

The flies in the ointment were Warsaw and Berlin. The Duce expressed his poor impression of Poland. If a Franco-Soviet agreement were to be signed, Poland would have no choice but to be reconciled. Mussolini thought that Germany's severing of its traditional friendship with Russia was reckless and could only weaken its international position. He emphasized that he frequently had told this to his friends in Berlin. At the end of the conversation, Mussolini asked that Potemkin, immediately upon his return from Moscow, tell him of the Kremlin's decision on his suggestion for an Italo-Soviet pact: "With great interest I will be waiting for you. . . . I hope that you will return here with good news."[6]

MOSCOW DECIDES

Three days later Suvich pumped Potemkin for details on the Soviet ideas for an agreement.[7] The plenipotentiary confidently replied that when he returned in a month, he would be carrying good news—the initiative was going to find favor in Moscow. Suvich, for his part, hoped that the initiative for the accord would appear to have come from Moscow. During the first two weeks of June, Attolico, despite his best efforts, discovered nothing more about the Soviet plans.[8]

Striving to smooth the way to an Italian pact, Litvinov addressed the problem of the Little Entente with the NKID.[9] He did not object to the Czech proposal that the Little Entente as an entity sign an agreement with the USSR—a procedure to which Romania agreed despite its unresolved problems with the Soviet Union. Assuming, however, that a pact with the Little Entente would make an agreement with Italy impossible, Litvinov proposed that Moscow negotiate simultaneously with Italy and Czechoslovakia, so that after achieving an Italian pact the USSR would be positioned to sign with the Little Entente.

The NKID agreed to negotiations with the Little Entente for a non-aggression pact and the simultaneous renewal of diplomatic relations with its members.[10] The commissariat also agreed to negotiate with Italy, and asked Litvinov whether he wanted the talks conducted in Rome through Potemkin, who would have to return there immediately, or in London through himself and Ambassador Grandi. Two days later Litvinov chose Rome and Potemkin, but added that the plenipotentiary ought to return immediately in either case.[11]

At the same time, when Litvinov inquired what such a pact would entail, Suvich told him that Rome was waiting for Soviet ideas, and that it could be along the lines of the Litvinov-Grandi discussions held in Milan. The foreign commissar replied positively.[12] Concerned that the signing of the Four Power Pact would affect Italy's relations with France and the Little Entente and hoping that news of the negotiations would moderate the latter's "fantastic" conditions for concluding a pact with the USSR, Moscow decided to accept what it described as Mussolini's offer to conclude a nonaggression pact.[13]

On June 20 in Moscow, Potemkin officially informed Attolico of the Soviet decision to accept the Duce's offer.[14] Responsible for the negotiations, he promised the Italians a draft nonaggression pact in short order. The ambassador "unofficially" tried to ferret out the character of the Soviet initiative. A "somewhat perplexed" Potemkin invoked, among other things, the Italo-Soviet conversations of 1924 to demonstrate that the proposed negotiations were an Italian idea. Attolico retorted that they ought to ignore such ancient precedents and remember instead the discussions in Milan, Geneva, Moscow, and Rome, wherein the idea of a pact had been a Soviet one. Potemkin did agree with the Italian ideas, except on matters, as Attolico put it to Rome, "of secondary importance." On the question of internal interference, the Kremlin wanted to delete the words "direct or indirect." The Soviets also wished to add a declaration used in its pacts with France, Poland, and the Baltic States that neither was tied to any previous pact with a third state requiring participation in aggression. Potemkin left for Rome on the evening of Monday, the twenty-sixth.

AMBASSADOR ATTOLICO'S ADVICE

Two days later, Attolico wrote the foreign ministry that he did not know the precise terms of the draft that Potemkin was carrying to Italy.[15] Contrary to the plenipotentiary's hopes, it had not been approved by the Politburo on Sunday. Attolico assured Rome that the Soviets remained interested; after all, Potemkin had postponed minor surgery for this initiative. It was to be approved by June 29, and Potemkin was ready to meet with Mussolini immediately upon his arrival in Rome.

Attolico readily offered his observations. The Soviet draft presumably differed from normal treaty proposals, which sought merely to improve relations and ameliorate problems. This one aimed, rather, to build on already strong ties, and the NKID thought it would be "the best pact so far concluded." The draft, the ambassador continued, ignored arbitration in case of conflict between the two countries. Moscow felt that ten years of good relations with Italy had shown that there was little chance of an issue arising that could not be solved diplomatically. In general, Moscow disliked arbitration, but agreed to such terms when the other party requested them. Moscow was especially pleased to include the principles of reciprocal nonaggression and territorial and economic neutrality.

Although there were no technical difficulties with territorial nonaggression—after all, the USSR and Italy shared no common border—Attolico felt that economic nonaggression posed problems. He feared that such a principle would limit Italy's freedom of action and might poison future relations with the USSR. For him, the only way to avoid this was to eliminate the issue by completely excluding all unnecessary economic and political stipulations. Economic matters could find sufficient protection in economic accords. Once every kind of nonaggression had been excised from the pact, something was needed to take its place. Attolico suggested a clause on reciprocal consultations, which could be manipulated according to mutual convenience.[16]

An Italo-Soviet pact, Attolico suggested, could be one in a series of accords following the Franco-Polish system, which the Kremlin would receive better than a nonaggression pact. He was also concerned about how the pact might affect Italy's relations in the Eastern Mediterranean. Further, if an Italo-Soviet pact contained consultation clauses, Italy ought to add similar ones to its agreements with Ankara, and he suggested that improved relations with Turkey might be the best result of an agreement with the USSR.[17]

On July 4, Deputy Foreign Commissar Krestinskii presented an unsurprising Soviet draft to Attolico.[18] Prodded by the recently signed London Conventions, the ambassador insistently repeated his warnings to Rome about the dangers of economic nonaggression obligations with a state having a foreign commercial monopoly. They would bind Italy unilaterally to too great a degree. Wanting to leave the details to a separate economic accord, he preferred a more general statement about maximizing economic possibilities. As before, he wanted the political obligations to be limited to reciprocal consultations.

Clearly, thought Attolico, the drive behind the Kremlin's desire to come to a political agreement with Rome lay in its uncertain relations with Berlin.[19] He requested that he be allowed to return briefly to Rome to explore how to negotiate an agreement with Moscow.

POTEMKIN PRESENTS THE SOVIET DRAFT

Back in Rome on July 8, Potemkin described to Suvich and Mussolini Moscow's favorable attitude on a political pact, and he showed them the draft proposal.[20] Soviet relations with Italy, he assured the Duce, remained immutable. Further, the London Conventions were not a response to the Four Power Pact, but had been made merely to facilitate the work of the Disarmament Conference and to extend the Kellogg-Briand Pact. Although the Soviet Union was not turning anti-German, it had to take all precautions and therefore was looking to those states, especially France, that opposed Germany. Suvich replied that he was ready to settle the negotiations quickly.[21]

Two days later Potemkin again spoke with Mussolini, this time for fifty minutes in the Palazzo Venezia.[22] He once more relayed Moscow's pleasure with the Italian desire for cordial relations, and the Duce assured Potemkin that the Four Power Pact would not be directed against the Soviet Union. The plenipotentiary explained that he had been given full authority to negotiate a political pact. He suggested that it ought to be supplemented with Franco-Soviet and Soviet-German accords to neutralize the four-power threat to the USSR. Emphasizing the Kremlin's good intentions, Potemkin invited the Four Power Pact members to join the London Conventions.[23]

Mussolini, Potemkin reported, fully agreed with his assessment of the world situation, but further blamed the French press especially for the suggestion that the London Conventions somehow opposed the Four Power Pact: "The attitude toward the Soviet Union of that press is permeated with irreconcilable hatred. . . . The Soviet Union ought not to put too much faith in the friendliness of France, a country of greedy peasants, misers, investors, and through-and-through bourgeois." The Duce hoped for a return of Rapallo-type relations between the USSR and Germany and promised to push Berlin in that direction—toward "reason." An Italo-Soviet pact, in Mussolini's opinion, would signal that fascist Italy would not support Germany in an adventure against the Soviet Union.

Mussolini thought that the Soviet draft proposal just handed him was essentially good. He suggested, however, a more positive statement calling for mutual action for the development of Italo-Soviet economic and political cooperation rather than the negative approach of the Soviet draft, which had merely spoken of nonaggression and neutrality. In other words, opined Potemkin, the Duce wanted more comprehensive obligations than did Moscow. Mussolini represented his statements as merely preliminary remarks prior to study by the foreign ministry's lawyers. He did, however, hope for the earliest possible conclusion of negotiations.

Ultimately, Potemkin's draft was adopted as the definitive text, with only a few changes. The relative ease of the ensuing negotiations suggests that both sides felt that the time was ripe for a more formal statement of their good relations—and so Mussolini told Ambassador Hassell.[24]

By July 11, rumors of the proposed pact already had leaked out. Much of the foreign press dramatized the irony that the two ideologically opposed powers were coming to a political agreement. It was noted that the Kremlin's first series of peace pacts in Central Europe had been designed in part to offset fascist diplomacy in that area. Thus to absorb Italy, the father of the Four Power Pact, into a neutrality system embracing states of such diverse interests as the Soviet Union, the states of the Near East (led by Turkey), and the Western and Central European nations (led by France) was a considerable success for Moscow.[25] The London *Times*, on the other hand, played down the significance of the impending pact, editorializing that in view of the good mutual relations of the previous nine years, the treaty held no great importance except to facilitate commercial exchanges.[26]

During Italo-French negotiations in the fall of 1933 on a Latin Mediterranean alliance, the French negotiating team urged Mussolini to help France keep Germany sandwiched between friends.[27] Noting that the Locarno Pact limited German expansion in the West, the French argued for another pact, with the Soviet Union, to stop any possible German expansion in the East. Once an Italo-Soviet treaty was signed, the French said that they could subscribe to it and then turn their attention to Italy's difficulties in the Mediterranean with an easy mind. Out of these talks grew the Rome Accords of January 1935. By signing the pact with the Soviet Union, Soviet historians have argued, Mussolini not only hoped to raise Italy's international weight, but wished to encourage a Franco-Soviet rapprochement as well.[28]

The Soviet press, however, did not quite know what to make of the incipient Italo-French rapprochement. In the last week and a half of July, *Izvestia* analyzed the controversies aggravating the two Latin sisters and concluded that "no accord between the two countries can stop the struggle between the French and Italian imperialisms."[29] On the other hand, numerous articles emphasized that Mussolini's negotiations with Hungary represented the first proof of Italo-French collaboration. Still, given Little Entente resistance, the press sadly predicted that it would be difficult for those specific talks, or the larger issue of Italo-French relations, to be worked out.[30]

In early August, *Izvestia* called one Hungarian statesman's visits to Berlin, Vienna, and Rome a "prism" reflecting Italo-French and Italo-German relations.[31] *Pravda*, stressing imperialist contradictions, concluded that the trip to Rome "represents new proof that the imperialists have no prospect of resolving peacefully the most complicated problems of Central Europe."[32] The *Izvestia* article above also noted that France and Italy, despite their competing imperialisms, had thwarted Hitler's plans for an immediate *Anschluss*. Toward that end, Rome was trying to unite Austria, Hungary, Bulgaria, and Greece. This grouping of revisionist powers, however, also opposed the Little Entente. Paris, meanwhile, was trying to glue Austria and Hungary together with the Little Entente into a Danubian bloc.

In the second week of August, the Soviet press emphasized Italy's position in the Austro-German conflict, and *Izvestia* editorialized that Rome knew its own best interests in the matter.[33] At the same time, Jacques Sadoul, *Izvestia*'s correspondent in Paris, reported on French irritation at Italy's "double game" of trying to hold Paris and London responsible for defending against *Anschluss*.[34]

Sensing dangers, especially in an economic nonaggression article, Attolico remained less hopeful about the value of a pact to his country than Mussolini.[35] Unrequited expectations could exacerbate a cooling in relations with the USSR, especially in case of an Italian entente with Central Europe, which the USSR surely would define as directed against it. Economic and political nonaggression between the Soviet Union and Italy could be better regulated by general conventions than a bilateral pact. He was also concerned at how an Italo-Soviet agreement would affect Poland, which was playing the Soviet Union against the Four Power Pact.

Attolico advised that in negotiating a pact, Rome ought to avoid every compromise on economic matters; it should establish some sort of political bond with the Soviet Union to counterpoise Polish policy now that Russia was reappearing in the Balkans; and it should make certain that the bonds being forged were such that they could be extended to Turkey. He repeated that these points would be better covered by a consultative clause. Several obligations ought to be included in a pact: mutual and absolute noninterference in domestic affairs, arbitration, neutrality and nonrecourse to force in case of third-party aggression, and an exchange of information on questions of common interest.

THE NEGOTIATIONS CONCLUDED

Potemkin visited Suvich on August 2 to see if the Italian comments on the Soviet project were ready, and he was promised unofficially that they would be by the end of the week.[36] The Soviet plenipotentiary suggested that Litvinov wished to meet Mussolini after the signing of an agreement, and he maintained that Berlin was pushing the Soviet Union into the anti-German camp. He feared that Britain and Japan were supporting Germany, where, Potemkin consoled himself, communism was growing.

Suvich explained Rome's views on the forthcoming accord in a long colloquy with Potemkin five days later.[37] Italy had no problem with a nonrecourse-to-force instead of a nonaggression pact if Moscow thought this better. Mussolini agreed with the proposed Soviet wording on doing all possible to improve economic relations. Potemkin argued that arbitration by third parties diminished sovereignty; only Soviet and Italian representatives should meet to dispose of contentious issues.

A week later Krestinskii responded to the Italian counterdraft and amendments to the Soviet draft.[38] Only two essential matters remained, he told Attolico. The first concerned the Preamble, which mentioned "the complete noninterference, direct or indirect, in the internal affairs of the other signatory power." Krestinskii maintained that because noninterference was a sacred part of Soviet policy, Moscow need not sign specific articles to that effect. His government did not object to fulfilling a pact recognizing mutual noninterference in internal affairs and agreed to the Italian suggestion, but without the words "direct or indirect."

The second matter concerned the Italian proposal that both countries should maintain their obligations assumed in previous agreements with other states. Krestinskii noted that Moscow had signed pacts containing similar articles and had no objection to signing such a pact with the Italians—but, of course, nothing in the new treaty should contradict earlier obligations. Not believing that the Soviet demands would cause any problem for Italy, he suggested that the negotiations could be quickly concluded.

Attolico responded that he foresaw no problems, but he defended the original Italian wording as merely putting into writing the extant relations between the two states. He added that Italy too hoped for a speedy conclusion of the negotiations. The Italian ambassador, partly misjudging the situation, opined to Rome that the Soviet government and especially Krestinskii were hurrying to conclude the pact because, with Litvinov absent from

Moscow, the credit for an accord would go to the vice commissar.[39] The Kremlin wished to conclude the pact before the imminent arrivals on Soviet soil of ex-Premier Edouard Herriot and Air Minister Pierre Cot, whose visits were to emphasize the Franco-Soviet rapprochement in progress.[40] Attolico perversely suggested that Italy not sign an accord until September 10—after Herriot's visit.[41]

The ambassador also inquired about Soviet contacts with Germany and stated that Mussolini was attentively following them.[42] The Duce, he continued, recently had told Papen that Italy did not approve of Berlin's ruining its ties with Moscow. Krestinskii responded that mutually satisfactory relations depended on Berlin, because the Soviets wanted friendship with all governments. There was no need, he continued, of additional agreements, but only that Germany abide in a friendly way with those already existing.[43]

At the end of August, Suvich and Potemkin were still debating minor points.[44] Although Rome had agreed to call the future agreement a "Pact of Friendship, Nonaggression, and Neutrality," the under secretary categorically refused Potemkin's last compromise formula, and he told the plenipotentiary that he was going to ask for instructions from Mussolini, who by now had returned from military maneuvers. The Duce, in fact, accepted the Soviet proposals without amendments and wished to sign the pact no later than September 2.

The plenipotentiary representative made it clear that Moscow, by reaching an agreement with Italy, had an eye not only on Central and Southeast Europe, but on East Asia as well. In effect, he drove home the points that *Pravda* had made a few days before: the Kremlin was considering a change in its policy toward Japan, and with this pact the USSR could now examine its policies toward that country in cooperation with Italy and France, and through them, with the United States as well.[45]

NOTES

1. *DVP* 16: no. 166; Mussolini memorandum, 5/28/33: AP URSS b8 f2.

2. Potemkin the day before had likewise complained about other articles that had shown no sympathy toward either the Soviet Union or communism. Suvich retorted that the Soviet press was more antifascist than the Italian press was anticommunist, but this was unimportant. Suvich memorandum 5/27/33: AP URSS b8 f2.

3. *DVP* 16: no. 166; Mussolini memorandum 5/28/33: AP URSS b8 f2.

4. According to Nina Dmitrievna Smirnova, *Politika Italii na Balkanakh: Ocherk diplomaticheskoi istorii, 1922-1935 gg.* (Moscow, 1979), p. 258, the difference was that the project for the regional Eastern Pact of mutual aid as an important element in a collective security system had become the subject of wide discussion. Franco-Soviet cooperation annoyed the fascist government, which saw it as part of the Gallic aspiration to hegemony in East Europe. Fearing any such alliance, Rome sought to prevent it—the result was the Italo-Soviet pact of September.

5. *DVP* 16: no. 166; Mussolini memorandum, 5/28/33: AP URSS b8 f2.

6. Ibid.

7. Suvich memorandum, 5/31/33: AP URSS b10 f1; Rome to Attolico, 6/6/33: AP URSS b8 f2.

8. Attolico to Rome, 6/14/33: AP URSS b10 f1.

9. *DVP*, 16: n.149.

10. Ibid., no. 183.

11. Ibid., n.150.

12. Suvich memorandum, 6/17/33: AP URSS b10 f1.

13. *DVP* 16: no. 186.

14. Ibid., no. 188; Attolico to Rome, 6/20/33, 6/20/33, 6/21/33, 6/26/33, 6/21/33, n.d.: AP URSS b10 f1.

15. Attolico to Rome, 6/28/33: AP URSS b10 f1.

16. Ibid.

17. Ibid.

18. Attolico to Rome, 7/4/33: AP URSS b10 f1.

19. Promemorial for Mussolini, 7/8/33: AP URSS b10 f1.

20. Suvich memorandum, 7/8/33: AP URSS b10 f1. For the various draft proposals and revisions presented by both sides, see the numerous documents in AP URSS b10 f1.

21. Suvich also assured Potemkin that rumors of Rosenberg's negotiations with the Japanese were exaggerated. Attolico relayed information on Moscow's preoccupation with Japan's military preparations in the East. Attolico to Rome, 7/4/33, 7/11/33: AP URSS b8 f3; *Izvestia*, June 30, 1933.

22. *DVP* 16: no. 230; Mussolini memorandum, 7/10/33: AP URSS b10 f1.

23. See also *DVP* 16: no. 227.

24. *DGFP* C, 1: 365.

25. Vera Micheles Dean, "The Soviet Union as a European Power," *Foreign Policy Reports* 9 (Aug. 2, 1933): 128; Edgar S. Furniss, "Soviet Diplomatic Successes," *Current History* 38 (Sept. 1933): 760.

26. *The Times* (London), Aug. 31, 1933.

27. Roy MacGregor-Hastie, *The Day of the Lion: The Life and Death of Fascist Italy, 1922-1945* (New York, 1963), p. 217.

28. Vladimir Petrovich Potemkin, ed., *Istoriia diplomatii*, 3 vols. (Moscow, 1941-45), 3: 476.

29. *Izvestia*, July 22, 1933.

30. See, e.g., ibid., July 27, 1933; Attolico to Rome, 7/31/33: AP URSS b11 f1.

31. *Izvestia*, Aug. 2, 1933.

32. *Pravda*, Aug. 2, 1933; Attolico to Rome, 8/2/33: AP URSS b11 f1.

33. *Izvestia*, Aug. 20, 1933.

34. Ibid., Aug. 11, 1933; Attolico to Rome, 8/15/33: AP URSS b10 f1. For an unflattering view of Sadoul's Stalinist mentality, see George Frost Kennan, *Russia and the West: Under Lenin and Stalin* (New York, 1961), pp. 53-54.

35. Attolico to Rome, 7/26/33: AP URSS b10 f1. Officials in Rome seriously discussed Attolico's reservations. See, e.g., Buti to Suvich, note, 8/2/33: AP URSS b10 f1. This document also clearly shows that Nazi Germany's dynamism lay behind the urge to cooperate among the sundry European states.

36. Suvich memorandum, 8/2/33: AP URSS b8 f5.

37. Suvich memorandum, 8/7/33: AP URSS b10 fl.

38. Attolico to Rome, n.d.: AP URSS b10 fl.

39. Ibid.

40. On September 22, the German counselor in Moscow spoke with Leon Gel'fand, the long-time counselor of the Soviet embassy in Rome. Regretting the deteriorating relations with Germany, he warned Berlin that the visits of Herriot and Cot to Moscow signified the complete normalization of Franco-Soviet relations. Because of Stalin's purges, Gel'fand eventually fled to the United States.

41. One Latvian paper saw things differently: reciprocal interests, not ideology, forms the basis of international relations, e.g., in the case of Italy and the USSR. The paper disputed the German thesis that Italy was hurrying to sign the pact before Herriot's visit to the USSR so as to weaken its importance. Rather, Herriot's visit, as well as those to Bulgaria and Turkey, was an attempt to create a favorable atmosphere to preserve the status quo. Therefore, an Italo-Soviet nonaggression pact served French policy. It would further isolate Germany. Ministry at Kaunas to Rome, 8/22/33: AP URSS b10 fl.

42. DVP 16: no. 270; Attolico to Rome, 8/15/33: AP URSS b10 fl.

43. For a colloquy between Suvich and Potemkin along similar lines, see Suvich memorandum, 8/14/33: AP URSS b8 f5. Potemkin again complained about several press articles that personally attacked Stalin, and he decried Italian help to cossacks wishing independence from the Soviet state.

44. DVP 16: no. 274; Suvich memorandums, 8/25/33, 8/28/33; Rome to Attolico, n.d.: AP URSS b10 fl. See also DVP 16: n.204.

45. Note for Suvich, 8/29/33: AP URSS b8 f3.

The Italo-Soviet Pact of Friendship, Neutrality, and Nonaggression, September 2, 1933

To French surprise and admiration, Mussolini and Potemkin signed the Italo-Soviet Pact of Friendship, Neutrality, and Nonaggression at noon on September 2 in the Palazzo Venezia in the Hall of the Map of the World.

THE PACT

Contents

Containing seven articles, the pact's terms followed closely those of the Franco-Soviet treaty of November 29, 1932.[1] The two signatories promised not "to declare war on the other Party or to attack it . . . and to respect the inviolability of the territory under its sovereignty." They promised neutrality if the other were attacked, and they allowed for denouncement without notice if either attacked a third party.[2]

While not voiding any previous agreement, to reassure Moscow about the Four Power Pact, the present pact forbade either state to enter into any political, economic, or military combination directed against the other. It provided for arbitration in matters not capable of resolution by ordinary diplomatic means, and the final article set a five-year life for the pact, after which it would remain in force for one year following its denouncement by either party.

At its signing Potemkin briefly emphasized the pact's importance, not only to its signatories but also to European peace. In reply Mussolini confidently declared that the pact represented "the logical development of a policy of friendship" and was "the basis for obtaining results still more useful."[3] Minor differences of interpretations and reservations were quickly settled, with

Litvinov acceding to the Italian interpretations.[4] The Central Executive Committee ratified the agreement on October 7; the Italian king followed on the nineteenth.

Italian and Soviet Attitudes toward the Pact

The pact was publicly lauded in Italy. A September 3 press communique celebrated its significance, as did Mussolini in *Popolo d'Italia*, wherein the Duce argued that it helped to prevent Europe from being divided into blocs; rather it worked "to stabilize politically" a large part of the continent.[5]

Italians seemed especially interested in the pact's economic implications. During the negotiations, for example, the journal of the Italian Touring Club published several articles on the work of Angelo Omodeo, who had earned a worldwide reputation for hydraulic and irrigation engineering. Invited in 1931 to Soviet Russia, he spent the next two years in Moscow, where he staffed an office with Italian engineers. Some speculated that after the pact Italy would send more such experts.[6]

Political benefits were expected as well. Italians celebrated that the pact was not only one of "nonaggression and neutrality," but "first of all, of 'friendship.' " It differed from others that the USSR had recently signed in that it expanded the already cordial relations between the two countries. Italy supported Russia's reintegration into Europe, and the September accord, in effect, had brought the USSR into the Four Power Pact, thereby short-circuiting any attempts to isolate the Soviet state. In other words, first Western and now Eastern Europe had been stabilized. Moscow's earlier pacts on defining aggression meant that if a communist revolt broke out in Poland or Romania, the USSR would not support it. Until the last year, Soviet policy had been oriented toward Germany, but Herriot's successful visit to the USSR was changing that. The pact was the logical conclusion not only of the Four Power Pact, but also of the 1932 Franco-Soviet pact. Many Italians believed that the French were happy with the continuing development of Mussolini's peaceful policies and welcomed *Izvestia*'s editorials claming that the contradictions between fascism and communism had not hindered a realistic policy. Mussolini himself picked up these themes.[7]

In *Giornale d'Italia* Virginio Gayda celebrated that the Four Power Pact had brought together once again the participants of the Locarno Pact; but collaboration also had to be established with other states demonstrating goodwill, principally the Soviet Union. The new diplomatic instrument with the Kremlin, therefore, was the natural development of the Four Power Pact. Clearly, without Moscow no political combination for a general accord was possible.[8]

Aloisi whipped off a circular telegram to inform Italy's diplomats of the pact's significance.[9] In effect confirming what the press had been saying, the royal government had felt it opportune to sign because of the USSR's recent diplomatic activities, that is, the conclusion of a series of accords oriented toward France and Poland, and the several tentative approaches to the Little Entente. Italy hoped to monitor and mold this activity. The pact, Aloisi emphasized, differed from others recently signed by Moscow in that it changed nothing in Italo-Soviet relations; rather it consolidated the existing mutual understanding as a foundation for the future and continued the Four Power Pact's policy of peace and cooperation, which had been limited to the Locarno signatories. Italy was following a realistic concept: collaboration with the USSR in problems concerning that state.[10]

Italy's representative at Geneva saw the pact as new proof of Moscow's desire to orient itself to the West and to develop the policy of European cooperation inaugurated by Mussolini's Four Power Pact.[11] He specifically mentioned the Kremlin's diverse negotiations with Paris and London. Pressured by Japan and Germany as well as by its internal situation, Moscow wished to break its political isolation and find agreement with its neighbors, the Little Entente, and Italy. Soon, he predicted, Moscow would be induced to join the League of Nations.

The Soviet press likewise wrote enthusiastically on the pact, and in the first half of September the USSR's growing ties with Italy and France dominated public comments by its leaders. Attentive to Italian and French sensibilities, the press saw the pact as analogous to the 1932 Franco-Soviet pact and found significance in Herriot's presence in the USSR when it was signed. Italy's growing international clout had made consolidating relations most valuable, and its lack of antisocialist vengeance had enabled peaceful economic and political collaboration, which would continue as long as Italy avoided active hostility against the USSR. The Four Power Pact was not anti-Soviet, and Soviet papers praised Italy for loyally honoring its earlier agreements and cited statistics on the growing economic cooperation between the two states. Further, the pact proved that Italian fascism differed from German fascism in that the former was not planning territorial expansion against the Soviet state. The contradictions between fascism and communism had not hindered a realistic policy. The pact proved that Moscow intended neither to isolate itself nor to get mixed up in imperialistic conflicts. It brilliantly confirmed Soviet peace policies and crowned the series of treaties with all of the chief European states except Great Britain.[12]

Despite the lack of official documents or memoirs revealing the deepest thoughts of the Kremlin's leaders, it is reasonable to guess that Moscow valued the pact for the multiple pressures it put on Berlin. Many powerful people in Germany disagreed with the Nazis' anti-Russian policy, and by emphasizing that fascist-communist contradictions need not inhibit realism, the Soviets were inviting Hitler to come to a similar *modus operandi*. Ideology need not get in the way of cordial relations. This was an especially sharp invitation, given Mussolini's attempts to mediate between Moscow and Berlin and his frequent criticisms of Nazi policy toward the USSR. It was an invitation made sharper yet by the complementary Franco-Soviet and Franco-Italian rapprochements then also being groped for. Presumably the Soviets hoped that all this would convince Hitler that Moscow was an ally worth courting, if not out of love, then at least to avoid driving it into the arms of another suitor.

Because of Italo-German "contradictions," Italy was the only power both geographically able and self-interestedly willing to oppose Austrian *Anschluss*. While certainly not wanting to support an overly strong Italy in Southeast Europe, with its defensive gaze focused on the Japanese in East Asia, the Kremlin was willing to encourage Italy to block the potentially much stronger German move into that area of Europe so vital to Soviet security. The pact and attendant military contacts honed to a sharp edge Rome's opposition to Nazi designs on Austria. They dramatized and enhanced Italy's ability to oppose Germany, and they implicitly opened up the possibility of Soviet diplomatic—and even military—support for Italy's defense of Austria.

Italian representatives had closely followed the Herriot-Cot visits of September to Moscow together with recent visits by Polish figures. That they took place simultaneously with the signing of the Italo-Soviet pact seemed auspicious. Herriot told Attolico that he loved Italy and wished to cooperate with Rome—the issues dividing the two Latin sisters were not insolvable. He feared that war with Germany would soon break out, and, as in 1914, that it would drag in all, including Soviet Russia. Attolico concluded that France and the Soviet Union had an equally strong fear of Germany.[13] France and the USSR were nearing anti-German military cooperation, and their political approaches were now independent of economics. To support his argument, the ambassador noted that the anti-German campaign was continuing in the Soviet press, and the government was supporting the French position on disarmament. Litvinov, he continued, believed that an agreement on disarmament was impossible, and there was a general feeling in Moscow that war was inevitable.[14]

Foreign Press Reaction to the Pact

Italy's representatives in the various capitals swamped Rome with reports on foreign reactions to the Italo-Soviet Pact. These accounts reflected the complicated and confusing nature of politics in East and Southeast Europe as well as the unknown quality of the new friendships and antagonisms being forged. Many Europeans saw the pact as directed against French hegemony in that area and thought that with Italian mediation, it might serve as a vehicle for Soviet-German rapprochement. Yet, to others, the Herriot-Cot tours of the USSR seemed an omen of future Italo-Soviet-French cooperation against Germany.[15]

The Italian ambassador in Paris, on the other hand, believed that despite French flattery of the Soviets, Paris was nurturing no illusions about having Soviet support in case of difficulties with Germany.[16] Herriot's supporters merely wanted others to believe that France exclusively had Soviet friendship.

Meanwhile, other Italian diplomats described similar Swiss opinions about French concern over the Italo-Soviet pact:

Litvinov, the man responsible for Russia's foreign policy, shows no intention of cutting short his vacation to meet in Moscow to shake the hand of the French statesman (Herriot); the simple reason is that Russian diplomacy is concentrating its principal interest not on Paris any more, but on Rome.[17]

Italy, in any case, was more important in containing Germany than was France. One paper suggested that the pact's goals were to apply political pressure against the Little Entente and to end French advantage in East Europe.

British papers, hewing yet another line, saw Italy as supporting Moscow's desire to reenter the European family. As the power responsible for the Four Power Pact, Italy could best bridge the differences between its signatories and the states bound to the USSR by nonaggression treaties. One British paper reported that the pact was welcomed in Paris "as another link in the chain of agreements designed to girdle Europe in the strait jacket of peace."[18]

The Turkish press offered yet another perspective. The pact, it wrote, had created little new, although it did impede both a Soviet-Little Entente and a Franco-Soviet deal against Italy on the one hand, and an Italo-German agreement against the USSR on the other. Italy's recent successes in Albania had damaged French influence in Southeast Europe.[19]

Yugoslavia, as could be expected, reacted harshly against the Italian success. Mussolini, *Politika* editorialized from Belgrade, deemed Russo-European collaboration to be an absolute necessity. But denigrating the pact, the paper continued that Soviet-fascist relations had never had much influence on Europe. Rather, Hitler was the major impetus in changing Soviet policy. Italy could fight a war only if supplied with grain, cotton, coal, oil, and so forth, shipped from the Black Sea. Rome therefore wanted to liberate the Dardanelles from the control instituted by the Lausanne Convention; the Italians could do this by creating a Black Sea bloc composed of Turkey, Greece, Bulgaria, Romania, and the Soviet Union. French influence in Southeast Europe threatened Italy. The paper wondered why the pact contained no clause defining aggression, a notable absence given that the Soviets always before had demanded such statements. Soviet antirevisionism and opposition to the Four Power Pact represented a huge failure for Mussolini.[20]

LITVINOV'S VISIT TO ROME, DECEMBER 2-5, 1933

Preparing for Litvinov's Visit

On October 27, Litvinov departed Moscow, heading for Washington, D.C. by way of Berlin to secure *de jure* recognition from the United States. The Soviets asked that on his way home he be allowed to meet the Duce in Italy. Rome's ambassador in Washington, Augusto Rosso, conferred with Litvinov on several occasions during the first half of November to firm up a schedule.[21] The United States recognized the USSR on November 17.

Moscow praised Rome for the attitude of the Italian press, which had welcomed America's recognition as the final blow against the old *Cordon Sanitaire*.[22] After smugly noting that President Franklin D. Roosevelt was merely following the Italian lead of nine years earlier, Italian papers ruefully acknowledged that America's political reconciliation inevitably had to lead to increased Soviet-American economic exchanges and possibly financial and technical assistance to Moscow. Italians feared that the United States would eat into their export trade with the USSR, which was already too small. Although Italo-French relations had recently improved, Rome remained concerned that a considerable portion of its raw materials imports funneled through Gibraltar, past a perennially hostile France; hence keeping the supply lines secure from Soviet Russia through the Dardanelles remained a cardinal point in Italian policy.[23]

Amid these ruminations, on Saturday, November 25, a happy Litvinov sailed from New York on the Italian liner *Conte d'Savoia* bound for Naples. He not only wanted to be invited as an official guest of the Italian government and to be interviewed by the press, he also wished to be presented to the king—a bizarre request for a revolutionary regicide to make, especially of a sovereign whose wife had lived at court in St. Petersburg. Even so, Rosso was instructed to issue a formal invitation to Litvinov to be a guest of the Italian government.[24]

The Italian government worked hard to prepare itself for the forthcoming colloquies by trying to understand Soviet positions and how best to deal with them. The year of 1933, one important memorandum pointed out, had been a special one for the USSR.[25] Dominated by fears of Japan and Germany, Soviet policy in Europe was no longer revolutionary, but conservative. And even though the Comintern was continuing its work, it was doing so at a slower pace. Moscow wanted peace, not by virtue of its idealism, but in recognition that war would bring about the fall of the communist regime in Russia.

This memorandum continued that Germany's anti-Jewish policy was greatly influencing the NKID, where many Jews were ensconced. The USSR was trying to improve its relations with its bordering states in case of problems in East Asia, and it was looking for a deeper relationship with France in case of problems with Germany and to pressure Berlin to return to Rapallo. Attempting to play Paris and Berlin against one another, the Soviets had signed nonaggression pacts with France and Poland, had signed the accords defining an aggressor, and had tried to deal with the Bessarabian question. Although the Kremlin had not yet approached the Little Entente, it had made moves toward Turkey and other Balkan states. At Geneva, Litvinov was siding with France on disarmament.

The memorandum continued that the Four Power Pact had upset the Soviets, who feared that agreements by the major European powers could only be directed against them. Thus they welcomed their Italian pact, which gave them the feeling of inclusion. It formed part of the series of agreements safeguarding the USSR.

Recognizing that the directions of Soviet policy were not yet settled, the memorandum discussed the topics that Litvinov could be expected to bring up. He would want to know if the USSR could count on Italian support in the event of difficulties with Japan.[26] It was suggested that he should be told that Italy, as a power with international concerns, worried about Japanese policy; East Asia, however, was not a vital interest. On the other hand, Rome could not remain indifferent to Japan's economic offensive, which was hurting Italian interests not only in foreign markets but in Italy itself. Discussion on this topic, however, was to be kept general with the idea of preparing the groundwork for future diplomatic contacts.

Litvinov, according to the memorandum, would want to know Italy's ideas on the situation following Germany's exit from the Disarmament Conference and the League of Nations, and would ask what Italy intended to do, especially as the Four Power Pact was the only vital agreement binding together the four major European powers. Not pretending to know what the USSR intended, the memorandum recognized that Moscow would follow the situation with "care and distrust." Although Italy did not want the USSR to enter a round of treaties with the Western powers, it was important to give the Kremlin the impression of not being excluded.

Litvinov would want to know Italy's judgment of German attitudes toward the USSR. Certainly, the memorandum continued, he would complain about Rosenberg and German policy in Poland and the Baltic States. In reply, Rome decided to stress its conciliatory action in Moscow and Berlin working toward restoring Rapallo-type relations.

What else should be said to Litvinov? According to the memorandum, he should be told to act moderately toward Turkey and that Bulgaria should not be pushed into Yugoslavia's arms. Litvinov should be probed concerning relations between the USSR and France. The Italians should also push for the exchange of military officers, which would be of great use in helping Rome to form an exact opinion of the military and political value of the Red Army. Points could be made on Yemen and Afghanistan that would form the basis of future diplomatic contacts. Finally, the Italians, in the most general way, could delve into the possibilities of Italo-Soviet economic co-operation in Asia.

The political rapprochement between Rome and Moscow, dramatized by Livinov's forthcoming trip to Rome, was played out against the backdrop of their economic relations. In mid-October, Mikhail Levenson had been re-called to Moscow. In reporting on the trade representative's consultations with his bosses, the Italian chargé, Berardis, stressed that the Soviet treasury faced tremendous difficulties.[27] For example, Moscow had not used even one-fourth of Italy's state-guaranteed credits for 1933. Despite growing com-petitiveness from other countries, Levenson was pushing the advantages of purchases in Italy. Berardis warned that if Italian competitiveness further declined, Levenson's position would be compromised. The trade repre-sentative was to stay at least several weeks in the Soviet capital to try to convince the Kremlin to purchase up to the credit agreement signed with Rome. At a dinner given at the Italian embassy for him, high officials swore that the agreement would be respected and that the USSR had eight months to accomplish this. Berardis reminded Rome that the Italian market for Soviet exports was third in importance and second in quantity; Italy absorbed many Soviet articles, because they were being sold for the most part at below cost.

Reports such as this concerned Rome. The day before Litvinov's arrival, a note on Italo-Soviet commercial relations was prepared for the Duce.[28] It lamented the one-million-lire trade advantage favoring the USSR. Despite Rome's efforts to increase Soviet purchases in Italy, the USSR had used only a small percentage of the state-guaranteed credits, while Soviet exports to Italy had not declined nearly so much.[29] The Kremlin justified this situation by noting that it had decreased purchases elsewhere as well; further, Italian goods had become more expensive than those from other countries. The note suggested that the truth was that, given the political approaches by the United States and France and the reestablishment of commercial relations with Britain, the Soviets thought that they had a free hand for purchases elsewhere. Soviet negotiators, rubbing salt in the wound, expressed their hope that Rome would grant permission for the USSR to export more to Italy than the total established by the commercial agreement, even though they expected that Soviet purchases in Italy would remain low. The note, in closing, stressed that Italy had much to gain from better equity in its economic exchanges with the Soviet Union.

Official Italian circles were ambiguous as to the meaning of Litvinov's coming visit. It was, at one and the same time, "nothing exceptional" and "of noteworthy practical importance." After all, visits to Mussolini by pre-mier statesmen had become part of the European political ritual, and nat-urally Litvinov should meet the Duce, especially when Soviet diplomatic activity was expanding and there remained many unresolved problems af-fecting both Italian and Soviet interests. Without authoritative information, the press opined that Italian officials would discuss with Litvinov the deadlocked Disarmament Conference and the possibility of Soviet entry into the League. Some wanted a discussion on prewar debts and claims of property nationalized by the bolsheviks. Others thought that Mussolini meant once more to reassure Litvinov of the Four Power Pact and that Italy regarded Soviet participation in all major European questions as indispensable. Some rumored that Roman Catholicism in the Soviet Union might be discussed, although direct contact between Litvinov and the Vatican was considered improbable.[30]

Only two days before Litvinov's arrival in Italy, Potemkin expressed his concern at press reports that Mussolini wanted to discuss an extension of the Four Power Pact.[31] If this was true, Litvinov wanted information from Rome so that he could get instructions from Moscow. Suvich reassured the Soviet plenipotentiary that no conversations on an extension of the pact were planned. Mussolini wished only to talk about those things of direct interest to the two countries.

The Conversations

The commissar arrived in Naples on Saturday, December 2, and was received by Potemkin, Attolico, the head of the ceremonial office, and others. After spending the afternoon at the Hotel Excelsior, Litvinov left for Rome, arriving at 7:20 P.M. to be greeted by Suvich and a number of other officials. Outside the Termini train station, a huge crowd cheered. Contrary to his original desires, Litvinov stayed at the Soviet embassy, and some pundits commented that he had rejected the Italian government's invitation to be its guest. And others attributed Mussolini's failure to greet the foreign commissar at the railroad station as revenge for this affront. Litvinov's decision, *The London Times* wrote, might have indicated that "the U.S.S.R., however anxious it may be to play a great part in European affairs, does not wish to be too much beholden to Italian chaperonage or to be stamped irrevocably into the Italian fold."[32]

On the morning of December 3, Litvinov spoke for seventy-five minutes with Mussolini in the Palazzo Venezia.[33] The Duce, scattering his thoughts about, expressed his hope that the Italo-Soviet pact would be fulfilled not only in letter but in spirit. He asserted that the Four Power Pact was not directed against the USSR, but was an instrument of peace. He nonetheless offered little solace for Litvinov's pet ploy, disarmament: German rearmament was a reality, and therefore it was better to regulate it than to face it unrestricted. Italy, he continued, had never loved the League, and although he had not known beforehand of Germany's departure from it, he approved of it. Without the Soviet Union, Germany, Japan, or the United States as members, the League could have no genuine meaning. Italy, however, would not leave the League but hoped to reform it. Praising the USSR's growing strength and influence, the Duce averred that without Soviet Russia, it was difficult to solve international problems.

Mussolini noted that relations with France and the Little Entente had improved, Paris having agreed to cooperate with the Italians in solving Danubian questions. Japan, he continued, threatened Italian interests by competing in the Mediterranean basin and in Abyssinia, where Tokyo had received economic, territorial, and immigration concessions. He promised to oppose Japanese aggression.[34] Mussolini neither posed questions nor made propositions except to ask if the Soviets wished to establish relations with Hungary.

To Mussolini's windy monologue, Litvinov responded that his government did not suspect the Duce's intentions in authoring the Four Power Pact, but was concerned that its signatories could decide matters affecting Soviet interests without Moscow's involvement. He also commented that, although Mussolini did not love the League, he continued to "cohabit" with it, while the Soviets always had spurned its offers. Moscow especially opposed the League's sanctions and judicial functions. At the same time, Moscow supported international cooperation and disarmament to secure peace; no one's rearmament would serve peace, and Germany's rearmament would only force others to do so. Japan was ruining all chances for disarmament.

Appreciating Italian policy in the Balkans, Litvinov rejected panslavism and, implicitly offering Italy room to advance, he relayed that Moscow was not particularly interested in the area. Promising to consider Turkey's interests, the commissar said that like Italy, the Kremlin wanted an agreement between Ankara, Athens, and Sofia. If Hungary wished to establish friendly relations, so did the Kremlin.

Thankful for Mussolini's declaration on Japan, Litvinov pointed out that Japanese militarism threatened not only the USSR but European countries as well. Much preoccupied with Japan, the USSR was willing to renounce its rights to the East Chinese Railway, but did want compensation for its capital investment. The Soviets were counting on the moral effect on Japan of America's recognition, and between the USSR and the United States there was an identity of views on East Asia. The Soviets felt that they had to support China against Japan.

The foreign commissar continued that Moscow wished to improve relations with Berlin but could not ignore Papen's propositions to France, Rosenberg's speeches, or Hitler's rantings about eastward expansion. He promised to try to stop any anti-Soviet, anti-Italian, Franco-German union by drawing closer to France. Litvinov strongly asserted his belief that Rome and Moscow could work together.

Mussolini agreed with Litvinov, recalling that he had advised Hitler that damaging relations with the USSR was dangerous. Denying that Hitler's ideology had much in common with fascism, he had told the Führer that he would never permit an Austrian *Anschluss*, which was contrary to the

Kremlin's interests as well. Litvinov credited Italy with stopping *Anschluss*. The Duce agreed in principle to Litvinov's request for an extension for a year of the May 6 economic agreement.[35]

After attending a private meal with Attolico, Litvinov spent the afternoon sightseeing. That evening at the posh Albergo Excelsior, the Italians hosted the foreign commissar at a banquet, after which he and Mussolini discussed only "extraneous themes."[36] The next morning, Monday, Litvinov followed his royal audience with a meal at the township of Littoria in the Pontine Marshes. That afternoon he attended a reception at Campidoglio given by Rome's governor, and later that evening he reciprocated the previous night's fete with a banquet at the Soviet embassy.[37]

Meanwhile, speaking with Potemkin, Mussolini called the League "a weapon in international mystification and force over the weak," and he now stressed the possibility of Italy's leaving it.[38] The Duce explained that German foreign policy under Rosenberg's direction desired expansion to the northeast and southeast and threatened both the USSR and Italy. He continued that Göring in his first visit to Rome had spoken of that "damned" Dollfuss and had prophesied that National Socialism would soon come to power in Austria. Italy, Mussolini promised, would decisively oppose *Anschluss* in any form. He then noted that the German-Polish rapprochement threatened the Soviet Union with war against Germany, Poland, and Japan.[39]

On Tuesday, Litvinov attended a luncheon at the American embassy and a tea at the Turkish embassy. He also found time to speak to the press, which, as usual, he charmed. Satisfied with Italy's policies, he continued:

For the 3 years of *de facto* relations and the 10 years of diplomatic relations between the Soviet Union and Italy, no conflicts and virtually no disputes have arisen. Nothing but benefit has resulted for both countries from their economic and political collaboration. We would therefore like merely to prolong and strengthen existing relations and forms of collaboration, and as my visit will undoubtedly further this, its purpose will be achieved.[40]

Concerning Italy's mediation in Berlin, which so fascinated European politicians and journalists, Litvinov wishfully denied any need: the USSR and Germany had normal diplomatic relations and a treaty of neutrality. He brushed aside as unimportant that he would pass through Berlin rather than Vienna on his return home. He also denied having had any contact with the Vatican and said that the USSR had made no special concessions to Soviet citizens on religious freedom. Nor was the USSR considering joining the League.[41] Having treated the journalists to a touch of Soviet openness, Litvinov left by train for the Brenner Pass at nine-thirty that evening.[42]

Only one cool spot disturbed the atmosphere surrounding Litvinov's visit. On Mussolini's instructions, Aloisi complained to Potemkin that on the very morning on which Litvinov had left Italian territory, Moscow radio had broadcast in French an outrageous attack on Italy, its king, and the fascist regime. A surprised Potemkin claimed that he knew nothing about it and surmised that it must have been a maneuver by Karl Radek and resulted from the excessive zeal of unauthorized individuals. When Aloisi turned back this answer as too vague for such a grave matter, Potemkin promised to telegraph Moscow immediately to stop similar incidents. A week later Potemkin telephoned Aloisi to say that Litvinov, after checking with Moscow's three radio stations, had determined that none had broadcast anything in French on the day in question regarding the Italian regime and the royal family. He attributed the broadcast to black propaganda by some unidentified private station using Moscow's call sign. Wishing to get to the bottom of the matter, Litvinov asked to know the exact date, hour, and wave length of the transmission.[43]

Practical results from the good feelings surrounding Litvinov's visit were few, but they were quick in coming. In the face of Italian complaints about the excessive trade imbalance and the unsatisfactory method of payments to Italian exporters, it was agreed on December 5 to prolong the May 6 agreement on export credits until the end of 1934. The Italian government was to continue to guarantee Italian exporters 75 percent of the value of Soviet orders in Italy.[44]

The ratifications of the Italo-Soviet treaty were exchanged in Moscow at midday on the fifteenth. *Izvestia* dedicated a long editorial to the event, and the Soviet press in general emphasized the possibilities of mutual friendship. Only Britain had not tied itself to Moscow. Italy, the papers continued, appreciated the USSR as an important factor for peace. And repeating the old refrains, the press stated that the pact with Italy was the natural development of preexisting friendly relations and proved that the USSR could maintain good relations with any capitalist state independently of its political regime.[45]

On February 8, 1934—the tenth anniversary of the establishment of relations between the two governments—Mussolini and Potemkin ratified the May 6, 1933, convention. The plenipotentiary seized the occasion to express his conviction that this friendship was essential for maintaining peace. He further offered Soviet thanks for Italian assistance in reestablishing diplomatic relations with Hungary. Mussolini replied that he intended to foster political and economic relations between the two states.[46]

The German Reaction

When Litvinov alighted the Rome Express in Berlin on the morning of December 7, 1933, he was met by the entire staff of the Soviet embassy plus representatives from the German foreign ministry and many members of the German and foreign press. His great successes in Washington and Rome apparently had impressed and shocked Hitler, and several editorials in the Nazi-controlled press invited Litvinov to establish closer contacts with Germany as he had with other states.[47]

That same day Mussolini described Litvinov's visit to Ambassador Hassell, who had just returned to Rome from Germany.[48] He insisted that no new agreements had been hatched, although the Duce admitted the economic and publicity value of the trip. Litvinov, he said, was much concerned about the international situation, especially in East Asia. He feared a possible German-Polish-Japanese conspiracy directed against the USSR, based in part on compensating Poland with Soviet territory. Mussolini reported that he had encouraged Litvinov's expressed desire for improved relations with Germany. Regarding disarmament, Litvinov had said that while he disliked German rearmament, he would not oppose it; after all, the Versailles Treaty did not involve the Soviet Union. Litvinov also had assured Mussolini that the USSR looked upon the peoples of Southeast Europe not as Slavs but as Balkan peoples; panslavism had been abandoned.

In the same vein, Suvich told Cerruti to assure Foreign Minister Neurath that Litvinov desired improved relations with Germany, which was something in Italy's interest, if only to impede further improvements in Franco-Soviet relations.[49] This argument likely appealed to Berlin. Back in Moscow on December 12, Litvinov reported the substance of his Rome conversations to the newly arrived German ambassador, Rudolf Nadolny.[50]

From Rome, Ambassador Hassell reported his impressions of Litvinov's visit, which he had garnered from Potemkin and "a reliable source."[51] He believed that Rome was unimpressed with its results, especially because of Litvinov's reserve. Italians nonetheless understood fully that the USSR feared Germany and would therefore welcome an understanding. Rome discounted Germany's handling of the Jewish question as an important element in Soviet animosity toward Germany.

Litvinov had told Mussolini, Hassell continued, that Japan obviously wanted a military solution to its problems in East Asia. The USSR, despairing of American help, feared that it would have to fight alone. Officials in Rome were saying that this anxiety about Japan, "which has grown almost to the proportions of a kind of psychosis," explained Litvinov's "strong reserve on the burning questions of European policy." Moscow had no aim in Europe other than safeguarding its western front while attending the volatile East. Therefore it was

entirely wrong to associate the visit of the Russian Foreign Minister in Rome with new European combinations to include Russia. Just as Mussolini desired no extension of the Four Power Pact which would deprive that treaty of its special character, so did Litvinov—at present at least—emphatically decline such opportunities. Russia wanted peace and security in the West, but no other political bonds in Europe.[52]

The impression left by the visit, Hassell thought, was one of a nonbinding exchange of views between leading statesmen, but without immediate practical consequences. Only time would tell if Mussolini had succeeded in warning Litvinov away from too close a tie with the Little Entente, or in inducing him to influence the Turks. "The only positively encouraging result [for Rome] lies in the satisfaction over the fact that Litvinov did not return home via Paris, but via Rome."[53]

On January 12, Mussolini told Hassell that since Litvinov's visit he had viewed Soviet policy with the greatest of misgivings.[54] He had tried, the Duce said, to make it clear that an anti-German policy could suck Russia into the orbit of France and the Little Entente and thereby involve it in serious European complications. Litvinov, in turn, had argued that the development was not Moscow's fault, and he brought up the old saws: the Hugenberg Memorandum, Rosenberg's Ukrainian plans, Rosenberg's negotiations with the Japanese in Berlin, and the German-Polish conversations. Mussolini told Hassell that the chief reason for the Soviet attitude was the destruction of communism in Germany, which made the Nazis a most dangerous enemy. On the other hand, Mussolini thought that Germany's attitude toward the Soviet Union was comprehensible only if Germany was sure that Japan intended to attack soon. Hassell responded that Germany could not change its Soviet policy and that courting Moscow would be a mistake. While agreeing, Mussolini also said that the chance of changing Soviet policy was not altogether lost. He warned that the Kremlin was behind the Turkish machinations in Southeast Europe, which were creating a bad situation for Bulgaria.

Soviet and Italian Accounts

On December 11, Litvinov summarized the meaning of his visit to Italy for his ambassador in France.[55] Mussolini had certified his love of peace and the Four Power Pact's harmlessness for the Soviet Union, and he had emphasized the improved relations between Rome and Paris. He remained opposed to Tokyo's aggression and promised not to render it or its allies any support. The Duce had assured Litvinov that he did not intend to solve international problems without Moscow. For his part, the foreign commissar said that he had stressed the danger of German aggression—a threat not only to the Soviet Union but to Italy as well. The Soviets, he had assured Rome, would be greatly pleased with an Italo-French rapprochement.

Amid reports that the Kremlin was pleased with Litvinov's trip to Rome, Attolico analyzed the speeches by Molotov and Litvinov as well as comments in *Izvestia*, all of which came in a three-day period at the end of December.[56] The foreign commissar publicly cast a positive light on things, characterizing Moscow's relations with Rome as having "special stability":

In the course of 10 years they have not suffered any vacillation, no conflicts either in the political or economic spheres. We have had in that time several instances of valuable diplomatic cooperation by Italy. We also have used Italian technical co-operation in several areas of our construction. Economic relations have developed to our mutual advantage. My recent visit to Italy and my reception there, witness the efforts of both countries to develop further our cooperation in all areas; the head of the Italian government, Signor Mussolini, and I came to this conclusion after an exchange of opinions of questions of current politics and on the best ways to preserve the general peace. Our efforts to maintain and develop relations with all important countries [i.e., Germany] is no small contribution in the matter of the general peace.[57]

Attolico emphasized the distinctions, to Italian advantage, that the Soviets were making between the Italian and German fascisms.[58] The year of 1933 had been most important for Russia's reintegration into Europe and recon-firmation as a great power. The Kremlin was maintaining a pacifist policy, especially now that the Soviets were convinced that they had the military/economic might to defend their country. Moscow was willing to ally with those states determined to maintain peace and was willing to abandon its political independence to enter into political combinations. The bolsheviks remained hostile to the Four Power Pact. Now that their enemies had departed the League, it had become a force for peace capable of inhibiting the aggressors, and the USSR was ready to join. "How much," he summed up, "and what has passed in 12 months!"[59]

Across the board, Italian publicists also waxed eloquent on the benefits of Italy's relationship with the USSR. Federico Curato was especially able in cutting to the core of Italo-Soviet cooperation, not, in any case, a radical break from the direction taken by prefascist governments. Liberal Italy, too, had seen the need for tying Central Europe and the Black Sea region to the port of Trieste and for creating markets to consume surplus production. Liberals had seen all this, but had done little; the fascist government had acted. Even while crushing internal communism, Mussolini had reopened diplomatic relations and had signed an economic accord. The trade level, although not high, was considerable; the major problem was to improve Italy's trade balance with Soviet Russia. At the political level, while Italy faced contentious issues with Germany, France, and Britain, no such prob-lems marred amicable relations with Soviet Russia. For its part, the USSR, faced with Germany, Japan, and the seemingly hostile Four Power Pact, was looking for points of support. Italy was working hard to soothe Soviet fears about the Four Power Pact's intent and hoped to mediate between Moscow and the powers surrounding it. The Soviet pact signified Italy's desire to expand peaceably its influence in the East.[60]

For all this, Rome refused to be excessively optimistic about either com-mercial or political relations with Moscow.[61] There remained, for example, the problem of Soviet demands for long-term credits. For the moment Italy could export industrial products in return for natural products, but with the successful industrialization of the FYP, Moscow predictably would have less need for Italian products, while Italy would always need Soviet raw materials and semiprocessed goods. Given the Soviet penchant for dumping, they would be competing vigorously in the Balkans if Germany, also practiced at dumping, did not conquer those markets first.

Although Italy had no need to fear either the Third or any other International, Soviet Russia's influence surely would grow in tandem with its economic expansion into the Balkans. For the moment the Soviet government had abandoned tsarist panslavism for its peace policy, but it could always revive that expansionism. This meant that Russo-Italian friendship before the war had been only conditional, and it had been Rome's fear of panslavism that had led to the demand for Dalmatia after the Great War. Whether Soviet expansionism was Slavic or bolshevist in nature, so long as it was directed to areas other than the Balkans and the Mediterranean, Italy was little concerned. Should it head in those directions, however, then Italy would become a bulwark of the West's defense against incursions from the East. Now, as before the war, Russia and Italy could either be good friends, or fierce enemies.

At the close of 1933, Attolico in a long and detailed report offered Rome his opinions on the directions of Soviet policy, dedicated to preventing a Franco-German alliance.[62] This, Moscow felt, theoretically could be done by working through either Berlin or Paris, but Hitler was pushing Moscow toward Paris. The Kremlin also worried that Germany might ally with Japan. Both France and the Soviet Union were obsessively preoccupied by security concerns—Moscow and Paris were at one in their psychology and their danger.

Attolico continued that Litvinov, when asked about rumors that France had offered the Kremlin a pact, had responded that his government was seeking only a regional pact of security with France, and that the USSR might enter the League of Nations. Litvinov maintained that, unlike a Franco-Soviet pact, a Franco-German agreement would also endanger Italy. Attolico, however, warned that the former might prove more dangerous than the German threat it was meant to contain. A regional grouping including Soviet Russia, France, Belgium, the Little Entente, Poland, and possibly Turkey, Estonia, and Latvia provided a good cover for what in earlier times would have been called a bilateral Franco-Russian pact. This, Attolico lamented, was to be feared because it would mean a return to the 1914 system of alliances and war.[63]

NOTES

1. Printed text in AP URSS b10 f1; *DVP* 16: no. 277.
2. Neither Rome nor Moscow took advantage of this last article despite subsequent Italian attacks on Abyssinia, Spain, and Greece, and despite Soviet moves on

Romania, the Baltic States, and Finland. See Rome to Grandi, 9/6/33: AP URSS b10 fl.

3. See Attolico to Rome, 9/11/33, 9/12/33: AP URSS b10 fl.

4. *The Times* (London), Sept. 4, 1933; *Izvestia*, Sept. 3, 1933; *DVP* 16: no. 278.

5. Federico Curato, "Italia e Russia," *Rassegna di politica internazionale* (May 1934): 182. The praise of the pact, however, was not universal. Some in the military feared increased bolshevik propaganda in the Italian colonies and in Italy through the Soviet commercial delegation in Milan. Mussolini to Attolico, 9/12/33: AP URSS b10 fl.

6. See *The Times* (London), Sept. 15, 1933, commenting on the articles by B.M. in *Le vie d'Italia e del mondo*: "Il Caucaso e le Alpi: Conversando con l'Ing. Angelo Omodeo," (Apr. 1933): 413-36; "Asia centrale sovietica: Conversando con l'Ing. Angelo Omodeo," (May 1933): 547-69; "Siberia: Conversando con l'Ing. Angelo Omodeo," (July 1933): 805–33; "Il Volgo: Conversando coll'Ing. Angelo Omodeo," (Sept. 1933): 1085-1118. Attolico, however, had no reason to hope naïvely for a dramatic spurt of trade. Less than a fortnight after the pact's signing, he asked Soviet authorities to increase the supply of Italian food products such as pasta, rice, olive oil, and citrus fruits to Italian technicians working in the USSR that winter. He was told that because of price and credit conditions, there would be no increase of purchases of Italian comestibles. MAE to DGAP, 9/28/33: AP URSS b12 f2.

7. *Il Telegrafo*, Sept. 5, 1933: AP URSS b10 fl; Benito Mussolini, "Italia e Russia," *Bibliografia Fascista* (Sept. 1933), no. 12: AP URSS b38 fl.

8. Carlo Lozzi, *Mussolini-Stalin: Storia delle relazioni italo-sovietiche prima e durante il fascismo* (Milan, 1983), pp. 110-11.

9. Aloisi circular 9/2/33: AP URSS b10 fl.

10. See *DGFP* C, 1: no. 420; and Cicconardi to Rome, 9/9/33: AP URSS b10 fl. Three weeks later, Mussolini wrote that the Four Power Pact was not an obstacle to the development of cordial relations with the USSR. Moscow was especially pleased that the Duce had published this article in a German newspaper. Berardis to Rome, 10/4/33: AP URSS b10 fl.

11. Bova Scoppa to Rome, 9/5/33: AP URSS b10 fl.

12. *Izvestia*, Sept. 3, 5, 1933; *Pravda*, Sept. 3, 1933; Stefani to Rome, 9/3/33, 9/4/33; Attolico to Rome, 9/4/33, 9/12/33: AP URSS b10 fl. The Kremlin backed up these press statements and praised Mussolini's article on the pact as well as the military and economic cooperation. Berardis to Rome, 9/26/33: AP URSS b10 fl. The communist press was not universally enthusiastic about the pact. Luidzhi (Luigi) Gallo, e.g., in "Sdvigi i treshchiny v massovoi base ital'ianskogo fashizma," *Komunisticheskii internatsional* (Sept. 20, 1933): 42-49, described the economic "crisis" in Italy and the antifascist movement of workers and peasants. Did this article represent Comintern upset to the signing of the Italo-Soviet Pact? Attolico to Rome, 11/7/33: AP URSS b11 fl; Grandi to Rome, 9/15/33: AP URSS b8 f3; Attolico to Rome, 9/5/33; Quaroni circular, 9/21/33: AP URSS b10 fl; *The Times* (London), Sept. 15, 1933. Attolico, not particularly pleased with the tenor of Karl Radek's article in *Izvestia* on September 5, complained to Litvinov, who weakly responded that the pact was too important to be tainted by one article. Attolico to Rome, 9/5/33: AP URSS b10 fl.

13. This opinion was backed up by the Poles, who saw German imperialism as pushing the Soviets and French together. They wanted to mediate between Paris

and Moscow. A strict Franco-Soviet accord would be a better guarantee of peace than was the Four Power Pact. Bellardi Ricci to Rome, 9/2/33: AP URSS b9 f8.

14. Attolico to Rome, 9/12/33, 9/18/33: AP URSS b8 f3; Attolico to Rome, 8/15/33, 8/29/33, 9/5/33, 9/19/33; Quaroni circular, 9/11/33; Consulate in Kharkhov to Rome, 9/15/33; Berardis to Rome, 9/26/33, 10/31/33, 11/28/33: AP URSS b9 f8; Berardis to Rome, 9/28/33: AP URSS b9 f9; Attolico to Rome, 9/18/33: AP URSS b10 f3; Bellardi Ricci to Rome, 9/5/33, 9/7/33; Attolico to Rome, 9/3/33: AP URSS b10 f1; Attolico to Rome, 9/23/33, 12/12/33: AP URSS b8 f4.

15. Political circles in Lithuania, satisfied with the pact, e.g., saw it as an avenue by which Moscow could approach Berlin. Stimulated by the Four Power Pact, the Italo-Soviet pact might serve as a model for a Soviet-German pact. Minister at Kaunas to Rome, 9/10/33; Grandi to Rome, 9/5/33; Stefani to Rome, 9/5/33; see Legation in Latvia to Rome, 9/28/33: AP URSS b10 f1. See also *Morning Post*, Sept. 5, 1933, and *The Times* (London), Sept. 4, 1933. Additionally, the Poles emphasized that the pact strengthened Rome in the Balkans and Moscow in East Asia.

16. Pignatti to Rome, 9/7/33: AP URSS b10 f1.

17. Marchi to Rome, 9/9/33: AP URSS b10 f1.

18. Grandi to Rome, 9/5/33; Stefani to Rome, 9/5/33: AP URSS b10 f1. The Kremlin had other fish to fry. Litvinov told his ambassador in London to pressure London by using the pact to wrench most-favored-nation status and guarantees. Britain, suggested Soviet representatives, was not pleased at this success for Soviet diplomacy. *DVP* 16: nos. 279, 280.

19. Embassy at Terapla to Rome, 9/8/33. The pact apparently did not interest Bulgarian political circles too much; Legation at Belgrade to Rome, 9/10/33; nor did the Danes seem too interested in the pact, but they did say that it was signed to prevent France from eclipsing Italy in the Balkans. Pansa to Rome, 9/14/33: AP URSS b10 f1.

20. Legation at Belgrade to Rome, "Politika," no. 9104, (Sept. 19, 1933), 9/19/33; another paper predicted that as soon as the Kremlin consolidated its internal situation, the USSR would return to its imperialistic policy; Legation at Belgrade to Rome, 9/11/33: AP URSS b10 f1.

21. Attolico to Rome, 6/13/33, 9/12/33: AP URSS b10 f1; Berardis to Rome, 10/28/33: AP URSS b9 f9; Note for Suvich, 10/22/33; Rosso to Rome, 11/10/33; Rome to Rosso, 11/15/33: AP URSS b8 f4; Quaroni to Suvich, 10/23/33; Rosso to Rome, 11/16/33: AP URSS b9 f3. There had been some talk that Litvinov would visit Italy while on his way to Washington, but the Kremlin rejected this idea for fear of antagonizing the Turks. Suvich memorandum, 10/27/33; Suvich circular, 11/2/33: AP URSS b8 f4.

22. Rome to Rosso, 11/19/33: AP URSS b8 f4.

23. The Soviets were not completely satisfied with the Italian press, however. The counselor at the Soviet embassy, Weinberg, complained about anti-Soviet books, pamphlets, and articles: Angelini, "Avvenire d'Italia," which dealt with the partition of the Ukraine; a series of short articles in *Popolo d'Italia*; Ciocca's book; and Bardi's *I soldati italiani nella Russia in fiamme*. Note for Suvich, 11/10/33: AP URSS b9 f3; Note for Suvich, 11/10/33: AP URSS b10 f1. *The Times* (London), Nov. 27, 1933. The Soviet press also commented on Göring's trip to Rome as an attempt to break Germany's isolation and warned that Italy would not be happy with Germany's commercial policies. *Pravda*, Nov. 10, 1933; Attolico to Rome, 11/14/33: AP URSS

b11 f1. For its part, Rome was upset at the propaganda activities of the Soviet consul in Milan. MAE Servizio Corrispondenza Uff. 3 promemorial, 11/3/33: AP URSS b10 f13.

24. Note for Suvich, 11/21/33; Rosso to Rome, 11/21/33, 11/24/33, 11/25/33; Rome to Rosso, 11/22/33: AP URSS b8 f4; Note for Suvich, 11/25/33; Attolico to Rome, 11/28/33: AP URSS b9 f3. The Soviets forwarded information on a possible attempt on Litvinov's life by Ukrainian circles and asked Italian authorities to take precautions. Note for Suvich, 11/27/33: AP URSS b9 f3.

25. Memorandum, 12/2/33: AP URSS b8 f4.

26. On October 27, Potemkin had told Suvich that Germany was trying to conclude an agreement with Japan at Soviet expense. Distrusting Britain in East Asia, Moscow wished to forge a pact between itself, Paris, Rome, and Washington to defend China against Japan. Suvich memorandum, 10/27/33; Suvich circular, 11/2/33: AP URSS b8 f4.

27. Berardis to Rome, 10/17/33: AP URSS b8 f4.

28. Note for Mussolini, 12/1/33: AP URSS b8 f1.

29. The trade statistics for the previous three years:

	Soviet Exports to Italy	Italian Exports to the USSR
1931	561,275,547 lire	275,663,030 lire
1932	333,484,503	237,000,090
1933 (9 mos.)	170,461,637	93,963,315

Source: Moscow embassy, Uff. Commerciale to Rome, 5/23/34: AP URSS b8 f1.

To this sorry picture had to be added that the Soviets were collecting in Italy merchandise for 100 million lire ordered in 1932. Because the projected purchases for 1933 would be 125.284 million lire, the actual new purchases for 1933 were only 25.284 million lire.

30. *The Times* (London), Nov. 27, Dec. 2, 1933; Marchi to Rome, 12/2/33: AP URSS b9 f3.

31. Suvich memorandum, 11/30/33: AP URSS b8 f4.

32. *The Times* (London), Dec. 4, 1933; Baratono to Rome, 12/2/33, 12/2/33: AP URSS b8 f4.

33. *DVP* 16: no. 405; Mussolini memorandum, 12/3/33: AP URSS b10 f1; MAE circular, 12/3/33: AP URSS b8 f4. The conversation proceeded along the lines of Krestinskii's December 2 telegram to Litvinov, which ordered that if Mussolini should begin to speak on disarmament, the League, or the invitation of the USSR, the United States, Germany, and Japan to a discussion of international problems, etc., Litvinov ought to hear him out but then protest that because of his continuing absence from Moscow, he was without instructions and could not answer. If Mussolini should broach the subject of German rearmament, Litvinov ought to say that in his

opinion the Soviet government would not agree to those demands because they were contrary to the interests of world peace. *DVP* 16: no. 400, n.291.

34. The world press picked up this theme of Italian upset at Japanese policy in the Far East. See *The Times* (London), Jan. 29, 1934, and "Business Abroad," *Business Week*, Dec. 16, 1933, 25, reporting rumors that Rome and Moscow had discussed ways of preventing Japanese inroads into their respective markets. TASS, noting "imperialist contradictions," reported on October 24 that Japanese economic expansion in Abyssinia and dumping in Austria and Hungary particularly upset Rome. Berardis to Rome, 10/31/33: AP URSS b11 f1. For its part, the Japanese press portrayed Mussolini as ready to lead the movement to ensure world peace and saw the possibility that discussions would bring about the entry of the United States, Germany, the Soviet Union, and Japan into the League. Auriti to Rome, 11/28/33: AP URSS b9 f3.

35. *The Times* (London), Dec. 4, 5, 1933.

36. *DVP* 16: p. 714.

37. MAE Cerimoniale, 12/4/33: AP URSS b8 f4.

38. *DVP* 16: n.299; *Izvestia*, Dec. 8, 1933. For Stalin's comments, see *DVP* 16: no. 438, and *Izvestia*, Jan. 4, 1934, wherein Stalin noted that the Duce talked extensively about League reform but offered few concrete proposals. Attolico to Rome, 1/5/34: AP URSS b12 f1.

39. *DVP* 16: no. 411; Memorandum, 12/4/33: AP URSS b9 f5.

40. *DVP* 16: no. 412; *Izvestia*, Dec. 6, 8, 1933.

41. Following Litvinov's Rome visit, rumors continued that he had effected a rapprochement with the Vatican. A lead article in *Osservatore Romano* (Jan. 19, 1934) clarified the situation: the Vatican, unsatisfied with Litvinov's declaration about religious freedom in the Soviet Union, was demanding special protection for clerical activities. The Soviets not only would make no such concession, but would even more closely regulate the activities of Catholic priests. *New World Review* 3 (Mar. 1934): 6.

42. Roy MacGregor-Hastie, *The Day of the Lion: The Life and Death of Fascist Italy, 1922-1945* (New York, 1963), pp. 218-19, without citation, claims that Mussolini told Litvinov that to stop Hitler their nonaggression pact ought to be extended to France and, if possible, to Britain. The Soviet Union had to be brought into the League to fill the gap left by Germany. Litvinov left it to Mussolini to see that these steps were taken, and he assured the Duce of the Kremlin's undying admiration. For his part, Hitler managed to persuade London not to join the Rome-Moscow axis. Having convinced the British that Germany was going to be as thick a shield as the West would ever need against bolshevism, more reliable and better placed than Italy, Hitler decided that Mussolini had to be placated. He said that he would support any Italian move in the Mediterranean. In the end Hitler stalemated Mussolini's plans for an Italo-Soviet-French-British alliance and gave nothing in return.

43. Aloisi memorandums, 12/16/33, 12/23/33: AP URSS b9 f3.

44. *The Times* (London), Dec. 6, 8, 1933; *DVP* 16: no. 409, n.296.

45. *Izvestia*, Dec. 16, 1933; Suvich memorandum, 11/6/33; Attolico to Rome, 12/19/33: AP URSS b8 f4; Note for Suvich, 11/10/33: AP URSS b9 f3; Berardis to Rome, 11/11/33; Attolico to Rome, 12/12/33, 12/15/33: AP URSS b10 f1; Attolico to Rome, 12/16/33: AP URSS b11 f1; *The Times* (London), Dec. 16, 1933.

46. *The Times* (London), Feb. 9, 1934.

47. *Izvestia*, Dec. 8, 1933.

48. *DGFP* C, 2: no. 104.

49. Rome to Cerruti, 12/10/33: AP URSS b9 f9.

50. *DGFP* C, 2: no. 122.

51. Ibid., no. 130.

52. Ibid.

53. Ibid.

54. Ibid., no. 178.

55. *DVP* 16: no. 419.

56. Stefani to Rome, 12/6/33; Attolico to Rome, 1/12/34. The future ambassador to Rome, Boris Shtein, accompanied Litvinov from Berlin to Moscow and let it be known that the trip had gone well and that he foresaw grand political developments. Tamaro to Rome, 12/27/33: AP URSS b9 f3; *Izvestia*, Dec. 30, 1933, Jan. 1, 1934.

57. *DVP* 16: App. 2; Attolico to Rome, 12/29/33: AP URSS b8 f6.

58. Attolico to Rome, 12/29/33: AP URSS b8 f4; Attolico to Rome, 12/29/33; Summary of Litvinov's speech on the foreign policy of the USSR n.d.: AP URSS b8 f6; Attolico to Rome, 1/3/34: AP URSS b12 f1; Attolico to Rome, 1/3/34: AP URSS b10 f1; Attolico to Rome, 1/6/34: AP URSS b14 f3.

59. Attolico to Rome, 1/3/34: AP URSS b13 f10.

60. Curato, "Italia," pp. 183-85, ignored the Bessarabian question. Other small matters did occasionally crop up, e.g., the *San Marco* incident at Theodosia on January 14, when police fired shots at the ship's crew. There is no indication that Rome wished to make a big deal of the matter. Garibaldi to Rome, 2/1/34; Barduzzi to Rome, 3/8/34, 4/4/34, 5/16/34; Ministero delle Comunicazioni to MAE, 3/9/34, 4/5/34, 6/1/34; Rome to Barduzzi, 3/13/34: AP URSS b15 f3. For the so-called Wrangel Fleet interned at Bisserta, a chronic source of Soviet disaffection with France, see AP URSS b11 f5 and b18 f7.

61. Curato, "Italia," pp. 173-74, 185-86.

62. Attolico to Rome, 12/27/33: AP URSS b10 f1.

63. Three weeks later Attolico opined that Soviet entry into the League was probable. The time was ripe to have a long talk with Litvinov to express Italy's views on the League and its reform. Attolico to Mussolini, 1/18/34: AP URSS b13 f10. See *Izvestia*'s comments on Mussolini's meetings with Simon on League reform and the disarmament negotiations on Jan. 8 and 9, 1934.

8

Military Contacts

Attolico's fears of a return to the prewar alliance system notwithstanding, a series of military visits, consultations, technical collaborations, and constructions palpably carried forward the Italo-Soviet political rapprochement of 1933 and 1934.[1] Moscow also thereby reminded the German military establishment and industrialists of the now lost value of their own Rapallo-era cooperation with the Soviets.[2] Further, paralleled by Franco-Soviet political exchanges, the military contacts presumably were thought useful in greasing the ways for Italo-French cooperation, which, together with Italo-Soviet and Franco-Soviet collaboration, would immobilize Hitler or—better yet—force Germany to return to Rapallo. For Rome these contacts were economically important. Additionally, they slightly improved Italy's ability to force Hitler toward moderation and, specifically, to thwart *Anschluss*.

MILITARY VISITS

As a tangible sign of the cordial relations developing between Rome and Moscow, and following up and symbolizing the economic accord of May 6, two Italian submarines—the *Tricheco* and *Delfino*—visited the Soviet Black Sea port of Batum later in the month. This, as TASS pointed out, marked the first visit of Italian submarines to the Soviet Union—just as Italo Balbo's 1929 trip to Odessa had been the first such flight of military aircraft. Ambassador Attolico, military attaché Aldo de Ferrari, the Italian consul at Tiflis, and the submarine captains met the Soviet naval command and were treated to banquets and tours. The Italians reciprocated with a reception of their own and visits to the submarines. The first foreigners to be so honored, Attolico and de Ferrari went aboard the modern cruiser *Krasnyi Kavkaz*, built completely in the yards at Novorossiisk and the pride of the Red Navy. After a four-day fete, the submarines put to sea early on the morning of May 27. That same day Attolico and de Ferrari boarded the *Armenia*, bound for Odessa, where they arrived three days later. At Sebastopol they honored the fallen of the Crimean War, and they were treated to visits to factories and a state farm. For the benefit of the press, Attolico found time to praise Soviet hospitality, industry, agriculture, and economic cooperation. Noting that Odessa was the most important maritime center on the Black Sea, the ambassador added that the recent economic accord of May 6 had extended the jurisdiction of the consulate general in Odessa to other Black Sea ports.

The Italians next stopped at Kiev, whence they departed for Moscow on June 1. In his report describing the tour, de Ferrari praised Soviet hospitality and naval construction. Although, thus far, no incidents had marred the trip, the Italians did note the incredible misery in the Crimea and Ukraine. They for example, passed on the claim by the German consul that 147 mothers had been imprisoned for eating their own children.[3] Curiously, the horror of this self-imposed suffering did not prompt Rome's representatives to suggest that the USSR was in any way an unfit partner for Italy.

The submarines were only the beginning. During August, as the final touches were being negotiated for the Italo-Soviet Pact of Friendship, Neutrality, and Nonaggression, Moscow made its approaches. Marshal Voroshilov, the Soviet Union's leading military figure, in a letter delivered August 7, informed Rome of his intention to send part of the Black Sea Fleet to Italy in September or October to return the visit made by the Italian submarines. Contact between the officers of the two countries, Voroshilov thought, would be useful, and he invited two infantry and one aviation officer to attend Soviet military maneuvers. Moscow also intended to invite Italians to its naval exercises and desired a reciprocal invitation to Italian maneuvers.[4]

Five days later V.P. Potemkin, the Soviet plenipotentiary representative in Italy, repeated Voroshilov's plea and invitation. Although Italo Balbo, now heading the Italian air force, threw cold water on the initiative, the other services proved more receptive.[5] A Soviet military mission visited Italy, and, on the occasion of its return to the USSR, *Izvestia* published the Kremlin's thanks for the "exceptional courtesy given the mission by the military authorities and by the Italian government."[6] An Italian mission, which included a brigadier general, arrived in Moscow on September 24 for a fortnight's feting and touring.[7]

Potemkin also told Suvich on August 12 that his government wished to send a flotilla from the Black Sea fleet to call on Italian ports to repay Italy for the recent submarine visit to Batum, and to demonstrate publicly the cordiality existing between the two countries. This was quickly arranged. Three Soviet vessels, the cruiser *Krasnyi Kavkaz* and the destroyers *Petrovskii* and *Shaumian*, left Sebastopol on October 17 and arrived in Naples thirteen days later. To dramatize Foreign Commissar Litvinov's forthcoming trip to Rome, the Soviets asked that the captains be allowed to go to Rome to call upon Mussolini. They did do so during their brief three-day stay, but otherwise they and their crews were amply celebrated and dined, and they visited shipyards, Mt. Vesuvius, and Pompeii.[8]

The Soviet press emphasized that the naval visit demonstrated the friendship between Italian and Soviet military and civilian authorities.[9] The Italian press merely recorded the festivities without political comment. *The Times* speculated that the official participation of the Turkish ambassador showed the good understanding developing between all three countries and that these friendly relations preoccupied Berlin, where it was noted that Moscow was anticipating the visit of yet another Italian military delegation. The Italians duplicitously denied this latter report.[10]

In fact, after a brief lull, the military exchanges picked up again. By mid-April 1934, plans were underway for visits by chemical warfare experts. Based on the success of this exchange in July, during which Potemkin presented the Soviet delegation to Mussolini,[11] Attolico called the mutual contacts a "tradition," and he emphasized their political as well as military utility. Both he and the Italian minister of war thought that the moment was propitious for improving relations and that new forms of military cooperation ought to be investigated. The ambassador, for example, suggested that the two aviation services cooperate in an exercise based on a problem of stratospheric navigation. This, he thought, would raise the prestige of the Italian air force in Soviet eyes.[12]

New military exchanges did quickly arise. To solidify mutually friendly relations, three Soviet military Tupolev TB–3 (ANT–6) aircraft officially visited Italy in repayment for Balbo's 1929 flight to Odessa. The planes, which recently had visited Warsaw, left Kiev on August 6, and traveled to Rome via Kharkov, Odessa, Istambul, and Athens. Commanded by General R.P. Eideman,[13] the planes carried thirty-nine, including five other generals plus civilian aviation figures—all met at the Rome airport by many Italian officials. Hoping to present the Soviet delegation to Mussolini, Potemkin delayed his vacation. The Duce, "with his usual cordiality," agreed, and on the hot afternoon of August 8, he, Under Secretary of the Air Force General Giuseppe Valle, and Under Secretary of State Fulvio Suvich, received the Soviet mission in the Palazzo Venezia. After the Duce praised Russian aviation, the Soviets shouted three "hurrahs."[14]

The Italians organized visits to military and industrial establishments, for example, FIAT in Turin, to encourage contracts to supply the USSR with military goods.[15] The Soviet fliers with General Poppo also traveled to Casserta and toured the city of Naples by automobile. Perhaps feeling lucky to have survived the latter excursion, the Soviets then were treated to a farewell banquet attended by five Italian generals and members of the Italian foreign ministry. They departed Rome in grand style on August 13. While General Valle watched, they circled the city several times—much as Balbo had circled

Odessa five years before—and then they flew near the Palazzo Venezia before heading to Vienna, whence they turned homeward on the sixteenth.[16]

By making the trip in one stage as an endurance test, Moscow wished to demonstrate the maturity of its air industry, personnel, and navigation, and the Soviet press reproduced parts of Italian articles on the quality of Soviet air activities.[17]

At the same time, another Soviet group had flown to Paris via Vienna and returned by way of Prague, dramatizing the political importance of the flight. The Soviet press for nearly two weeks avidly followed both flights and almost always placed the stories emanating separately from Rome and Paris under one large headline. Clearly they saw the two separate military visits as one diplomatic event publicly demonstrating the close cooperation flowering between Italy, France, Austria, Poland, Czechoslovakia, and the USSR. Extolling the events and attendant ceremonies, the press further stressed, in a flight of hyperbole, that the visits had helped to consolidate universal peace.[18]

These military contacts of 1934 culminated in the fall, when Moscow and Rome exchanged observers to their annual military maneuvers. The Italians again organized the program for the Soviet mission, headed by General Utitskii, to include visits to military and industrial establishments so as to encourage contracts for supplying the USSR with military goods. In return, General Grazioli headed a mission to observe the maneuvers around Minsk held from September 6 to the 10th. Given "particular attention and honor" by the Soviets, he told Attolico that the Red Army's enormous progress had impressed him. The ambassador, for his part, again stressed the political importance of the whole series of military contacts.[19]

Even as tensions were building in 1935 over Italy's mobilization against Abyssinia, an Italian delegation attended important Soviet military maneuvers to the west of Kiev from September 12 to the sixteenth. Given the city's strategic sensitivity and the concurrent attendance of observers from France and Czechoslovakia, countries with which Moscow recently had signed mutual assistance pacts, the Italian chargé in Moscow credited the Soviet invitation to Italy as having special political significance.[20] Headed by General Monti, the Italians saw heavily motorized units, many planes, and five-hundred parachutists. After the exercise the Italians, along with the French and Czechs, attended a reception. Later they visited a factory complex and then went to Moscow, where they arrived on the twenty-second to attend another party with the French and Czech representatives.[21]

In return, Soviet military men headed by General Gordovikov and three other generals, including Kmelnitskii, who had been part of the Soviet mission to the Italian maneuvers of 1932, attended Italian exercises. The Soviets especially wanted the mission to tour Italy after the maneuvers.[22]

Moscow proved quite determined to preserve its military contacts with Rome. Even while wallowing in the mud slung at one another during the

Abyssinian conflict and the first four months of the Spanish Civil War, on November 10, 1936, twenty high Soviet figures, including marshals M. N. Tukhachevsky and S. M. Budnenny, visited the Italian embassy to see films of Abyssinia's conquest. Tukhachevsky was especially impressed, and asked if he, Voroshilov, and others could see additional films.[23] This request presumably reflected his own professional interests as well as the Kremlin's larger hope of suggesting that it held no insuperable grudge because of Italy's colonial conquest of that African nation.

The screening of these films, however, proved to be the last gasp. As political relations withered, so too did the *raison d'état* of the military exchanges.

NAVAL CONSTRUCTION

Productive as these exchanges were for their symbolism and practical support for diplomacy, the Soviets wanted more. Despite the rapid industrialization of the USSR by virtue of the Five Year Plans, the Soviets continued to lack the skills and industrial capability necessary to produce the technology of modern weaponry. Stalin sought foreign offers for naval machinery, armor plate, heavy guns, and even complete battleships.

Soviet Needs

Reviving a significant prewar connection in design and technical expertise,[24] in 1925 the Russians sought Italian help for their naval program, a relationship celebrated by the visit of Italian naval units to Odessa in that year. The new submarine construction, begun in 1927 and 1928, was designed by Cantieri Riuniti dell'Adriatico (CRDA) and resulted in the *Dekabrist* (D)-class, for which the *Fratelli Bandiera*, built by the same yard at about the same time, may have been the prototype. The first six of these oceangoing submarines appeared in 1929.[25]

In April 1929, the 16th Party Congress accepted Stalin's First FYP for developing the Soviet economy and creating the factories necessary for rearming the army and navy. Simultaneously a five-year ship construction program (1928-1933) was confirmed. Much wider than the 1926 program, it foresaw the construction of small ships of all classes, including transports, merchant vessels, barges, and, especially, submarines. In 1932 the Central Committee and government resolved to create new shipbuilding enterprises.[26]

With the Second FYP Stalin moved closer to the concept of a large, balanced fleet strategy in line with the tradition of Alfred Thayer Mahan. The naval staff, however, informed him that Soviet heavy industry, unlike tsarist factories and yards, could not construct capital ships on its own.

Tenders thus were sought abroad for complete battleships as well as machinery, armor plate, and heavy guns for hulls to be built in the USSR.[27]

Much of the outside help came from fascist Italy. The era of the Kremlin's close association with Italian shipbuilding, begun in 1925 and embracing all types of warships, ended only after the Second World War. In seeking Italian yards, designs, motors, armament, equipment, and engineers—and in purchasing Italian ships—the Soviets were demonstrating yet another continuity with their tsarist past.

But the key advantages were real, not historic. With an outstanding reputation for warship design and arsenal labor cheaper than France's and Britain's, Italy was getting a higher return for its naval expenditure than was any other major power. While the depression racked other nations' yards, Italian yards were keeping their labor in a higher state of efficiency with regular work. Enviably, they were receiving more foreign than domestic orders, and without labor discord they contrasted strikingly with the practically idle French and British yards.[28]

The commercial agreement of 1931, however, limited Soviet naval purchases to $5 million.[29] Why? The Italian ship subsidy law, designed to stimulate the growth of a merchant marine serviceable in peace and war, also applied to the construction of foreign ships. These subsidies, although limited to 114 million lire a year from 1930 to 1934, were sufficient to allow Italian shipbuilders to compete comfortably, but not without limits, with other nations. So, while the USSR wanted to place more orders in Italian yards, Rome limited shipbuilding for the Soviet Union to 25 percent of total Soviet orders.

Despite the artificial limit, this commercial nexus proved attractive to the Soviets, in part because the technical requirements of both navies were remarkably similar.[30] Both operated on closed, shallow, relatively sheltered seas, close to home ports, air support, and repair and resupply facilities. Neither, therefore, needed ships with long cruising ranges or extreme endurance. This permitted high, fuel-consuming speeds, increased maneuverability, and reduced protective armor. Further, these ships could afford to mount heavy guns requiring more frequent replacement because of their heavier shells fired at higher muzzle velocities. In addition, although the Soviet Union had no treaty displacement limitations on its warships, the relatively shallow depths of the Baltic and Black seas limited permissible drafts just as effectively. Historically, in any case, the Russian navy rarely had ventured great distances from its coastal waters.

Both powers faced the stark conundrum of balancing naval capabilities with foreign necessities and economic realities. The Italian peninsula was like an island, vulnerable to combined air and naval attack, cursed with having its critically important sea communication routes run through an enclosed sea with outlets controlled by others.

All Soviet routes to open seas were likewise controlled by foreign powers, but even more evidently hostile ones than in the Italian case. Compare the persistent Soviet-Japanese enmity to the traditional Anglo-Italian amity; consider that when Germany was not bottling up the USSR in the Baltic, Britain was. Even with a friendly Turkey, the Black Sea leads only to the Mediterranean, which was blocked by Great Britain at either end. The Allied Intervention following the Bolshevik Revolution had proved Soviet Russia's vulnerability to naval attack and invasion on many fronts. And last, while the Soviets did not need to keep alive the bonds of overseas expatriates as the Italians did, the Allied blockade during the Intervention demonstrated the importance of sea routes even for a continental power such as the Soviet Union.

Italian Construction and Technical Assistance to the Red Navy during the First Years of the Second FYP

Lured by Italian technology and designs, which so well fitted Soviet strategic needs, the Kremlin actively sought a close association with Italian shipbuilders. This dependence on Italian ship design during the 1930s suggests how little Soviet naval construction was directed toward high-seas operations.

Early Negotiations. In April 1932, a Soviet economic delegation negotiating in Italy asked about collaboration on naval warships.[31] The chief of Soviet naval construction attempted to work out an arrangement, but the firms of Ansaldo and CRDA refused to talk, pleading that their technical officials were overburdened and lacked authorization from Admiral Giuseppe Sirianni, the naval minister, to conduct such negotiations. Only after the Soviet representatives had left for Berlin did Moscow receive a letter from Sirianni, dated January 26, 1933, satisfactorily resolving the matter.

In late March, on the occasion of the arrival of the new Soviet naval attaché to his post in Rome, the Soviets indicated that they intended to order fast, light cruisers of six to seven thousand tons, as well as a smaller type of vessel used in the Italian navy.[32] Toward this end they proposed a technical mission to visit Italian shipyards. For political reasons, they did not want these ships to be built entirely in foreign yards, and therefore they wished to order the essential parts in Italy and assemble them in the USSR with Italian technical assistance. In Moscow, Attolico unsuccessfully pressed the Soviets for more than the 50 million lire they were offering to spend.

At the beginning of June, a commission headed by a Professor Andreev arrived in Italy to conclude the negotiations, but after two and one-half months they came to nothing.[33] CRDA and Ansaldo, Potemkin complained, had presented neither detailed offers nor prices for either the technical collaboration or the material orders. Despite some last-minute hints of progress on the problem of the firms guaranteeing the results of their technical collaboration, the Soviet commission returned home, not wishing to tarry in Italy while waiting for all the documents necessary for a contract. Potemkin suggested that to eliminate obstacles the two firms ought promptly to communicate prices and precise guarantees relative to technical collaboration and to compile by the end of August all of the materials necessary for contracts. Attolico urged Rome to move quickly.

Admiral Sirianni explained to the foreign ministry that negotiations between the Soviets and the naval yards, begun in 1932, had not been completed, because Moscow had requested ships with unrealistic specifications.[34] The problem was the ratio of desired speeds to displacements. For the next phase of negotiations, begun in January 1933, Sirianni further explained that he had intervened indirectly for a positive solution of the Soviets' technical collaboration request. And the latest talks, those begun in June with Professor Andreev, had failed to work out the details because the yards had no previous experience in translating the Soviet desires into contractual language. Referring to Potemkin's promemorial, Sirianni argued that the first two points could be explained by the contract's complexity and newness. As for the third, the yards did not want to give full guarantees because, although the designs were Italian, the motors were to be built in the USSR. In any event, the last problem had been resolved; Ansaldo had agreed to give partial guarantees for the construction of its machinery by Soviet firms. CRDA would follow Ansaldo's lead on this matter, and Sirianni believed that the other problems could be solved as well.

Still, the negotiations for collaboration ground on slowly, with the high prices asked by the Italians a major, but not insuperable, stumbling block.[35] Then on February 13, 1934, the chief of the Soviet naval general staff attempted to break the logjam by suggesting to Attolico that he approach Marshal Voroshilov and Ordzhonikidze to get their support for the negotiations already begun by engineer Enrico of Ansaldo. Attolico took the hint and asked the foreign ministry to tell Ansaldo that the Soviets were prepared to reopen negotiations.[36] The problem of price, however, still haunted the negotiations. Levenson insisted that his government would not pay more than 27 million lire, while Ansaldo was asking for 37.76 million lire for the material and the group of engineers and technicians who were to remain in Soviet Russia for five years.[37]

Within five weeks Attolico was able to secure a meeting with Voroshilov.[38] The marshal said that although his government was negotiating with French industry for the construction of torpedo boats, he preferred to see a contract concluded in a friendly way for Italian motor torpedo boats. He lamented, however, that it seemed that Ansaldo did not want to come to a deal, an assertion that Attolico denied. The ambassador guessed that Moscow would compromise enough on price so that a deal could be struck for these boats. This opinion was confirmed by Rosengolts, the foreign trade commissar, who told Attolico that price was less important than the conditions of payment.[39]

On April 30, 1934, Ansaldo signed a contract for technical consultations and the supply of naval motors to the USSR for 34 million lire. Attolico told the Kremlin that the price reduction conceded by Ansaldo had resulted from the intervention of the royal authorities responding to Voroshilov's appeal. The company and Mussolini praised the ambassador for his assistance.[40] For his part, Voroshilov expressed satisfaction with this and other contracts with other firms, and he suggested that they would help advance Italo-Soviet political relations. In relaying Voroshilov's sentiments to Rome, Attolico added his conviction that Italy ought to work diligently to fulfill its military contracts with the USSR, not only because Voroshilov sincerely appreciated them, but also because they were then the only significant commercial opportunities that Italy had to offer the Kremlin.[41]

Ansaldo's Contracts with the USSR. One of the Italian firms most active in working on military contracts with the Soviet Union was Ansaldo of Genoa.[42] Among its contracts, the firm built two *esploratore* (escort vessels) designed to protect Soviet fishing smacks in the Vladivostok area. As they neared completion, the questions of their transfer to Soviet nationality and their physical move from Genoa to Vladivostok raised minor legal and political problems.

Fearing that the trip would cause political complications under the Soviet flag, Moscow wanted the ships to be transferred under the Italian mercantile flag with Italian captains and crews. After all, the two ships would have to traverse oceans and use ports controlled by the British and Japanese empires. The problem was that according to Italian maritime law, no foreign national could fully own Italian commercial vessels unless he had resided in the kingdom for five years. The ships would pass to the ownership of the Soviet government upon their consignment in Genoa. Rome, desiring to accommodate the Soviet request, batted the problem about.

One possible solution was to have an Italian consul at Vladivostok formally transfer the nationality of the ships, but this would relieve the Soviet Union of any financial-insurance responsibilities during the trip. Alternatively, Ansaldo could consign the ships to the commercial representative, who had more than the five years' residency.

To the additional legal problem of a warship flying a commercial flag, the Soviets replied that the ships could go unarmed to Vladivostok, where they would be armed with their weapons and munitions carried as cargo. The enrollment of such vessels in the merchant marine temporarily removed their military character, and Italy previously had adopted this solution when furnishing warships to other foreign states. Small arms, however, would be carried, in accordance with mercantile practice, to guard against pirates in the eastern seas.

The absence of an Italian consular agent in Vladivostok at that time created still another problem. The acts of transferring nationality, flags, and documents would have to be done by the captains of the two ships, who would then have to give the papers to the first Italian consular official they should meet on their way home. Mussolini himself ultimately intervened to ensure that the ships were transferred according to Soviet desires.[43]

The two diesel ships, the PS 8 and PS 26, weighed anchor in Genoa on October 27 manned by probably eighty-seven Italians commanded by officers of the Lloyd Triestino Co. and, learning the ropes, eighteen Soviet officers and men.[44] The latter included Admiral Kukel, who had served as the Soviet representative at Ansaldo. Capable of making twenty knots and armed with twelve rifles, they passed through the Suez Canal less than a week after departing Genoa and reached Colombo, Ceylon, on November 13. Between Singapore and Hongkong they survived a violent monsoon. The long trip, in effect a shakedown cruise, was not marred by the few repairs needed along the way, and the Soviets were pleased with their purchases.

The Italian captains, too, were pleased with the cruise and their treatment at Soviet hands. Together they had celebrated on board the fascist and bolshevik holidays of October 28 and November 7 respectively. At the transfer ceremonies the Soviets even shouted "long live" for both the king and Duce, and they saluted the Italian tricolor. Returning home via the Trans-Siberian Railroad, the Italians spent two days in Moscow, where again they were shown every courtesy. The group left for Warsaw on December 26, the captains carrying a military report for Rome. The two escort vessels were now armed with three 100mm guns.[45]

Thereafter, the naval design office of the Ansaldo group of companies maintained a lively business relationship with the USSR. In October 1934, an Ansaldo delegation attached to the construction office "Bolshevik" completed forty guns of various calibers for the Soviet navy. Notwithstanding the obstacles, especially the deficiencies in the Soviet plant, they had done their job brilliantly and cordially, at least according to the Italian consul in Leningrad. At the same time the consul reported that another Ansaldo delegation of about forty had been sent to Leningrad and the Marti shipyard to complete various jobs, among them to construct a ship of the *esploratore* class. For its projects Ansaldo asked for and, because there was no political objection, received state guaranteed-credits.[46]

GENERAL UMBERTO NOBILE AND THE SOVIET AIRSHIP PROGRAM

The famous Umberto Nobile as a technical consultant to Dirizhablestroi lent the Soviets critical support in the construction of dirigibles.[47] Nobile, upon his return from an Arctic expedition aboard the *Malyghin*, arrived in Moscow at the end of August 1931. While there he spoke with Abramo Holtsman, the head of civil aviation, and Purmal, the head of its subsidiary organization, Dirizhablestroi. Attending were also two famed Soviet air engineers, Flaxermann and A.N. Tupolev. It quickly was made clear to the general that the Soviets wished to expand their civil airship program.[48] Effusively interested, Nobile stressed that a dirigible program had to be just that, a program comprehensively incorporating all the technical and managerial skills necessary, from blueprints to functioning air routes.

Nobile was preaching to the converted, and the Soviets quickly asked him to head up such a program and promised that there would be enough money to finance it. Nobile prudently made his acceptance of a long-term obligation contingent upon his government's approval and Moscow's promise to provide him with the means to complete his work. Before leaving for Italy, on September 30, Nobile stipulated a preliminary accord with Holtsman for scientific cooperation. Nobile's contract called for the construction of dirigibles of 37,000 cm, 7,000 cm, and 1,000 cm as well Arctic exploration by dirigible.[49]

Pressed to return quickly, before leaving Moscow the general wrote his wife, asking her to find his designs for the dirigible "N," which his government had rejected in 1927, and those of the dirigible "Mr" of 1,000 cm. Nobile planned to use this smaller ship to familiarize Soviet engineers with the construction of the Italian-type of semirigid dirigibles.[50]

When Nobile started his work, for all intents and purposes there were no Soviet facilities, materials, or personnel for an airship program. All had to be done from scratch. That year and the next, with Nobile's assistance, the Soviets constructed three dirigibles of the soft type to serve in a pilots' school. In the spring of 1932, again under Nobile's direction, the Soviets began the study and construction of dirigibles of the Italian type, and later they began to study the construction of rigid dirigibles. In 1932 Nobile executed a study for a stratospheric dirigible of 100,000 cm, and, spurred by Soviet desires for high-altitude ships, he continued to work on this project into 1935. Nobile's V–5, a small semirigid dirigible, made its first flight in April 1933.

The entire program, however, suffered several unfortunate accidents. One ship the Italians were helping to build with Dirizhablestroi in 1933 was accidentally destroyed.[51] In 1934 another was built, but it and another dirigible, the V–7 constructed by Felice Trojani, were consumed by fire along with the wooden hanger housing them.[52] A new ship, substantially a copy of the Italian airship *Italia*, was then constructed according to Nobile's plans. His activities, including pilot training, were circumscribed, however, by appendicitis, hospitalization, and a long vacation in Italy.[53]

By 1935, despite these setbacks, a well-furnished site had been set up about 25 km from Moscow, and another aerial facility was under construction at Sverdlovsk to provide anchorage pylons.[54] At Dirizhablestroi there were one-hundred qualified engineers and many specialized workers, who had learned to construct and mount dirigibles of the semirigid type. The Soviets were projecting the construction of such dirigibles of 2,300, 9,500, and 20,000 cm in the next three years. And there were plans for a semirigid dirigible of 50,000 cm. The construction of a hangar large enough to contain such a giant was slated to begin in 1936.

The maiden flight of the V–6, one of the Italian-designed dirigibles, with Nobile aboard left Moscow on the afternoon of April 21, 1935, and arrived in Leningrad that evening. Two days later it returned to Moscow. The second flight, again under Nobile's personal direction, departed Moscow on May 16, flew to Archangel, and returned to the Soviet capital on the eighteenth.[55]

By late July 1935, Soviet engineers completed the V–7 bis. with Nobile's and Trojani help. This dirigible and the V–6 were to establish regular air service between Moscow and Sverdlovsk. In one of the trials, which lasted forty-one hours, the airship reached the White Sea from Moscow despite bad weather. On the night of October 23 to 24, 1935, the V–7 bis. hit an electric line during a forced landing and was destroyed in the ensuing fire.[56]

The V–6 had little better luck. After setting a world-record flight for duration in October 1937, in February of the next year it was destroyed during a test flight in the Murmansk region. Thirteen crewmen died. Responding to the tragedy, numerous diplomatic representatives at Moscow, including the English, French, and German, sent their condolences to the Soviet government. Ambassador Rosso explained to Rome that he had refused to follow the German lead because it did not seem to him that the catastrophe was sufficient to justify official condolences.[57]

Nobile's contract with Moscow was to end in February 1936.[58] Eight months before then, the head of Dirizhablestroi tried to convince him to renew it. Nobile had several reservations and made his acceptance contingent on participation in an Arctic expedition. The Soviets agreed and asked him to prepare voyages for 1936 and 1937 in the Arctic region with a dirigible of 20,000 cm. This ship was to be of the Italia-type with some significant improvements. The V–8 was completed by Soviet engineers and first flew in 1938.

Meanwhile, in a personal letter to Mussolini, the general placed himself at the Duce's disposal. By November 1935 he had decided not to stay, and he wrote the Italian ambassador in Moscow, "At this time [during the war with Abyssinia] . . . it seems intolerable that I should serve a foreign government rather than my own."[59] In that same letter, Nobile asked for the ambassador's help in case the Soviets, anxious for his expertise, decided to keep him after the expiration of his contract. He got out without difficulty.

By that time, however, Soviet relations with Italy in all fields had begun to crumble, buffeted first by the Italo-Abyssinian War and then all but destroyed by the Spanish Civil War.

NOTES

1. A shortened version of this chapter first appeared as "Manifestations of Cordiality," *Naval History* (Spring 1989): 25-28.

2. On January 13, 1934, at a farewell dinner given by the Red Army for the departing Italian military attaché, Lt. Col. Aldo de Ferrari, the Soviets told the German military attaché that they desired a return to military cooperation. To put an edge on this wish, they intimated that they were considering equipping their submarines with Italian torpedoes. *DGFP* C, 2: no. 191.

3. De Ferrari to Rome, 6/6/33; Attolico to Rome, 6/6/33: AP URSS b8 f2; Suvich memorandum, 5/31/33: AP URSS b10 fl.

4. Suvich memorandum, 8/7/33: AP URSS b10 fl.

5. Rome to Attolico, 9/13/33; Suvich to Baistrocchi, 8/12/33; Sirianni to Suvich, 8/17/33; Baistrocchi to Suvich, 8/19/33; Balbo to Suvich, 8/30/33: AP URSS b10 fl. Balbo was flush with honors from his transatlantic flight to Chicago and back in early July. *Izvestia* congratulated the Italians for their trans-Atlantic flight and said that the Soviets were studying Italian aviation. The paper also noted French upset that Balbo, fearing antifascist demonstrations, had refused to visit France after his flight. It concluded that the Italo-French rapprochement was politically and psychologically difficult. *Izvestia*, July 27, Aug. 12, 22, 1933; Attolico to Rome, 8/15/33, 8/29/33: AP URSS b10 fl; *The Times* (London), July 17, 1933.

6. *Izvestia*, Sept. 10, 1933; Attolico to Rome, 9/11/33: AP URSS b10 fl.

7. Berardis to Rome, 10/9/33: AP URSS b10 fl. Suggestive of the web of political possibilities inherent in these military exchanges, in November a Polish flight went to Moscow. *Izvestia*, Nov. 4, 1933.

8. Rome to Attolico, 9/13/33: AP URSS b10 fl; Suvich to Baistrocchi, 8/12/33; Sirianni to Suvich, 8/17/33; Berardis to Rome, 9/26/33, 9/28/33, 10/21/33; Potemkin to Rome, 10/14/33; Salerno Mele to Rome, 10/22/33; Rossoni to Rome, 10/23/33; Note for Suvich, 10/23/33; Baratono to Rome, 10/31/33, 11/1/33, 11/2/33: AP URSS b11 f4. Only two small matters slightly soured the taste of the visit. The Società Rimorchiatori Napoletani had some problem in receiving payment of 431.80 lire for work done on the *Krasnyi Kavkaz*. A complaint to the foreign ministry, which in turn remonstrated to the Soviet embassy, quickly settled the matter. MAE to Puppini, 1/11/34; Puppini to MAE, 12/9/33; Potemkin to Rome, 12/19/33: AP URSS b11 f4. Of even less consequence, the Italians arrested an individual, born in St. Petersburg, who had tried to distribute antibolshevik propaganda to Soviet sailors in Naples. Rome to Attolico, 11/27/33: AP URSS b11 f2.

9. *Pravda*, Nov. 1, 1933; *Izvestia*, Nov. 4, 1933; Attolico to Rome, 11/7/33, 11/14/33: AP URSS b11 fl. Potemkin thanked Suvich for the "excellent welcome" given the Soviet ships. Suvich memorandum: AP URSS b8 f4. From Rome TASS also recounted the reception given at the Soviet embassy celebrating the sixteenth anniversary of the Bolshevik Revolution. *Izvestia*, Nov. 10, 1933; Attolico to Rome, 11/14/33: AP URSS b11 fl.

10. *The Times* (London), Oct. 31, Nov. 3, 1933. As an example of that good understanding, Voroshilov was made an honorary citizen of Turkey at the beginning of 1934. Attolico to Rome, 2/1/34: AP URSS b15 f10.

11. Attolico to Rome, 4/19/34; Aloisi to Baistrocchi, 5/7/34; Baistrocchi to MAE, 5/11/34, 7/9/34; Rome to Attolico, 5/15/34; Baratono to Rome, 7/9/34, 7/18/34, 7/20/34; Suvich to Baistrocchi, 7/11/34; MAE to Baistrocchi, 7/11/34: AP URSS b15 f5; *DVP* 17: no. 248; *The Times* (London), July 13, 1934.

12. Attolico to Rome, 6/7/34, 6/30/34; Suvich to Baistrocchi, 6/23/34: AP URSS

b14 f1; Attolico to Rome, 7/3/34, 7/4/34; Baistrocchi to Suvich, 8/13/34: AP URSS b15 f5.

13. Robert Petrovich Eideman, among his many activities, worked to train and equip Soviet military forces with Marxist theory and modern technology. His reward was to perish along with most of his cohorts in the military purges of 1937.

14. *DVP* 17: no. 248; Attolico to Rome, 7/4/34, 8/2/34, 8/5/34; Valle to MAE, 7/9/34; Suvich to Balbo, 7/9/34; Aloisi to Balbo, 7/31/34; Potemkin to Mussolini, n.d.: AP URSS b15 f14; Attolico to Rome, 8/9/34: AP URSS b14 f8; *Pravda*, Aug. 2, 1934.

15. *Pravda*, Aug. 11, 1934. The Italians did find success in selling to the Soviets, who purchased, e.g., FIAT A–24R and A–6 engines. *Izvestia*, Aug. 18, 1934.

16. *Pravda*, Aug. 13, 15, 16, 17, 1934; *Izvestia*, Aug. 16, 18, 1934.

17. *Pravda*, Aug. 9, 10, 1934. The all-metal, heavy TB–3 bomber was also used to carry freight and parasite fighters as well as to drop parachutists. Some of these bombers were adapted to carry armored cars and light tanks between the main undercarriage legs. Over 250 of these planes flew over Red Square during the 1934 May Day parade. This tremendous output of the only effective four-engined, heavy bomber force in the world in the 1930s was taken to prove the industrialization of the USSR. See John W.R. Taylor, ed. and comp., *Combat Aircraft of the World from 1909 to the Present* (New York, 1969), pp. 613–15; *Izvestia*, Aug. 19, 1934.

18. *Izvestia*, Aug. 8, 9, 10, 11, 12, 14, 15, 17, 20, 1934; *Pravda*, Aug. 8, 11, 13, 15, 16, 17, 18, Sept. 28, 29, 30, Oct. 2, 1934; Attolico to Rome, 8/23/34, 8/16/34; Berardis to Rome, 11/4/34: AP URSS b15 f2; Berardis to Rome, 11/4/34: AP URSS b15 f4. Praising collective security, the Soviet press stressed Italo-French cooperation in opposing Nazi activities in Austria, where the Nazi coup had so recently failed, thanks to Italy. *Pravda*, July 29, 30, Aug. 11, 13, 1934; *Izvestia*, Aug. 11, 27, 1934. The press extolled a French flight to Italy in September as dramatizing the growing triangular Italo-French-Soviet friendship. Ibid., *Izvestia* Sept. 28, 1934.

19. Attolico to Rome, 8/9/34; MAE to Baistrocchi, 8/24/34: AP URSS b15 f6; Attolico to Rome, 9/6/34, 9/13/34; Buti to Suvich, 8/23/34; Aloisi to MAE, 8/29/34; Rome to Attolico, 9/2/34: AP URSS b15 f7.

20. The Soviets originally had offered the Italians the opportunity to see special maneuvers in the absence of other foreigners. They then lamented that the reciprocal Italian invitation had asked them to attend only regular exercises in the presence of all foreign military attachés. Moscow righteously complained that by being treated by the Italians merely as one of the many, they did not understand the greater value of seeing "true," full maneuvers, as opposed to "special" and "truncated" ones. Attolico to Rome, 8/8/35: AP URSS b17 f2.

21. Chargé d'Affaires in Moscow to Rome, 8/15/35; Arone to Rome, 9/26/35: AP URSS b17 f2.

22. Attolico to Rome, 8/8/35: AP URSS b17 f2.

23. Rosso to Rome, 11/11/36: AP URSS b21 f5. Mikhail Nikolaevich Tukhachevsky, 1893-1937, was a leading military strategist. His arrest and execution in June 1937 was a crucial event in Stalin's purge of the military. Semen Mikhailovich Budnenny, 1883-1973, had great success with Red cavalry forces during the Civil War and was named a marshal in 1935. Although one of Stalin's cronies, he was out of his depth in modern warfare and was removed for incompetence in September 1941.

24. Paul W. Martin, "The Russian Navy—Past, Present, and Future," *United States Naval Institute Proceedings* 173 (June 1947): 658; Jurg Meister, *Soviet War-*

ships of the Second World War (New York, 1977), pp. 16-17; René Greger, *The Russian Fleet, 1914-1917*, trans. Jill Gearing (London, 1972), pp. 9-11.

25. Siegfried Breyer, *Guide to the Soviet Navy*, trans. M.W. Henley (Annapolis, 1970), pp. 21, 28-30, 143. Not surprisingly, Soviet propagandists, memoirists, and historians rarely, if ever, mention the role that foreign technology and expertise played in the development of the Soviet fleets in the 1920s and 1930s. See, e.g., Vasilii Ivanovich Achkasov and Nikolai Bronislavovich Pavlovich, *Soviet Naval Operations in the Great Patriotic War, 1941-1945*, trans. U.S. Naval Intelligence Command (Annapolis, 1981), pp. 1-43 and Sergei Georgievich Gorshkov, *Morskaia mosch gosudarstva* (Moscow, 1976), pp. 212-29.

26. Achkasov and Pavlovich, *Soviet Operations*, p. 5.

27. Robert Waring Herrick, *Soviet Naval Strategy: Fifty Years of Theory and Practice* (Annapolis, 1968), p. 29.

28. In *United States Naval Institute Proceedings*, see: "Where Italy Leads," (Sept. 1933): 1361; "Italy: Cruiser Performance," (Aug. 1935): 1176-1177; "Italy: Brief Notes," (Nov. 1933): 1650; "Italy: Italian Building," (Jan. 1934): 128-29; "Italy: Italy Sees Menace," (Mar. 1934): 427; "Italy: New Battleships for Italy," (Sept. 1934): 1316-1317; "Italy: Mussolini Speaks," (Aug. 1934): 1163; "Italy: Various Notes," (Dec. 1934): 1779; "Italy: Various Notes," (Feb. 1935): 279; and "Italy: Current Building Program," (Dec. 1935): 1866. The journal suggested that Italy wished to fortify its navy with battleships because of its alarm over the possibilities of a Franco-Soviet alliance, which would have required a strong naval presence not only in the eastern Mediterranean, but also in the Black Sea.

29. Hubert Renfro Knickerbocker, *Fighting the Red Trade Menace* (New York, 1931), pp. 21-22. Italian law provided for a basic subsidy of 32 lire per gross ton for all metal hulls. This was increased by 30 percent if the vessels could reach 14 knots and was scaled upward to 235 percent for a speed of 27 knots. A drawback of 100 percent was offered on all customs duties for metal materials imported for ship construction. To promote labor-saving devices, there was a premium for fuel efficiency running from 16 lire to 12 lire per 100 kilograms of weight for all auxiliary machinery installed.

30. William H. Garzke, Jr., and Robert O. Dulin, Jr., *Battleships: Allied Battleships in World War II* (Annapolis, 1980), p. 315.

31. Promemorial, 8/14/33: AP URSS b17 f1.

32. Attolico to Rome, 3/20/33; Suvich memorandum, 3/29/33: AP URSS b8 f1.

33. Rome to Attolico, 10/9/33; Potemkin to Suvich, 8/14/33; Suvich to Sirianni, 9/13/33: AP URSS b17 f3. For construction figures, see Attolico to Rome, 8/9/33: AP URSS b11 f4.

34. Suvich to Sirianni, 9/13/33: AP URSS b11 f4; Sirianni to Consulenza Tecnica all'URSS, 9/24/33; Sirianni to Suvich, 9/29/33: AP URSS b17 f3.

35. Berardis to Rome, 10/22/33; MAE to Sirianni, 11/6/33: AP URSS b17 f3.

36. Attolico to Rome, 2/14/34; MAE to Asquini, 2/18/34: AP URSS b17 f3.

37. Rome to Attolico, 3/3/34: AP URSS b17 f3.

38. Attolico to Rome, 3/24/34; for an early rumor that France would help build super dreadnoughts for the USSR, see Attolico to Rome, 9/23/33: AP URSS b17 f3.

39. Attolico to Rome, 3/28/34; for more on Ansaldo's negotiations for the supply of motors and technical consultation, see Suvich to MAE, AP Uff. 4, 3/28/34: AP URSS b17 f3.

40. Aloisi to Attolico, 4/15/34; Attolico to Rome, 4/25/34, 5/10/34; Ansaldo to Rome, 5/1/34; Rome to Attolico, 5/3/34; MAE to Sirianni, 5/22/34: AP URSS b17 f3.

41. Voroshilov to Attolico, 5/16/34; Attolico to Rome, 5/17/34: AP URSS b17 f3. For one of the other contracts, between Silurificio Italiano and the USSR, as well as Sirianni's indignant response that Attolico's advice was unnecessary because Italians dealing with foreign states already had been admonished to fulfill their contracts scrupulously, see Suvich to Sirianni, 5/28/34; Sirianni to Suvich, 6/4/34: AP URSS b17 f3.

42. In late April, 1934 Attolico sent Rome a list of Italian military contracts on the account of the Soviet government.

1. Ansaldo was building, along destroyer lines, two coast guard/escort vessels of 776 tons displacement, each 76 meters in length. Endowed with Tosi motors and costing 18.65 million lire, the ships were to be consigned about April or May. These were the PS 8 and PS 26, described below. Ansaldo also was building factories for the construction of complete motors for cruisers. The firm was to supply technical collaboration for cruiser construction as well. These contracts were worth 34 million lire and resulted from the negotiations described above.
2. Odero-Terni-Orlando of La Spezia was building twelve twin-barrel anti-aircraft cannons.
3. Società S. Giorgio of Sestri had finished in March the consignment of 46 range-finding devices of 4 meters at the base and detachable in three parts.
4. Officine Galileo of Florence was in the process of supplying four complete fire-control systems including searchlights, range finders, sight mechanisms, and gyrocompasses for four torpedo boat destroyers. Three of these had been delivered, and the fourth had passed its trials and was ready. Officine Galileo also was supplying fifteen attack periscopes for submarines. Of these, five already had been sent, four had passed their tests, and the rest were 90 percent completed. Additionally, Officine Galileo was supplying fourteen range finders, of which ten were of 6 meters and four were of 8 meters. Some were undergoing testing and some were being mounted. Finally, Officine Galileo was supplying one-hundred mirrors for 150mm searchlights, of which thirty had been sent and the others were being tested or were still under construction.
5. Silurificio Italiano of Naples was in the course of consigning fifty torpedoes of 533mm x 7.5 and forty-five of 533mm x 7.27, as well as two 3-tube torpedo launchers of 533mm.
6. Silurificio Whitehead of Fiume was delivering eighty torpedoes of 533mm, of which twenty-five were as yet incomplete, and fifteen torpedoes of 450mm, none of which was completed.
7. Ditta Isotta Fraschini of Milan was supplying spare parts for Asso 750 motors for 606,850.72 lire, plus 51 marine units of the type Asso 1000 MAD.
8. Ottico Meccanica Italiana of Rome and Aeronautica Macchi of Varese had made offers of aeronautical material for Soviet aviation, but no concrete orders had yet come to pass.
Attolico to Mussolini, 4/25/34: AP URSS b15 f4.

43. For the ships the Soviets owed Ansaldo 18,645,770 lire, with payments spread over fifty-one months from the date of consignment. Italy guaranteed payments to 65 percent. Puppini to MAE, 7/13/34; MAE to Sirianni, 7/21/34; MAE to Giannini, 7/31/34; Potemkin, note verbale, 7/23/34; MAE to Sirianni, n.d.; Campioni to MAE, 7/25/34, 8/4/34; Suvich to Sirianni, 7/31/34; Suvich to Puppini, 8/18/34, 11/3/34; Puppini to Mussolini, 10/25/34; Rome to Attolico, note verbale, n.d.: AP URSS b17 f3.

44. Consul at Port Said to Rome, 11/2/34; Puppini to Suvich, 11/7/34; Campioni to MAE, 11/16/34; Consul at Colombo to Rome, 11/22/34; Bianconi to Mussolini, 1/

3/35: AP URSS b17 f3; Attolico to Rome, 12/27/34: AP URSS b18 f10; Puppini to MAE, 2/2/35: AP URSS b18 f12.

45. Other vessels of the same pattern possibly were built in Soviet yards. Three *Albatross*-class ships in the Black Sea may have been of this type. Not until 1938 did the Soviets independently develop a class of escorts. In dimensions and gun armament they resembled the Italian-built class, but they proved significantly faster and their torpedo armament was more like that of older destroyers and torpedo boats. Breyer, *Guide*, p. 100; Meister, *Soviet Warships*, p. 144; John Campbell, *Naval Weapons of World War Two* (Annapolis, 1985), p. 363. The Soviets also inquired for help in building a salvage vessel to raise sunken ships. Consul at Leningrad to Rome, 11/6/34; Quaroni to Puppini, 11/21/34; Puppini to MAE, 11/29/34; Quaroni to Consul at Leningrad, 12/4/34: AP URSS b15 f4.

46. Consul at Leningrad to Rome, 10/24/34; DGAE, Uff. 1 to DGAP, 9/1/34; Quaroni to DGAE, Uff. 1, 9/8/34: AP URSS b17 f3.

47. Nobile to Mussolini, 8/11/35: AP URSS b22 f13; "New Dirigibles Constructed," *Economic Review of the Soviet Union* 9 (Aug.-Sept. 1934): 182. Nobile, in his *Quelo che ho visto nella Russia sovietica* (Rome, 1945), expressed a profound sympathy for the Soviet experiment. This reflected his genuine, not come-lately, antifascism as well as his admiration for the Soviet war effort. He maintained that fascist censorship had muted his true opinions before the war. He was awed by the "heroic" temper of the 1930s and the self-denying spirit of Soviet youth striving to create a new world. This despite the often poorly organized system that adversely affected his work and his having seen things that repulsed him—after all, his Moscow apartment lay across from the infamous Liubianka. Finally, Nobile's claim that he had never worked on military matters or even set foot in a military office must be taken as at least somewhat naïve.

48. The Soviets were then building a flexible ship of 7,500 cm, the *V–4*, the last of their pre-Nobile construction. For the earlier *V–1*, *V–2*, and *V–3*, the last of 6,500 cm, and plans for a Moscow-Gorky-Moscow route, see *Izvestia*, Mar. 24, 1933; for a flight to Murmansk, see ibid., Apr. 28, 1933; see also *Pravda*, Apr. 7, 1933 for comments on foreign, including Italian, dirigible construction.

49. Ovidio Ferrante, *Umberto Nobile*, 2 vols. (Rome, 1985), 2: 159-63.

50. Ibid.

51. Attolico to Rome, 5/21/33, 6/19/33, 8/21/33, 9/25/33: AP URSS b11 f11.

52. Attolico to Rome, 2/14/34, 6/19/34, 8/21/34; Balbo note, 2/23/34: AP URSS b15 f14.

53. Berardis to Rome, 11/13/34: AP URSS b15 f4. For Nobile's health problems, see the documents in AP URSS b15 f9 and Nobile, *Quello che ho visto*, pp. 17-25. Doctors at the hospital serving the Kremlin's leadership operated on Nobile, and among them was Levin, Maxim Gorky's doctor, who was later shot during the purges. Nobile was much impressed with the quality of his care--despite a postoperative infection requiring a second operation and leaving him hanging between life and death for a week. He was in the hospital for a month and a half.

54. Nobile to Mussolini, 8/11/35: AP URSS b22 f13.

55. Attolico to Rome, 4/25/35, 5/24/35, 7/24/35: AP URSS b18 f14; Nobile to Mussolini, 8/11/35: AP URSS b22 f13.

56. Ambassador Pietro Arone implied that the poor quality of Soviet engineers and pilots had caused the accident. Arone to Rome, 10/30/35; Attolico to Rome, 4/

25/35, 5/24/35, 7/24/35: AP URSS b18 f14; Nobile to Mussolini, 8/11/35: AP URSS b22 f13. For Soviet dirigible construction and the establishment of an airship line between Moscow and Irkutsk, see *Pravda*, Aug. 13, 16, 1934.

57. The Polish, Japanese, Hungarian, and Austrian representatives similarly refused to offer their respects. Rosso to Ciano, 2/12/38: AP URSS b29 f1.

58. Nobile to Mussolini, 8/11/35: AP URSS b22 f13.

59. Nobile to Arone, 11/27/35: AP URSS b22 f13.

9

Successful
Collective Security?

The collapse of good relations, however, was for the future. For the moment, the Kremlin continued to seek to erect a structure of collective security, a structure designed to preserve first and foremost the political, economic, and military integrity of the Soviet Union. The critical area was Southeast Europe, where the Nazi gaze fixed on Austria.

REGIONAL PACTS AND OTHER AGREEMENTS

In the tangled traces of friendships and antagonisms in East and Southeast Europe, Italy was the one power best able to straighten out the reins and make collective security work. Not an easy task. In the end it proved impossible.

The Little Entente, 1921-1933

Following the collapse of the tsarist, Ottoman, Austro-Hungarian, and German empires at the end of World War I, the Danubian and Balkan peoples had their opportunity for self-government. The French fostered there an association of smaller states—Czechoslovakia, Romania, and Yugoslavia—to maintain the frontiers established by the peace treaties, and they did their utmost to strengthen the latter, an especially important block against German and Italian expansion into Southeast Europe.[1]

Contrary to common illusions, however, except for the number of men under arms, this "Little Entente" had none of a major power's attributes, and its common objectives little concerned the outside world. On major issues the three disagreed even among themselves: Czechoslovakia wanted support against Germany, while Romania and Yugoslavia were sanguine in that direction; Romania worried about the Soviet Union, while Czechoslovakia and Yugoslavia saw no threat there; and, although its two partners maintained perfectly correct dealings with the Duce's regime, Yugoslavia's relations with Italy nearly always strained to the breaking point.

After 1928, as revision became a recognized instrument of Italian national policy, Rome branded the Little Entente as nothing but an obedient lackey of a selfish and reactionary France obstinately deaf to Rome's new gospel. Only as Mussolini came to recognize the German danger did he seek rapprochements with both France and Yugoslavia, but it was not until after the turn from 1934 to 1935 that he swallowed his pride sufficiently to contemplate any serious, practical concessions.[2]

Fearing that Hitler might forge a revisionist bloc to compel France to grant territorial concessions at the expense of the countries of Central and East Europe, the Little Entente countries drew closer together. On February 16, 1933, the Czech, Yugoslav, and Romanian foreign ministers signed a Pact of Organization. In important renunciations of individual sovereignties for the commonweal, the three sought to coordinate their general economic and political policies.[3]

This stronger, more formal grouping greatly concerned Ambassador Attolico in Moscow.[4] He felt that this French-controlled reorganization was directed against both Hungary and Italy, and he asked Rome about its repercussions on Italy's relations with the USSR, especially given the 1932 Franco-Soviet nonaggression treaty. Predictably, Rome, Berlin, and Budapest denounced the Little Entente pact as a French-inspired reversion to the prewar system of political blocs, which the League's inception supposedly had terminated.

In April and May 1933, rumors spread that the Italians were seeking to glue Greece, Turkey, and Bulgaria into a rival formation, which Austria and Hungary might adhere—a solution to the problem of countering French hegemony in the Balkans without countenancing *Anschluss*. Reacting to this activity and encouraged by the Italo-French détente accompanying the four-power pact negotiations, Italy took up with Paris the question of reorganizing the Danubian area.[5] Their summer exchange of views culminated on September 29 with an Italian memorandum.

This ingenious and self-serving document sought to obtain Italy's preeminence in Central and Southeast Europe. Rome's proposed system would have embraced itself, the Little Entente, Austria, and Hungary, and it would have countered the increasingly vigorous German economic campaign against Austria by removing tariff barriers separating Austria from its neighbors. Italo-French interests coincided in erecting a common front to check Germany's eastward expansion, but Paris's good wishes were not enough to ensure its acceptance by its East European protégés, who feared that France might sacrifice their interests to prevent an Austro-German union.[6]

The Soviet rapprochements with Italy and France and the burgeoning Italo-French friendship were important, even critical, to the Kremlin's leaders. But they were not enough. Germany, already too strong, had the potential to dominate Central, East, and Southeast Europe, and by drawing upon the resources of their neighbors, the Nazis could threaten the very existence of Soviet Russia. Already imperiled by the Japanese in the East, the Soviets felt that keeping Germany out of Southeast Europe, and first and foremost Austria, could stop this nightmare in its tracks. And, finally, if frustrated, the Nazis might be tempted to return to the Rapallo tradition.[7] Thus, to ensure Soviet security, the triangle encompassing Rome, Moscow, and Paris had to be squared by bringing in East Europe, those states bordering on the Soviet Union and lying between it and Germany.

Rome's mediation and pressure on the Hungarians, to the extent that the negotiations between them and the Soviets even took place in the Italian capital, proved significant in getting Budapest to recognize the USSR. All ended well despite Potemkin's illness in January 1934, which could have delayed the negotiations, and despite Hungarian fears that the USSR would recognize the Little Entente. Moscow was suitably grateful.[8]

Back in March 1933, Attolico had spoken with Litvinov on Soviet attitudes toward the Little Entente as well as the Baltic bloc, and the USSR was shoring up its relations with the three Baltic States separating it from hostile Poland and Germany. The foreign commissar emphasized that Bessarabia remained the stumbling block as far as better relations were concerned. He did, however, assure Attolico—in English—that "we may however put on record that if we knock at the door of the Little Entente it will be opened."[9] The ambassador attributed Litvinov's confidence to the Kremlin's blossoming collaboration with France.

A year and some months later, on June 9, 1934, Czechoslovakia and Romania extended *de jure* recognition to the Soviet Union. Not wanting to sanctify the existence of the group, the Kremlin carefully recognized the Little Entente members as individual states. The USSR also entered into diplomatic relations with Bulgaria on July 23 and Italian-dominated Albania on September 17.[10]

Ambassador Attolico told Rome that Litvinov's definition of aggression had helped make possible the Soviet rapprochements with the countries of the Little Entente and their possible insertion into the Moscow-Ankara system. This, of course, concerned Rome because it meant that Moscow was being drawn into the French security system and possibly that panslavic policies in Southeast Europe were reviving.[11]

Rent by their own antagonisms and fearing Soviet Russian imperialism, the diverse peoples of Eastern Europe found it difficult to cooperate against the German danger to themselves and the Soviet Union. Moscow worked consistently and logically in the early 1930s to overcome these problems. Its growing cooperation with Paris made possible the rapprochements with the countries of the Little Entente, just as its friendship with Rome had helped make possible recognition by Hungary, Albania, and Bulgaria. The trick was to get the Italophile and Francophile groups to work together. Hence the importance to Moscow of the cooperation between Rome and Paris.

Pravda's summary in November 1934 of Italo-French controversies since the war hopefully concluded that there existed the "possibility for a long-lasting reconciliation between the two countries," which would strengthen peace.[12] The paper warned that discord between the Latin sisters could only weaken their influence in the Danube to Germany's advantage, and it noted that settlement of Rome's problems with Belgrade was the necessary premise to reconciliation. Two weeks later *Pravda* returned to these themes, suggesting that if France could satisfy Italy's colonial claims, then Italo-Franco-Little Entente cooperation would be possible despite Yugoslavia's hostility toward Italy and Hungary. Further, to slow German expansion toward Austria, Italy would support France in the Saar.[13]

The Balkan Pact, February 9, 1934

When the Nazi revolution in Germany brought the question of treaty revision to a head, Romania sought to strengthen the status quo. Bucharest's first step was to put its relations with the Soviet Union on a better footing, which it did by signing a nonaggression pact in July 1933. Romania then turned its attention to guaranteeing its southern frontier through a Balkan federation.[14]

Bulgaria, however, refused to join any system supporting the status quo. Irredentist and revisionist, the Bulgarians were alarmed not only because of the signing of the Greco-Turkish Pact of September 1933 in which Italy had played a prominent part, but also because of the new Little Entente Statute consolidating the antirevisionist forces. The Four Power Pact also affected Bulgarian interests, and the Italo-French rapprochement, which had made the pact possible, appeared likely to alter the whole situation in Southeast Europe and to remove the motive for Italy's support of Bulgaria. The Italians, however, took pains to convince Sofia that they remained friendly.[15]

The London Conventions also directly concerned Bulgaria, because the definition of an aggressor covered the case of a state supporting armed bands that invaded the territory of another. That Sofia had failed to curb the Macedonian Revolutionary Organization clearly brought Bulgaria within the scope of this definition. Thus its relations with the Soviet Union also deteriorated.[16]

Despite Bulgaria's objections, the governments of the other four Balkan states decided to proceed. At the beginning of January 1934, the Greek foreign minister visited Rome, London, and Paris to explain the Balkan pact project. He obtained formal Anglo-French blessing. In Rome the task was more delicate. Would Mussolini support a project designed to reduce Italy's influence in Southeast Europe? Despite official assurances that Italy would not oppose the Balkan Pact, an unenthusiastic Italian press suggested that the proposal would have hurt Italian interests but for Bulgaria's persistence in standing aloof—which made it superfluous.[17]

Also suspicious, Litvinov feared that the proposed pact intended to guarantee the Bessarabian border and therefore was directed against the USSR. Moscow therefore counseled Ankara that the true danger was not a weak Bulgaria attacking Turkey, but rather Italian penetration of Turkey through Bulgaria. Upon learning from the Turks that Suvich had spoken of a possible agreement binding Italy, Germany, Turkey, and the USSR, Litvinov assured them that a month before in Rome he had found Mussolini in a decidedly anti-German mood. He suggested that perhaps Italy wanted to use the proposed Balkan Pact to draw Turkey away from other courses of action.[18]

The Balkan Pact, signed in Athens on February 9, 1934, aimed at repressing Bulgarian revisionism and bound the countries of Greece and Turkey, plus Romania and Yugoslavia from the Little Entente, to maintain the Balkan's territorial order. The participants were to assume no political action or obligation toward any nonsignatory Balkan state without the consent of the other contracting parties. They declared that any Balkan state could join, thus entertaining the possibility of Bulgaria's and Albania's participation. To be sure, the Italo-Albanian alliance precluded the latter from joining, and Italy counseled Bulgaria's abstention.[19]

The pact was in line with other manifestations of regional consolidation, for example, the Little Entente, the Italo-Austro-Hungarian Pact, and the Baltic Pact, all reactions against comprehensive revision of the peace treaties, such as Nazi Germany was demanding. Not merely an *ad hoc* measure to safeguard the status quo, this pact also expressed the need for federative cooperation in Southeast Europe, which would free its members from great-power interference and patronage.[20]

In spite of the enthusiasm for the pact among its members, neighboring governments were disquieted. While the negotiations for the pact had been in progress, the Soviets questioned Turkey about its implications. In the event of hostilities between the USSR and Romania, Bulgaria might be drawn in on the Soviet side. In that case Turkey would be obliged to support Romania against Bulgaria and therefore also against Soviet Russia. Such action would contravene the 1925 Soviet-Turkish treaty of neutrality. A written declaration from Bucharest that it would expect no aid from Turkey in the event of a conflict with the USSR overcame this difficulty.[21]

After the pact's signing, the Greek opposition party attacked the government for not taking precautions to ensure that Greece would not become involved in an Italo-Yugoslav war. Athens asked for, and received, assurances from the other three governments that the pact's application would not involve Greece in hostilities against a great power, that is, Italy. Greece thus contracted out of its obligations in that very eventuality most critical to Yugoslavia, as Suvich, "not without malicious pleasure," noted to Potemkin.[22]

Opposition from Italy and the USSR, the abstentions of Albania and Bulgaria, and the qualifications on military obligations demanded by Greece and Turkey robbed the Balkan Entente of its full potential. This new grouping, nonetheless, was a major defeat for fascist Italy. It liquidated the temporary effect recently achieved by the signing of the Greco-Turkish agreement and the development of an Italian combination in the eastern Mediterranean basin. Greece and Turkey now had crossed over to the hostile French camp, and Bulgaria drew closer to Yugoslavia, whose position improved vis-á-vis Italy. Only Albania formally entered into the Italian sphere. Frustrated in sufficiently extending its influence in the Balkans, ultimately Italy ominously shifted its aspirations elsewhere, to Northeast Africa.[23]

For the moment, however, the Soviets continued to show a confident face to the world. *Izvestia*, for example, continued to praise the Italo-French rapprochement, "caused in great measure by aggressive German fascism."[24] German expansionism, the paper continued, threatened the Danubian basin and especially Austria, and was driving Italy toward friendship with the countries of the Little Entente. The approval of the Rome Accords of January 1935 by the French Camera, the paper concluded, demonstrated the success of the rapprochement between Italy and France.

MORE SIGNS OF ITALO-SOVIET FRIENDSHIP

In his speech to the 17th Party Congress in early 1934, Stalin described Moscow's relations with Italy as "indisputably satisfactory," certainly better than those with France or Poland.[25] Attolico called the speech "moderate" and, finding the key to Soviet policy in the thirties, noted that it confirmed "the tendency of not definitely closing any door."[26] Clearly Moscow hoped for Rome's support not only against Germany in the Danubian area, but also in the East. Rejoicing at the worsening Italo-Japanese relations, for several weeks the Soviet press found great sport in reproducing articles from the fascist press, especially those contrasting the Soviet defensive posture against aggressive Japanese military preparations in East Asia. It rejoiced at Mussolini's comments placing Italy among the powers threatened by Japan. Of equal interest were Italian reflections on Japanese-American antagonisms in the Pacific and Japanese upset at Italy's criticisms.[27]

At the end of June 1934, *Izvestia* reviewed the previous six months of growing Italian press fulminations against Japanese imperialistic expansion. According to the paper, the Italians were especially concerned over textile competition and other Japanese activities in Abyssinia. *Izvestia* pointed out Mussolini's article provocatively entitled, "The Yellow Danger," and then called attention to a recent article in *Popolo d'Italia* that intimated, unlike earlier Italian comments, that the Japanese threat to Italy had a political and military dimension beyond the purely economic. *Izvestia* wondered how this new alarm would be translated into policy.[28]

In mid-August *Pravda* discussed the development of Italian interests in China, especially in the Tientsin concession, Catholic missions, and collaboration in aviation. Italian imperialism, the party paper concluded in a thankful tone, was limiting Japanese expansion. It also reproduced several articles from the Italian press on the need to establish barriers against Japanese aggression and a unified front against Japanese dumping.[29]

Nor did Central Asia pose any problems for relations between Moscow and Rome. In April 1934, Attolico reported on the visits of Italian officials to the Soviet capital, where they discussed Afghanistan and Persia with NKID personnel. Attolico opined that these contacts had stabilized, naturally and without force, an understanding with the Kremlin. Soviet officials echoed these sentiments and said that they preferred Italian influence in the area to that of others.[30]

Beyond the military connections, the Italians and Soviets in a number of small ways worked to improve their ties in 1934. For the tenth anniversary of recognition, the Soviets celebrated with a grand reception, attended by a high-powered group including Litvinov, Krestinskii, Molotov, Rosengolts, Voroshilov with his general staff, B.S. Stomonyakov, and A.I. Mikoian; Attolico remarked to Rome on their sincere deference to Italy.[31] Conventions regulating judicial relations were signed in July 1934, at which time Attolico reminded Rome that the Kremlin attached political significance to every agreement. That same month saw the signing of a convention regulating the exchange of postal packages.[32]

Exchanges of tourists and other visitors picked up. The Soviet tourist agency, *Intourist*, opened an office in Rome on the picturesque Piazza del Porto di Ripetta and successfully promoted tourism to the USSR in the summer of 1934. Italian authorities suggested that to avoid incidents, Italian agencies had to get contracts clearly stating their obligations to *Intourist*, the organization of such trips, and the norms to be observed by Italian citizens. Evidencing no worry at moral contagion, the Italians were concerned, however, that because Soviet tourism to Italy would be virtually nil, there was an inherent balance of payments problem involved with increased tourism.[33]

There was talk about staging theatrical and concert shows in the USSR by Italian artists, and as late as October 1935, just as the fascist army was marching into Abyssinia, an Italian orchestra entertained Odessa's culturally attuned with Italian music. In July 1934, Professor Marsoni of the press office toured wide areas of Russia, the Ukraine, and the Caucasus. The next month Professor Beonio Brochieris arrived in Moscow to tour across the wide expanse of the Soviet Union. In late 1934, upon the visit of Stoppani and Corrado to Odessa, *Izvestia* celebrated their recent world record for straight-line flight of a seaplane.[34] Meanwhile, a Soviet delegate to the Theater Congress in Rome praised the superior preparation and organization of the affair, and the Soviet press extolled the grand success of Soviet films at the international film festival in Venice. More mundanely, a Soviet agricultural mission was to visit Italy.[35]

This good feeling culminated with the Soviet entry into the League of Nations in the fall of 1934. Throughout that year, Moscow had asked that Rome sound out other League members concerning its possible entry, and Rome gladly agreed to Moscow's request that it, along with Paris, sponsor the invitation to join.[36] On the evening of August 1, Litvinov explained to Attolico that his government wanted to participate in events and therefore wished to join the League. He suggested that Soviet entry would ease the fears of the Little Entente and the Baltic States about the proposed Eastern Pact. The commissar saw the League as an instrument of peace, that same peace so recently preserved in Austria by Italian bayonets.[37]

AUSTRIA AND COLLECTIVE SECURITY

One of the reasons for this tightening of relations was that tensions over Austria were persisting.[38] Despite German denials to Italian diplomatic representatives, Berlin knew of "renegade" plans of Austrian Nazis for a coup. Italy adamantly opposed these activities and began negotiations with Vienna and Budapest with an eye on forestalling them. At the beginning of 1934, *Pravda* praised Suvich's trip to Vienna as representing an Italo-French front in the defense of Austria's independence.[39]

The Rome Protocols, March 17, 1934, and Tripartite Cooperation over Austria

But it was Italy that brought matters to a head in Austria. Acting on the Duce's advice to strike at Austria's Social Democrats, Chancellor Engelbert Dollfuss in February 1934 dissolved all political parties except his own Fatherland Front, and crushed the socialists in a three-day civil war. A Pyrrhic victory; Dollfuss had little support left in his country.[40] Austria then appealed to Italy, Britain, and France, and the three powers officially declared on February 17 their common interests in maintaining Austria's independence.[41]

As a further warning to Germany, on March 17 Italy, Austria, and Hungary signed the Rome Protocols, which reasserted the right to independence of every state. Providing for commercial, economic, and political cooperation, the protocols called for collaboration among all European states. Italy insisted that the protocols had not created a new bloc nor solved general Danubian problems, either politically or economically. Italy further assured Berlin that the door remained open to initiatives from other quarters and that others could join. Berlin, nonetheless, promised to obstruct the working out of the protocols.[42]

In effect, Rome had established a protectorate over Vienna and Budapest. The rise of Balkan cooperation and the failure of the Four Power Pact had pushed Rome to knit together this pro-Italian bloc in the Balkans and Danubian Europe, which perhaps could have counterbalanced the Little and Balkan ententes as well as Germany. The Rome Protocols thereby divided the Danubian states into two sharply defined groups working at cross-purposes on the issue of territorial revision of the peace treaties. And although both sought to bar the Third Reich's expansion into Southeastern Europe, the fact that each followed separate policies in pursuing their identical aims weakened the other's efforts.[43]

On the other hand, reassured that the Italo-French and Italo-Little Entente accommodations had taken place concurrently with increased Italo-German coolness and taking into account Rome's cooperation with London and Paris, Czechoslovakia accepted assurances that the Rome Protocols were not directed against the Little Entente. The Czechs hoped to fit Austria into a new political and economic Central European system.[44]

The Soviet press reacted quickly to the Italian initiative, and especially the French relation to it. In the days preceding the signing, the newspapers supposed that France was hoping for an entente with Italy and therefore was trying to ease Italo-Little Entente relations.[45] Three days after the signing, *Pravda* editorialized that the accords

testify only that the imperialist struggle for predominance in Southeast Europe has entered a new phase. Notwithstanding that at present there is a tendency toward a certain "union of forces" between Italy and France, the general situation of Danubian and Balkan Europe is characterized by a sharpening of imperialist contradictions.[46]

Hardly more optimistic was *Izvestia* in examining Mussolini's speech in Rome in which the Duce had said that no great Italo-French postwar problems had been resolved. This, the paper judged, was an invitation to Paris to join Italy in supporting Hungarian revisionism against its friends in the Little Entente and to combat Nazi machinations in Austria while promoting Germany's right to rearm. *Izvestia* concluded that if France should settle these questions in Italy's favor, then Rome would change its position.[47] Nine days later, the paper lamented: "The Rome Accords do not seem to lead to the complete tranquility of Central Europe. To the contrary, they constitute a point of departure for a major worsening of the contradictions between the European imperialist states."[48]

Italian diplomats got to the heart of the matter by quoting *Vecherniaia Moskva* to the foreign ministry in Rome: "Italy is planted, like a wedge, between France and the Little Entente, supplanting German capital, pushing it back from the Balkans, and in the end obliging Germany to renounce, at least for the immediate future, *Anschluss*."[49] Rome, the evening paper predicted, next would launch a diplomatic offensive against Germany and look for strategic points against France.

In mid-May Soviet papers again brought up the ties binding Italy, Austria, and Hungary.[50] *Za industrialisatsiu*, the organ of the Commissariat of Heavy Industry, maintained that the accords represented growing economic collaboration between the three countries. This marked the success of Italy's Central European policies, answering not only the French plan for a Danubian federation but also German plans for *Anschluss*. The paper concluded that the signing represented a new period in the struggle between the great European powers for predominance in the Danubian basin.[51]

Indeed, the Rome Protocols had placed Rome once again at the center of Europe's international politics. France, having obstructed every Italian ambition since the war but now absorbed with internal problems, had come to feel that either Italy or Germany was going to step into the area. Paris preferred that Rome bring the Danubian states under its economic control. Yugoslavia, chaperoned by France, had stood in the way of effective Italian penetration of Balkan markets. With Hungary and Austria moving toward the Italian orbit, with Albania under the Italian thumb, and with Bulgaria long friendly to Italy, Mussolini had almost completely encircled Yugoslavia, which now was cut off from its Little Entente friends. Italy's success reestablished its equality with its western partners and preserved a little of its patronizing attitude toward Germany. Yet Mussolini, in maneuvering for a stronger diplomatic position, had made heavy financial and commercial sacrifices.[52]

Although Italy had closed the door to Germany in Austria and Hungary, the paradox was that Rome needed German economic help in the Danubian-Balkan area. Mussolini, now feeling more confident and secure, also wanted to cooperate with Germany in the Danube, ideas that Hassell continued to push on Berlin. The Nazis, in response, became increasingly interested in setting up a meeting between Hitler and Mussolini.[53]

The Mussolini-Hitler Colloquy, Venice, June 14–16, 1934

Throughout the spring and early summer of 1934, Austria's internal tensions increased. Attempting to reach a direct settlement with Germany on the Austrian question and other issues, Mussolini invited the Führer to Venice for conversations. Berlin, for its part, hoped to offset the Rome Protocols.[54]

The prospective talks greatly concerned Moscow, and several days before the meeting, Potemkin met with Suvich, who explained that it was a long-admiring Hitler who had been seeking to meet with the Duce and the latter who had put it off.[55] Suvich believed that the discussions would remain general and that nothing important would come from them. Mussolini planned to press Hitler on only one matter—Austria, whose independence was an absolute condition for European peace. The plenipotentiary concluded in his report to Moscow that Mussolini, although enraged at Nazi terrorism in Austria, had swallowed his pride and was going to meet with Hitler because he did not wish Europe to think that he had helped to sabotage the Disarmament Conference. Potemkin also felt that because the Italian government had accepted the French foreign minister's visit to Rome, it could not refuse to meet with Hitler.

The two leaders met from June 14 through the sixteenth. The languid, summertime beauty of Venice and the pomp and circumstance of the attendant ceremonies contrasted vividly with their tempestuous wranglings over Austria.[56] Mussolini refused Hitler's request to withdraw his protecting hand. The Duce tried to convince Hitler that Dollfuss was not anti-German and that getting rid of him would not necessarily improve Berlin's position in Vienna.

Mussolini sympathized with the German position on disarmament. On the related question of Germany's return to the League, Mussolini resurrected his idea of a consortium of powers, that is, the extension of the Four Power Pact or some sort of League reform with German cooperation. Concerning the USSR's imminent admission to that august body, both dictators held that the Soviets would use it as a propaganda platform. Suspicious of any Soviet initiative supported or suggested by France, Mussolini disparaged Moscow's proposed treaty system, arguing that it would mean merely a return to the old prewar alliances; Italy would not join any such combination.[57] On Italo-French relations, Mussolini said that his repeated attempts to come to amicable terms had failed: he would continue to try, but predicted nothing positive. Hitler gained the impression that the Danubian question little concerned the Duce.

Official Italian reports, not easy to compile because Mussolini relied on his memory to relate his colloquies to his subordinates, spoke only in general terms of collaboration and clarification of the European situation. Galeazzo Ciano, head of the Italian press bureau and future foreign minister, claimed that Hitler had agreed to give up the idea of an Austrian *Anschluss* and that the Duce had invited Germany to join the Italo-Austro-Hungarian economic accord. The two had found many avenues for collaboration.

The semiofficial spokesman, Virginio Gayda, saw in the meeting the development of an understanding that would offset French influence in Central Europe and the Balkans; further, Mussolini and Hitler had reached a "gentlemen's agreement" to call off the Nazi terror campaign and to preserve Austrian independence. Hassell complained that Gayda had written based on his impressions and not with his usual impartial precision. The foreign newspapers, he continued, "simply abound in sensationalism."[58] Berlin insisted that all had gone well: "The Reich Chancellor's visit to Venice went off with exceptional cordiality and most harmoniously, and made a great impression on the public as well. . . . . Hitler and Mussolini got on extremely well together and conceived feelings of personal friendship over and above their mutual esteem."[59]

Despite these official and public claims of a successful meeting, the reality was quite different, and so Attolico told a relieved Litvinov.[60] Nothing had been settled.

On the basis of information received from an Italian official, Potemkin wrote the NKID on July 5 that Mussolini had tried to bolster Italy's prestige, shaken as it was by foreign-policy failures and growing domestic dissatisfaction with the fascist regime.[61] Despite the theatrical organization of the visit and the hullabaloo raised by the fascist press, the meetings had produced no serious, positive results, but rather had pointed up disputes that could not be painted over by official communiqués and inspired press accounts. Conducted helter-skelter, the meetings frequently had degenerated into brutal debates on matters such as disarmament and the League of Nations. After the first conversation, an irritated Hitler had decided to fly back to Germany, but was dissuaded by Neurath and Hassell. Surely Moscow was pleased with this part of the report.

Both leaders, however, had agreed on the status of equality on which Hitler was conditioning his return to the League. Potemkin, continuing his report, supposed that this was in Rome's interests, fearing as it did that without Germany and with Soviet entry, the League could become a tool of anti-German and anti-Italian policy. The plenipotentiary continued that Rome was pushing Germany to reenter the League should its parity in armaments be confirmed by international decree.

According to Potemkin, Suvich had criticized the Führer for dealing not in concrete formulations, but in abstractions on which he could talk for hours on end. Mussolini had not managed to convince Hitler to return to the League or to demand it be reformed. Both deliberately obfuscated the Austrian issue. Hitler denied plans to invade Austria, but he condemned the Dollfuss government and its increasingly violent repression of those advocating national self-determination, that is, the ethnic unity of all Germans. Mussolini strongly supported Dollfuss and rejected elections in Austria in the face of Nazi terrorism. Potemkin thought that Mussolini was publicizing his friendship with Dollfuss to prevent Austria from looking to French patronage. He also relayed Mussolini's fear that his Danubian partners believed that Germany's economic help would be more profitable than cooperation with a poorer and weaker Italy. In the end all that they could do was to paper over their disagreements, because each had come away convinced that the other would not compromise on the Austrian question.

One week later, on July 13, Potemkin tried to reassure the Duce about the directions of Soviet policy.[62] Particularly solicitous about the Italian public's reaction to the Franco-Soviet rapprochement, he assured Mussolini that it had been dictated by Hitler's animosity. Unfortunately, not only was he not working to improve those relations, the Führer had established a threatening friendship with Poland. To this Mussolini noted that Warsaw was hoping to divert Germany's attention southward, toward *Anschluss*, and therefore German-Polish cooperation threatened Italy as well as the Soviet Union. He went on: "I think that it is in both our best interests to watch Poland closely. We could give you some information on their plans in the Ukraine. We would appreciate it if you shed some light for us on their domestic politics." The upshot was that the USSR had to provide for the security of its western borders, and the best way to do this was through friendship with France—the most powerful nation in Europe and the one most capable of threatening Germany and taking effective measures against Poland. The rapprochement with Paris, Potemkin promised, would not alter the Kremlin's friendly stance toward Italy.

In this context the plenipotentiary took particular care to reassure Mussolini that his government was normalizing its relations with the members of the Little Entente as individual states, not as a collective entity. Therefore, no tripartite Franco-Soviet-Little Entente arrangement directed against Italy was in the works. The USSR, strong enough not to fall prey to French influence, was prepared to cooperate actively with all states in the struggle for peace.

The Foiled Nazi Putsch, July 25, 1934

Hitler failed to implement whatever agreements Mussolini thought he had gotten at Venice and Nazi violence in Austria continued unchecked. These outrages culminated in late July with a putsch, carried out by Austrian Nazis inspired from Berlin, which led to the assassination of Dollfuss, whose wife was Mussolini's guest at the time.[63] An indignant Italian press attacked Germany, and with Italian troops at the Brenner, Hitler faced an Italo-French-Little Entente coalition. He backed down and recognized Austrian independence. A new government put down the rising, quashing the last armed Nazis resistance in southern Austria by the end of the month. This was collective security's single outstanding success in the 1930s, although the fascist apologist Luigi Villari has pointed out with some sophistry the limitations of even this:

The action to safeguard Austria, in order to be effective, should have been international. Although the presence of Italian troops on the Brenner did save the situation for the time being, Great Britain and France should have cooperated closely with Italy. . . . A secret military agreement between Italy and France . . . had been concluded with the view to joint action in the event of a German invasion of Austria, but Great Britain would not undertake any engagement. So, in the end, Italy was left unsupported. This fact forced the Italian Government to abstain from any further measures, for it could not act alone.[64]

Mussolini's second thoughts did not come until later. In the meantime, on August 21 in the Villa de Marinis in Florence, Mussolini spoke with the new Austrian chancellor, Kurt von Schuschnigg. They agreed to cooperate in maintaining Austria's "independence and integrity to which appertains also complete internal autonomy, and which, moreover, represents a concrete European interest and an element favourable to the maintenance of tranquility in the Danubian sector."[65]

The Soviet press, as could be expected, closely followed the meeting and, seduced by what it took to be the glow of cooperation, repeated the chancellor's declaration that Italy was the principle guarantor of peace in Europe.[66]

Seemingly confirming this optimism, the Austrian chancellor conferred with the British, French, and Italian representatives at Geneva and impressed upon them the grave situation in his country, where Nazi intrigues still smoldered. Responding on September 27, France, the United Kingdom, and Italy promised that their February 17 declaration "retains its full effect and will continue to inspire their common policy."[67] Mussolini sharpened this point on October 6, telling the workers of Milan that Italy would defend Austrian independence: "We have defended and will defend the independence of the Austrian Republic, an independence consecrated by the blood of a Chancellor, small in stature but great in soul and heart."[68]

European statesmen continued to discuss the Austrian problem until the close of the year. It formed the foundation for the Franco-Italian rapprochement of December, which received concrete form in the Rome Accords of January 1935. That fateful pact provided for cooperation in Europe against Germany in exchange for French support for Italian expansion in Northeast Africa.

The Soviet press rejoiced at length at this course of events. In mid-August 1934 *Pravda* excitedly editorialized that Italy was firmly committed to preserving Austria.[69] According to Litvinov's mouthpiece, the *Journal de Moscou*, recent events had delivered a grave, perhaps irreparable, blow to Italo-German relations. That friendship, in any case, had no serious basis in mutual interests. Rome merely was using Germany to pressure France to make concessions on matters left over from the Great War. An Italo-French rapprochement was possible.[70] Two days later *Pravda* joyfully reproduced an article from the German press lamenting that the Austrian situation could drive Italy away from Germany and into French arms, and at the end of the month the press reproduced Italian articles denouncing Rosenberg's anti-Italian speeches.[71] At the end of September *Izvestia* cheerfully acknowledged that "the English and French recognize the preeminence of Italian interests" in Austria.[72]

The Soviet press, however, reflected not only the Kremlin's fond hopes, but also its profound fears. For example, it had dramatized the pointed coincidence in time between Louis Barthou's trip to Belgrade and the anti-

French naval demonstration by an Italian squadron at Durazzo, Albania, in June 1934. In an editorial at the end of the month, *Pravda* emphasized the contradictions between the French and Italian blocs in the Balkans.[73] By August the party's paper was warning that Italo-Franco-British cooperation in Africa was running into problems because of Italy's pretensions, and a month and a half later *Izvestia* regretfully passed on Aloisi's belief that it would not be possible for Italy and France to reach an agreement on the Austrian issue.[74]

As the year 1934 drew to a close, Moscow's confidence returned. *Pravda* again played up anti-Italian tendencies in Germany and declared that Italy would not permit *Anschluss*.[75] Another paper analyzed Italo-French controversies such as colonial borders, relations with Yugoslavia, and naval armaments, and thankfully concluded that an agreement with French concessions was quite possible.[76] In December Litvinov told Cerruti that he had high hopes for the happy conclusion of an Italo-French accord and for continued close Italo-Soviet cooperation.[77] Several days later, *Izvestia* again announced optimistically that France was prepared to find agreement with Italy over Tunisia, and that both London and Paris were disposed to make concessions on Abyssinia. In return, France wanted Italy's guarantee to come to agreement with the countries of the Little Entente, especially Yugoslavia.[78]

Henri's Analysis of the 1934 Austrian Nazi Putsch

In 1936 Ernst Henri, that curious and often self-contradictory Soviet publicist and intelligence operative, wrote that an ardent Italo-German friendship had existed immediately following Hitler's rise to power, but the Austrian events of July 25, 1934, had almost led to an Italo-German war.[79] Called "the best account of their thinking,"[80] *Hitler over Russia?* argued that the break represented a rational conflict between the German and Italian capitalisms. The former was highly intensive and the latter mildly industrial and still predominately agricultural; one produced coal, iron, machinery, guns, chemicals, locomotives, electrical plants, and airplanes, while the other supplied fruits, vegetables, wine, silk, cotton, and musical instruments; one was obsessed with the means of production, and the other focused on consumption; one had the Atlantic for an outlet, and the other the Mediterranean. But, in the capitalist, imperialistic world, even this symbiotic balance could explode. Mussolini logically could and should have combined with Hitler to form a new European dominance for political, economic, tactical, military, and ideological reasons; but capitalist disputes, especially in the Danubian basin, prevented this.

Despite Hitler's earlier promises to make Italy the cornerstone of his foreign policy and the deals between Italian and German capitalists, when Hitler came to power, the German industrialist Thyssen double-crossed

Mussolini. The Germans made Austrian *Anschluss* and a push through the Balkans their most important foreign-policy goal. As they squeezed Rome's economic interests out of Southeast Europe, they threatened to turn Italy into a vassal.[81]

To stay this eventuality, Mussolini concluded the Rome Protocols of March 17, 1934, which presaged a complete economic, political, and military federation between Italy, Austria, and Hungary under the Duce's leadership. This union sought to create a new, consolidated political empire stretching from the Alps to the Black Sea, from Vienna to Sicily. It would dominate the Balkan peninsula through Italy's old friends, Albania, Bulgaria, and Romania, and would reach to equatorial Africa via Abyssinia and perhaps some of British Africa. This would mean no less than the restoration of the Eastern Roman Empire![82]

Mussolini began his decisive counterattack on Thyssen's economic and political position in Austria, Henri continued, immediately after the Rome Protocols. The first blow was the transfer, enforced by the Austrian government, of the Alpine Mining Company from Thyssen to Italian industrialists. The ensuing grotesque struggle between a government and a private concern in the same country, reminiscent of the internecine wars between the nationalizing central powers and the feudal territorial dukes, led to the Austrian civil war of July 25 through the twenty-eighth.[83]

In characteristic Marxist analysis of the economic substructure of things, Henri pictured Thyssen as desperately fighting Toplitz's Banca Commerciale for heavy industrial hegemony of the whole of Danubian and Southern Europe. Thyssen's strategy was twofold. Economically, he planned to monopolize the Styrian iron ore for the Ruhr's blast furnaces, to occupy Vienna and the Danube as a transit station for the new German export assault on the Balkans and the Near East, and to blackmail Italy by controlling Italy's coal and iron supplies. Politically, Thyssen planned to fortify Austrian national socialism to safeguard these economic aims and, beyond this, to foment new Balkan fascisms of the German hue through the Romanian Iron Guard, the Bulgarian Mikhailovists, the Croatian Ustashi, and so forth. This would bring German control of Southeastern Europe to Italy's very borders.[84]

The Italian strategy, on the other hand, was to reverse the operation: aggression from south to north, using Italian capitalists instead of German, Italophiles and Austro-clerics instead of Austro-Nazis, Roman glory instead of Germanism, and civilized Mediterranean Fascio instead of the barbarous Nazi swastika.

In 1934 the Nazi insurrection in Austria was killed and so was the Alpine Mining Company—from Thyssen's standpoint. There were no longer any heavy industrial Ruhr possessions in Austria. Mussolini and the Alpine financial oligarchy, for now, had defeated Hitler and the Ruhr's oligarchy. Henri, however, perspicaciously predicted an inevitable German victory in Southeastern Europe.[85]

NOTES

1. Maxwell Henry Hayes Macartney and Paul Cremona, *Italy's Foreign and Colonial Policy, 1914-1937* (New York, 1938), pp. 208-09.

2. Bruce F. Pauley, *The Habsburg Legacy, 1917-1939* (New York, 1972), pp. 126-27; Vladimir Konstantinovich Volkov, *Germano-iugoslavskie otnosheniia i rasval Maloi Antanty, 1933–1938* (Moscow, 1966), pp. 33-57; Filipo Filipovic [B. Boshkovich], "Italo-iugoslavskii konflikt," *Kommunisticheskii Internatsional* (May 10, 1933): 32-40; *Izvestia*, Aug. 18, 1934. Benito Mussolini, *Opera omnia di Benito Mussolini*, ed. Edoardo and Duilio Susmel, 36 vols. (Florence, 1951–63), 21: pp. 158-72.

3. Macartney and Cremona, *Italy's Policy*, pp. 192-200, 209; Arnold Joseph Toynbee, *Survey of International Affairs, 1934* (London, 1935), pp. 328-29, 539-50, 557-58.

4. Attolico to Rome, 2/22/33, 2/24/33: AP URSS b8 f1.

5. "Italian Policy in South-East Europe," *Economist* 116 (May 13, 1933): 1014; *Izvestia*, on Apr. 25 and 26, 1933, discussed the Italo-French struggle in the Balkans and Central Europe: despite the recent Italo-French rapprochement, their imperialist competition continued and so too the tendency to form two continental groups; see also May 6, June 21, 30, 1933. On May 9, *Izvestia* discussed Italy's attempts to reconcile with the Little Entente. Attolico to Rome, 5/3/33, 5/16/33: AP URSS b11 f1.

6. Macartney and Cremona, *Italy's Policy*, pp. 202-03; Toynbee, *Survey, 1934*, p. 493.

7. Attolico to Rome, 9/23/33: AP URSS b8 f4.

8. Ramaro to Rome, 12/12/33; Aloisi to Mussolini, 1/8/34; Suvich to Rome, 1/14/34; Lomacono to Rome, 1/15/34; Attolico to Rome, 1/16/34, 2/27/34; Note for Suvich, 1/22/34: AP URSS b15 f15; Suvich memorandum, 2/7/34: AP URSS b12 f1; *DVP* 17: nos. 13, 27; *Izvestia*, Feb. 11, 1934.

9. Attolico to Rome, 3/21/33; see also Berardis to Rome, 11/6/33: AP URSS b8 f4.

10. *DVP* 17: nos. 193, 194, 196; Attolico to Rome, 4/19/34; Suvich memorandum, 6/11/34: AP URSS b12 f2. A. Sheviakov, "Ustanovlenie diplomaticheskikh otnoshenii SSSR so stranami tsentral'noi i iugo-vostochnoi evropy," *Voprosy istorii* (Jan. 1975): 32–48. Austria had recognized the USSR in 1924.

11. Attolico to Rome, 7/12/34: AP URSS b12 f3.

12. *Pravda*, Nov. 5, 1934.

13. *Pravda*, Nov. 17, 18, 1934; Berardis to Rome, 11/21/34: AP URSS b15 f2.

14. Toynbee, *Survey, 1934*, pp. 521-25.

15. Ibid., pp. 512-13, 519-20.

16. D.B. Mel'tser, "Bolgaro-sovetskie otnosheniia (ianvar'-noiabr' 1935)," in I.N. Chempalov, ed., *Politika velikikh derzhav na Balkanakh i Blizhnem Vostoke (1933-1943)* (Sverdlovsk, 1977), pp. 29-43.

17. Toynbee, *Survey, 1934*, p. 526.

18. Nina Dmitrievna Smirnova, *Politika Italii na Balkanakh: Ocherk diplomaticheskoi istorii, 1922–1935 gg.* (Moscow, 1979), p. 205; *DVP* 17: n.17. For the Czech, Polish, and Italian points of view, see ibid. 17: nos. 48, 56, 89, and *Izvestia*, Mar. 18, 1934.

19. Robert Joseph Kerner and Harry Nicholas Howard, *The Balkan Conferences and the Balkan Entente, 1930-1935: A Study in the Recent History of the Balkan and Near Eastern Peoples* (Berkeley, 1936; reprint, Westport, CT, 1970), pp. 116-49; William Miller, "The Balkan Pact", *Contemporary Review* 145 (May 1934): 531-39; Norman Judson Padelford, *Peace in the Balkans: The Movement Towards International Organization in the Balkans* (New York, 1935), pp. 90-137, 186-89; *Izvestia*, Feb. 11, 1934; *DVP* 17: nos. 1, 49.

20. Angelo Piero Sereni, "Piccola Intesa, Intesa balcanica e Intesa baltica," *Rivista di Diritto Internazionale* 15 (Apr. 1-Sept. 30, 1936): 172-208; Toynbee, *Survey, 1934*, pp. 508-11, 529.

21. *DVP* 17: no. 14.

22. Ibid., 17: no. 137. Suvich also stressed his regret at the distancing of relations between Turkey and Italy, and he asked for Soviet help in calming down the Turks.

23. Macartney and Cremona, *Italy's Policy*, pp. 210-13; *Izvestia*, Sept. 28, 1934; Smirnova, *Politika Italii*, p. 211. See Federico Curato, "Italia e Russia," *Rassegna di Politica Internazionale* (May 1934): 173-86.

24. *Izvestia*, Apr. 4, 1935.

25. *DVP* 17: no. 28.

26. Attolico to Rome, 1/29/34, 2/1/34, 2/7/34, 2/13/34, 2/16/34: AP URSS b13 f8. The first secretary at the Soviet embassy in Rome complained that the fascist press had not stressed Stalin's speech—particularly galling because the Soviet press always amply reproduced Mussolini's speeches. Note for Suvich, 2/1/34: AP URSS b14 f1.

27. *Pravda*, Jan. 8, 9, 15, 16, 18, 1934; *Moscow Daily News*, Jan. 9, 16, 1934; *Izvestia*, Jan. 18, 21, 22, Feb. 23, 1934; Attolico to Rome, 1/16/34, 1/25/34: AP URSS b15 f2.

28. *Izvestia*, June 27, 1934; Attolico to Rome, 7/4/34: AP URSS b15 f2.

29. *Pravda*, Aug. 13, 1934; Attolico to Rome, 8/16/34: AP URSS b15 f2.

30. Attolico to Mussolini, 4/26/34: AP URSS b14 f1. For similar conversations dealing with Turkey, see Attolico to Mussolini, 1/23/35: AP URSS b17 f2 and Quaroni circular, 1/26/35: AP URSS b16 f1.

31. Attolico to Rome, 2/21/34: AP URSS b14 f1. A native Bulgarian, Boris Spiridonovich Stomonyakov was the Soviet trade plenipotentiary in Berlin from 1920 to 1935. Arrested in 1938, he died in prison in 1941. Anastas Ivanovich Mikoian, a trade official, eventually came to head the foreign trade establishment.

32. Rome to Attolico, 4/2/34; Attolico to Rome, 3/8/34, 5/9/34; Aloisi to De Francisci, 6/13/34, 7/16/34; De Francisci to Aloisi, 6/30/34: AP URSS b17 f2; Rome to Attolico, 7/12/34: AP URSS b14 f1.

33. Carmine Senise to MAE, 12/10/33; MAE circular, n.d.; MAE to Servizio Corrispondenza, Uff. 3, 2/21/34; Romanelli Fasano promemorial, 2/27/34: AP URSS b13 f10; DGAP to DGAP, Uff. 1, 2/28/34; Quaroni to DGAP, Uff. 4, 3/3/34: AP URSS b14 f1. Soviet merchant sailors did occasionally get off their ships to tour. The *Dimitrov*, e.g., bound for New York, laid over in Civitavecchia for about one month. Rome granted Potemkin's request that the crew be allowed to go to Rome. Occasionally, small diplomatic problems arose, especially over customs, but nothing of importance. Potemkin, note verbale, 7/12/34, 7/20/34; Babuscio to Buffarini Guidi, 7/14/34; Montecchi-Renucci to Buffarini Guidi, 7/20/34: AP URSS b14 f8; Servizio Corrispondenza, Uff. 3, to DGAP, 7/31/34: AP URSS b17 f3.

34. Rome to Attolico, 7/12/34; DGAE, Uff. 1, to DGAP, Uff. 1, 2/17/34; Quaroni

to DGAE, Uff. 1, 2/20/34: AP URSS b14 f14; Barduzzi to Rome, 11/20/35: AP URSS b18 f16; Attolico to Rome, 7/4/34, 8/16/34, 8/23/34: AP URSS b15 f2; Attolico to Rome, 7/7/34: AP URSS b14 f1; Attolico to Rome, 7/7/34: AP URSS b12 f3; *Pravda*, Aug. 8, 13, 1934; *Izvestia*, Nov. 2, 1934.

35. *Izvestia*, June 24, Aug. 8, 11, 20, Nov. 5, 1934; *Pravda*, Aug. 11, 1934; Berardis to Rome, 11/7/34; Attolico to Rome, 8/16/34, 8/23/34: AP URSS b15 f2; Attolico to Rome, 2/27/34: AP URSS b14 f8.

36. Promemorial for Suvich, 5/14/34; Attolico to Mussolini, 5/24/34, 6/18/34, 7/11/34; Note for Suvich, 5/28/34; Bastianini to DGAP, 5/30/34; Suvich memorandum, 8/2/34; Buti to Suvich, 8/29/34: AP URSS b13 f10; Suvich memorandum, 5/25/34; Suvich circular, 5/30/34: AP URSS b12 f2.

37. Attolico to Mussolini, 8/2/34: AP URSS b13 f10.

38. *DGFP* C, 2: nos. 160, 166, 188, 213, 225, 229, 247, 257, 258, 260, 278, 279, 308.

39. *Pravda*, Jan. 19, 1934; Attolico to Rome, 1/25/34: AP URSS b15 f2.

40. A. Shenau, "Vooruzhennoe vosstanie v Avstrii," *Kommunisticheskii Internatsional* (Mar. 10, 1934): 39-47.

41. *Izvestia*, Feb. 20, 22, Mar. 6, 14, 1934; *DGFP* C, 2: nos. 286, 290, 292, 299, 300, 311, 313, 327, 328.

42. Ibid., nos. 332, 333, 334, 338, 339, 341, 344, 345, 346, 349, 389; *DVP* 17: no. 137.

43. Smirnova, *Politika Italii*, p. 239.

44. Gerhard Schacher, *Central Europe and the Western World* (London, 1936), esp. pp. 161-218.

45. *Izvestia*, Mar. 15, 18, 1934; *Moscow Daily News*, Mar. 16, 1934.

46. *Pravda*, Mar. 20, 1934.

47. *Izvestia*, Mar. 20, 1934; see also Mar. 14, 1934, and Attolico to Rome, 3/21/34: AP URSS b15 f1.

48. *Izvestia*, Mar. 29, 1934.

49. Attolico to Rome, 3/28/34: AP URSS b15 f1. *Moscow Daily News*, Mar. 21, 1934, reassuringly editorialized that in the complicated Central European political situation, Italy was working against *Anschluss*. Il'ia Ehrenburg penned a four-part series of articles on the Austrian civil war that stressed Italo-German enmity. *Izvestia*, Mar. 6, 8, 12, 15, 1934.

50. *Izvestia*, May 16, 17, 1934.

51. Attolico to Rome, 5/16/34, 5/24/34: AP URSS b15 f1.

52. In *Business Week* see: "Europe," Mar. 17, 1934, 28; "Europe," Mar. 24, 1934, 32; and "Europe," May 19, 1934, 24; Smirnova, *Politika Italii*, pp. 250-51.

53. *DGFP* C, 2: nos. 263, 368, 377, 380, 393, 394, 409, 420, 431, 432, 446, 449, 462, 472, 492.

54. *DGFP* C, 2: nos. 333, 334, 338, 344, pp. 63, 64; Smirnova, *Politika Italii*, p. 252; Gerhard L. Weinberg, *The Foreign Policy of Hitler's Germany: Diplomatic Revolution in Europe, 1933-36* (Chicago, 1970), p. 99.

55. *DVP* 17: no. 196.

56. *DGFP* C, 3: nos. 5-7, 10, 19, 26.

57. On the proposed Eastern Pact, see *DGFP* C, 2: no. 48, and V.-I. Mikhailenko, "Proekt vostochnogo pakta i positsiia Italii," in Chempalov, ed., *Politika velikikh derzhav*, pp. 43-58.

58. *DGFP* C, 3: no. 26; *The Times* (London), June 16, 1934.

59. *DGFP* C, 3: no. 10.

60. *DVP* 17: nos. 221, 228. The *Journal de Moscou*, June 20, 1934, editorialized that Hitler had received nothing he wanted and that *Anschluss* had been thwarted. A week later TASS reported from Rome that the results of the meeting were insignificant. *Moscow Daily News*, June 27, 1934. On July 3, 1934, *Pravda* and *Izvestia* reported that the Venice meeting showed the profound differences separating Italy from Germany in foreign policy. See also Attolico to Rome, 6/28/34: AP URSS b15 f2, and Weinberg, *Foreign Policy*, pp. 99-102.

61. *DVP* 17: no. 237; Smirnova, *Politika Italii*, pp. 254-55.

62. *DVP* 17: no. 248.

63. Petr Alekseevich Lisovskii, *Voina v Afrike* (Moscow, 1935), p. 28; Petr Alekseevich Lisovskii, *Italo-abissinskii konflikt* (Moscow, 1935), p. 23; Sergei Danilovich Skazkin, K.F. Miziano, and S.I. Dorofeev, eds., *Istoriia Italii*, 3 vols. (Moscow, 1970-71), 3: 116-17.

64. Luigi Villari, *Italian Foreign Policy Under Mussolini* (New York, 1956), pp. 113-14. See Mussolini, *Opera*, 27: pp. 18-21.

65. John Wheeler Wheeler-Bennett and Stephen Heald, eds., *Documents on International Affairs, 1934* (London, 1935), p. 295; *The Times* (London), Aug. 22, 1934.

66. Attolico to Rome, 8/30/34: AP URSS b15 f2.

67. Wheeler-Bennett and Heald, eds., *Documents, 1934*, pp. 273, 298.

68. Mussolini, *Opera*, 26: p. 358.

69. *Pravda*, Aug. 10, 1934.

70. *Journal de Moscou*, Aug. 11, 1934.

71. *Pravda*, Aug. 13, 1934; Attolico to Rome, 8/30/34, 11/29/34: AP URSS b15 f2.

72. *Izvestia*, Sept. 27, 1934; Berardis to Rome, 10/4/34: AP URSS b15 f2.

73. *Pravda*, June 28, 1934; *Izvestia*. June 30, 1934; Attolico to Rome, 6/29/34: AP URSS b15 f2.

74. *Pravda*, Aug. 9, Nov. 5, 24, 1934; *Izvestia*, Sept. 28, Nov. 20, 1934; Berardis to Rome, 10/4/34; Attolico to Rome, 11/29/34: AP URSS b15 f2.

75. *Pravda*, Nov. 23, 24, 1934.

76. Attolico to Rome, 11/29/34: AP URSS b15 f2; Attolico to Rome, 8/16/34; Berardis to Rome, 10/4/34: AP URSS b15 f2.

77. Cerruti to Rome, 12/13/34: AP URSS b12 f4.

78. *Izvestia*, Dec. 16, 1934; Attolico to Rome, 12/20/34: AP URSS b15 f2.

79. Ernst Henri [Henri Rostovskii], *Hitler over Russia? The Coming Fight between the Fascist and Socialist Armies*, trans. Michael Davidson (London, 1936), pp. 82, 86, 91-93, 96. The overall thesis of this book is that under Hitler's aegis, there was forming in the middle thirties in Central and East Europe a bloc of fascist states whose object was to conquer the USSR. The USSR, however, would turn the tables on this scheme.

80. Jonathan Haslam, *The Soviet Union and the Struggle for Collective Security in Europe, 1933-39* (New York, 1984), p. 236.

81. Henri, *Hitler Over Russia?* pp. 100-01.

82. Ibid., p. 101.

83. Ibid., pp. 103-04.

84. Ibid., pp. 105-08.

85. Ibid., pp. 108-20; see also pp. 38-53 and Henri, *Hitler over Europe*, (New York, 1934) p. 183. In 1939 Thyssen broke with Hitler and went into exile. After the Nazi conquest of France, Thyssen ended up in a concentration camp. Walter Zeev Laqueur, *Russia and Germany: A Century of Conflict* (London, 1965), p. 228.

Epilogue

Collective security, that capstone of Soviet public diplomacy in the 1930s, was eloquently proclaimed by Litvinov from the podium of the League of Nations and elsewhere.[1] Its essence can be summed up in the ideas that an attack against one should be considered as an attack against all, and that multilateral, collective action could stop aggression with its first, tentative steps against the weak, before it could muster its strength to attack the strong.

Near the end of 1934, Litvinov forthrightly told Ambassador Cerruti that he believed that an Italo-French agreement was the most solid assurance of peace in Western Europe and that agreement of those two powers with Soviet Russia would likewise guarantee the security of Eastern Europe. Finally, if Great Britain could be brought to cooperate, then world peace could be secured. From the Soviet perspective, collective security had proven successful in Austria in 1934; Moscow's policy seemed to be working well.[2]

Then why was it that the Italo-Soviet diplomatic, commercial, and military cooperation, so essential to successful collective security, first fizzled and then collapsed? Not from a lack of effort—to the contrary—by the Kremlin.

ANTAGONISTIC PRESSES

Before the crash in relations, even while Moscow was working toward a tight political relationship with Rome and was encouraging Italo-French cooperation, the Soviet and Italian presses began to attack each other. *Pravda*, for example, in March 1934 reproduced an article from *New States-man and Nation* on the condition of Italian workers. This was a common ploy by the Soviet press, which might have wanted to publish criticisms without taking responsibility for them—after all, *Pravda*, in this case, was merely reporting what others already had published.[3] Next, *Ekonomicheskaia zhizn'* noted that the fascist regime had worsened the proletariat's position and concluded that Italy could not be a developmental model for other nations.[4]

Il'ia Ehrenburg, the famous Soviet journalist, turned his Marxist-Leninist glasses on Italy. In mid-February he examined literature and arts under the "fascist dictatorship and white terror."[5] He claimed that few books were published in Italy, because fascism meant action, not intelligence. The middle schools were closed to the children of workers and peasants, who attended special schools where they were taught arithmetic and obedience, and the catechism and church history, but not the Latin necessary to continue their studies. Amid social and economic contradictions, concluded Ehrenburg, fascism had been called upon to save a bourgeois class destined for death.

Attolico generously explained Ehrenburg's position to Rome. A member of the privileged intelligentsia, the Soviet regime had left him some latitude in his movements and attitudes. Although he resided in Paris, he returned every so often to Moscow, and this article constituted "a precautionary act of homage to the regime."[6]

Several months later in a series of articles, Ehrenburg described the various countries he had seen in his travels. About Italy he wrote that contrary to fascist claims, the trains still ran late. Lightly denigrating other fascist pretentions, he also noted that German-Aryan tourists lurked everywhere. Leaving behind Italy and its militarism, Ehrenburg was most happy to cross the border into France, "the last democracy in Europe."[7]

Attolico in May and June complained of continued antifascism in the Soviet press, although he did concede that by "fascism" Soviet publicists were not alluding specifically and solely to the Italian party. After the 1923 Munich putsch, he explained, the term had come to describe various racist, nationalist, monarchist, republican, Catholic, and socialist movements. A wide generic umbrella indeed! The ambassador found particularly noteworthy an article by Karl Radek, wherein the Soviet publicist reassured his readers that fascism was not an inevitable historical stage, because such terminology implied a new set of economic relationships. Fascism had not fundamentally changed the economic systems of the countries where it ruled, but merely had reinforced monopoly capital's domination in its attempt to stave off the proletariat's inevitable victory.[8] Radek again attacked fascism the following month by poking fun at the March on Rome, which had brought Mussolini to power in 1922.[9]

The Italians of course responded to these press attacks. In the first week of June Potemkin complained to Suvich about the opening of an anti-Soviet campaign by the Italian press and radio.[10] Especially offensive were the personal attacks on Litvinov. Potemkin promised that when Italy decided to repay the commissar's recent visit to Rome, the Italians would see how willingly the USSR would nurture its friendship with Italy. Potemkin wanted the mutual presses to manifest that friendship. Responding, Suvich blamed the objectionable stories on individual journalists. The one concession that the royal government was willing to make was to have the foreign ministry write an article in the *Giornale d'Italia* to inform everyone that Rome favored Soviet entry into the League of Nations.

On June 29 Litvinov conveyed his irritation to Attolico over recent articles in *Giornale d'Italia*.[11] Two weeks later, Litvinov again complained about Italy's anti-Soviet press campaign. The ambassador retorted that the commissar was overly sensitive and lacked a sense of proportion. Believing, however, that Litvinov was sincere, he advised the foreign ministry in Rome that the situation was important for Italy's relations with the USSR; it was a "most delicate moment."[12]

With his report Attolico included articles from the Soviet press that complained about Arnoldo Cipolla's story appearing in *Gazzetta del Popolo* in June 1934.[13] Cipolla had claimed that Soviet plans for conquering Central Asia, India, Afghanistan, and the Himalayas had sparked British defensive measures. Potemkin and Litvinov complained directly to Mussolini that the Italian press attacks were out of line with friendly relations and were due to Italy's upset at the ties established between the USSR and the Little Entente. Attolico, feeling the heat in Moscow over this article, again asked that the Italian press be told to behave itself.[14]

In June and July of 1934, the Polish press blamed the worsening of Italo-Soviet relations on Moscow's wish to draw closer to France without paying sufficient attention to Mussolini's desires and tactics.[15] The Kremlin had noted that Italian efforts to mediate between Moscow and Berlin had failed and that the Franco-Soviet rapprochement had sapped Moscow's friendship with Rome. The Soviets were showing that they did not need Italy's support. Feeling the sting of this rebuff, the Italian press began to attack the USSR. Soviet representatives, the Polish press continued, had made several formal approaches for an explanation of the anti-Soviet attitude of the fascist press. Although Moscow preferred to remain friends, the Soviet press had begun to respond in kind.

As part of this counter-offensive, *Pravda* published a letter from the Afghan ambassador denying that the USSR had any aggressive designs directed against India. The party paper also published a copy of a telegram sent by the ambassador to the editor of *Gazzetta del Popolo* denying his charges.[16]

This matter, however, was slow to die. On the first day of August, Litvinov expressed his surprise to Attolico for an article by General Alberto Baldini that had reopened Cipolla's claim of an aggressive Soviet gaze on India through Afghanistan. Actually, the commissar said, Anglo-Soviet relations were good, and therefore there was no need to move south against the British Empire. At the same time, Litvinov also complained about Luigi

Barzini's "tendentious" article in *Popolo d'Italia*, especially objectionable because it had come so soon after Potemkin's colloquy with Mussolini and Suvich. Yet again Attolico requested that the Italian press be instructed not to hinder the development of good relations with the Soviet Union.[17]

Back in the first week of July, the Soviet representative to Finland, Boris Shtein, had approached his Italian counterpart, Attilio Tamaro, to try to dissipate the bad atmosphere that had developed between their two countries.[18] Shtein, while not alluding to specific incidents, did draw attention to Litvinov's feeling at Geneva of a coolness, as if Italy suspected the USSR of fomenting anti-Italian policies. Shtein assured Tamaro that the Kremlin was not hostile toward Italy. Further, the USSR wanted to see the problems between Paris and Rome solved as part of its collaboration with France and the Little Entente. To Tamaro's insistence that the Four Power Pact was not anti-Soviet, Shtein replied as Soviet diplomats had for the last year: the USSR had never believed that Italy harbored anti-Soviet thoughts but feared that others in the group might transform it into something hostile to the Soviet Union. Shtein repeated that the USSR had abandoned revisionism and that nothing could make his country turn against Italy. Turning aside Shtein's accusation that Italy was friendly with one of the aggressors, Germany, Tamaro replied that no one spoken out more forcefully against Japanese aggression than had Italy, and no one opposed Germany in Austria more actively than Italy. Shtein agreed.

A couple of weeks later, Attolico passed on to Rome his comments on the Tamaro-Shtein conversation. He emphasized the discrepancies between what Shtein had said and what Litvinov had been saying. Attolico recognized that the Soviets were disturbed by Italy, but on the other hand, he continued to believe that they saw the possibility of a moderating Italian influence on Germany. The ambassador again suggested that it would be a good idea for the presses of both countries to calm down for the sake of mutual friendship.[19]

Rejecting such advice, at the end of December 1934 Mussolini explained to the Kremlin: "The Italian government cannot silence its press and forbid it to write against communism because the communist press of the USSR and the entire world is conducting a campaign against fascism."[20] The Soviet chargé who received this statement in turn objected to the "frenzied campaign" directed against the USSR and its leaders and rejected the notion that his government was in anyway responsible for the world communist press.

Litvinov protested the Duce's attitude to Attolico and threatened that the Soviet press would take up the challenge of Mussolini's "declaration of war."[21] The commissar feared that the campaign reflected a change in Rome's policy. Attolico denied these allegations. Litvinov instructed Shtein not to protest further, but to watch calmly as events unfolded.

Despite the attempts at goodwill, this strange schizophrenia marking the two presses continued throughout the rest of 1934 and the next year as well.

For each article praising the other country, another launched aspersions. This anomaly is not easily explained beyond simple generalities. Perhaps the positive articles reflected Moscow's hopes and encouragement to Italy, while the negative ones represented Moscow's fears and warnings. Surely, in such times, Soviet leaders can be allowed some confusion until Italy's true intentions settled out of the wort.

THE ABYSSINIAN ADVENTURE

Press articles, however, in and of themselves lay on the periphery of the larger skein of Italo-Soviet relations. Both Rome and Moscow were equally worried about Nazi revisionism, and for a while the Soviet design to fashion collective security, with Italy as a key actor, continued to do well.

The Rome Accords, January 7, 1935

With the Rome Accords of January 7, 1935, Mussolini and French Premier Pierre Laval reaffirmed the obligation to respect the independence and territorial integrity of other European states, and they specifically agreed to maintain Austria's independence and to collaborate with the Little Entente toward that end. Italy would join France to prevent further German rearmament and to assure its containment. In exchange, Mussolini received concessions in Africa.[22]

France's strategic position, buttressed by the Franco-Soviet treaty in May, was now more favorable than at any other time between the two wars. This was especially true because the accords spawned secret military talks between the two Latin sisters. Only four days after their signing, Mussolini grabbed the initiative, and Marshal Pietro Badoglio quickly entered into talks, which centered around cooperation over Austria. As early as May 13, the general staffs of the two air forces signed an agreement, and at the end of June the two governments signed a pact of general military cooperation. Such diplomatic negotiations seldom move so fast, and, suggesting possibilities for the future, these talks implied that Mussolini favored moving directly to an alliance with Paris.[23]

The Kremlin appreciated the Rome Accords and Italo-French military cooperation for the very reasons that Berlin found them obnoxious.[24] Even as tensions were building before the Italo-Abyssinian War, the Soviet publicist P.A. Lisovskii wrote with understanding of the strategic necessities driving France toward Italy, the one power with both the need and the ability to act quickly and significantly against any German move on Austria. Beyond wanting to pander to a Paris seeking agreement with Rome, both important to any collective security scheme, the Soviets had their own anti-German stake in Southeast Europe, which by their own admission was more important than were any revolutionary interests in Northeast Africa.[25]

Although Moscow was emphasizing that only it could take an impartial position in conflicts between the white race and others, Attolico in February 1935 noted that for some time the Kremlin had taken a reserved attitude toward the brewing Italo-Abyssinian conflict. According to their verbiage and ideology, the ambassador continued, the Soviets should have been enjoying the conflict of African peoples against a great power.[26]

Aside from not wanting to go against France on this issue, the Soviets overcame their natural desire to support the Abyssinian people against imperialism because they believed that the principal cause of those hostilities was Japanese expansion in Abyssinia. One long article, after affirming that Abyssinia was threatened by Italian occupation, declared that the African state had maintained its independence thanks only to the tripartite Italo-Franco-British rivalry. Italy now had its chance to improve its position, because the advance of Japanese capital in Abyssinia and Japanese dumping in that country economically and politically threatened all three Western powers. Italy had received the tacit support of London and Paris to establish with force the economic privileges that the African state had not voluntarily conceded to Italy.[27]

In short, the Soviets were willing to swallow any ideological embarrassment to support anyone consuming Tokyo's attentions and thereby deflecting, however slightly, Japanese appetite away from Manchuria and Siberia. Certainly, too, the Kremlin was willing to use any hook—in this case the Japanese threat—to latch onto allies that might be gotten into the habit of stopping aggression, or at least that aggression perpetrated by Moscow's enemies. Other than Great Britain, Italy was the only power—a much weaker one to be sure—that could serve Soviet interests against both of the USSR's two enemies, Germany and Japan, and certainly Britain could not be counted on for long to risk the diplomatic quicksand of East and Southeast Europe. Although the Kremlin could not have thought that the Italian navy could oppose the Japanese in the Pacific, at least Rome was actively opposing Japanese expansionism somewhere, which was more than Moscow would have been willing to concede to either Great Britain or the United States.

In mid-March, *Izvestia* at length analyzed the history of colonialism in Abyssinia and concluded that the latest events showed that Italy's policies had entered a new phase.[28] Its position was especially favorable following the Rome Accords. With no small degree of wishful thinking, the paper continued that Britain and Italy were rebuilding their cooperation in Abyssinia, which had existed before the Great War. Fearing Japanese expansion in the area because of the threat to its communications with India and Singapore, Britain again was using Italy to its own ends in Northeast Africa, with Abyssinia as the payment. Although Rome was not expecting difficulties in its colonial conquest, *Izvestia* perspicaciously stressed the enormous topographical, climatic, and strategic problems in any military operations against Abyssinia.[29]

The Stresa Meeting, April 11-14, 1935

Following quickly upon the heels of the Rome Accords, Italy and France met with Britain at Stresa in April 1935.[30] Giving urgency to the matter was Germany's unilateral denunciation on March 16 of Versailles's military restrictions and introduction of compulsory military service. The three powers at Stresa agreed to follow a common line in the League of Nations concerning the German action. They confirmed their tripartite declarations of February 17 and September 27, 1934, supporting Austria's independence and integrity.[31]

The Soviet press believed that the tight collaboration defined at Stresa between Italy and France had surprised London. It was this cooperation, that had made the decisive impact on the conference. The French were satisfied with the support they had received from Mussolini; the political independence and integrity of Austria represented a promise for Europe's tranquility through international cooperation. The German threat, the Soviets felt, had consolidated the conference's success. The stand of the three powers taken at Stresa, however, would be made more decisive in the League—a forum where the Soviets could participate.[32]

The Soviets clearly distinguished between the decisions, which they appreciated as necessary to oppose Germany, and the way they had been created. The *Journal de Moscou* declared that the USSR demanded to be recognized as a great power and to be admitted into the European councils. The paper threatened that it would be a terrible mistake to ignore this "fixed point in international Soviet policies."[33]

Even so, the agreement formed another brick in the wall being raised against German expansion, and Moscow appreciated it as such.[34] Although Mussolini was most forceful in denouncing the German danger and in expressing his hope that Stresa would mark effective action against Berlin, the fundamental weakness of the arrangement was that Italy's contribution depended upon a free hand in Abyssinia. Rome warned the western powers of this and underscored that warning with Mussolini's personal assumption of leadership of the colonial ministry.[35]

The French made their position on Abyssinia quite clear to the Soviets. Their ambassador in Italy told Potemkin on June 19 that Laval had explained to Mussolini that France had no interests there and did not oppose a *de facto* Italian protectorate over the country.[36] Moscow did not object, presumably because Italo-French military talks pointing toward collective security were proceeding nicely. In fact, in later June the Soviet representative, Shtein, told Suvich that the USSR did not intend to interfere in Italian plans for East Africa.[37] Stresa marked the flowering of Italy's temporary shift from archrevisionism in Europe to the status quo, a process begun with the Four Power Pact. But Britain, whose policy became increasingly counterproductive after the mid–1930s, downgraded Italy's international stature and dismissed its ability to counter the Hitlerite threat. Further, having but a limited interest in Austria anyway, London proceeded to tear apart the Stresa front, with its implicit Soviet connection. Britain first concluded on June 18 the Anglo-German Naval Agreement behind the backs of its Stresa partners and then insisted on League-imposed economic sanctions to punish Italy for invading Abyssinia.[38]

The Soviets clearly worked to soothe any threat to collective security by Italian action in Abyssinia. Anxious to appease Rome, the Kremlin appeared willing to trample the League Covenant. Moscow's job was greatly eased by Litvinov's fortuitous presidency of the eighty-sixth session of the League Council, and behind closed doors he pressed hard for a peaceful settlement. When told, for example, that London was pushing for a Council meeting for July 29 to discuss the dispute, the commissar instructed Shtein to warn the Palazzo Chigi and to suggest that Italy formally request a delay, which he would support. Aloisi thanked Shtein for Litvinov's friendly gesture.[39]

The last thing that Litvinov wanted was a confrontation between Britain and Italy, which would paralyze all efforts to form an anti-Nazi united front. Prepared to delay discussion at Geneva, on the afternoon of July 31, Litvinov told Anthony Eden that "he thought it would be difficult for the Council to decide here and now to discuss broader aspects of the dispute . . . since Italy would demand an adjournment to prepare her case and that would be difficult to refuse."[40] Litvinov went on to suggest the beginning of September as the proper time for a public session on the matter. He hoped that before then Italy might recognize the "serious crisis" it was racing toward. Eden continued in his report to London that Litvinov

thought it would be helpful if the Council could declare as a body that in this dispute it was prepared to carry out its obligations under the Covenant. There was the memory of Manchuria and this no doubt had encouraged Italy. If the Council could show clearly that Manchuria would not be repeated [the] effect might be salutary. I asked M. Litvinov whether he was prepared to take part in such [a] declaration; he stated that he was, though he had not of course as yet consulted his government and had made [the] proposal to me in the first instant.[41]

The key to Soviet policy throughout the entire Italo-Abyssinian War was clearly set forth here, and Litvinov would repeat it many times in the League's public forum. The commissar, for example, on September 14, 1935, complained:

If we had before us from Italy, instead of a declaration on liberty of action, a formal and well-founded complaint against acts of aggression committed by a neighbouring Ethiopia, falling under a definition of aggression adopted by the League of Nations, I venture to assure the representative of Italy that not only would he have obtained from the League full justice, but also convinced himself of the amount of the sympathy to which the noble Italian nation is entitled.[42]

In other words, if Italy had only presented its case differently, then both the League and Moscow would have accepted its claims. Form, not substance, lay at the heart of Soviet dissatisfaction with the Abyssinian adventure.

Litvinov concluded that the conflict

does not shut out for me the whole international horizon with other looming dangers behind it. . . . You may be assured that, if all efforts for conciliation fail and the Italo-Ethiopian conflict comes before the Council again or before the Assembly, the Soviet delegation will pass its judgment with impartiality and also with courage. . . .

As you know, the Soviet government is, in principle, opposed to the system of colonies, to the policy of spheres of influence and of mandates, to anything pertaining to imperialistic aims. For the Soviet delegation there is only a question of defending the Covenant of the League as an instrument of peace. This instrument has already been somewhat damaged by previous attempts and we cannot allow a new attempt which would put it completely out of work.[43]

This speech *in toto* remarkably blended a Marxist outlook on colonial problems with the dictates of Soviet expediency necessitating peace. It stressed not only an abstract Soviet admiration for the League as an instrument to stalemate aggressive states, but also the Kremlin's efforts to make it a workable and effective instrument.

But again, the most impressive thing about this statement is its mildness, its desire to put off the day when the Soviets would have to condemn directly, and on their own terms, Italian aggression in Abyssinia. Moscow clearly was more interested in potential aggression elsewhere, first and foremost by Germany and Japan against the Soviet Union itself, than in the specific plight of the Abyssinian people. Their fate merely threatened the League's ability to deal with aggression elsewhere, and for that reason alone was their struggle worth the energies of the League's representatives. If collective security in or out of the League—it is hard to imagine that Stalin truly cared where—caved in to a weak aggressor, what would happen when the aggressor was strong? And given the Kremlin's earlier support to the Rome and Stresa accords, if Italy's aggression could have been carried off without calling it aggression, Moscow would have been just as content.

It was London that insisted on that definition and thereby forced a resentful and unhappy Moscow to make its choice. Was Italy or Britain ultimately more useful in opposing Germany and Japan? The answer was obvious. Thus it was London that sucked Paris and Moscow into the vortex of anti-Italian League action. Just when the USSR, Italy, and France seemed to be moving toward one another, Britain shifted toward Germany and forced the USSR and France away from Italy. The Italian government responded on December 28 by denouncing the Rome Accords and its Stresa commitments.[44]

Comintern activity reflected the bitter pill the Kremlin had to swallow, even though as an international agency it had its own constituency only imperfectly directed from Moscow. Throughout the summer of 1935, international communists, echoing the Soviet press, expected the war to become an Anglo-Italian conflict,[45] with the implication that the USSR should not get involved. The Comintern therefore carefully refrained from criticizing Anglo-French or Italian policies in Africa. In short, the Soviets, in both their diplomatic and their revolutionary garb, were willing to swallow any ideological embarrassment to support anything deflecting Tokyo's interests away from Manchuria and Siberia and Berlin's away from East and Southeast Europe.

Even the Italian Communist Party (PCI) only slowly reacted, and not until February 1935 did it launch the slogan of "Hands Off Abyssinia!" Comintern activity, however, did not reflect even this unenthusiastic campaign, as Italy's diplomats noted. One sure sign of Moscow's reluctance to unleash international communism against Italy was the wave of arrests in 1935 that swallowed up Italian communists living in exile in the USSR. They suffered no less than other foreign nationals as the Great Purges began to unfold.[46] Ultimately the PCI did receive permission to agitate on the Abyssinian issue, while the French Communist Party was granted authority to mobilize the leading socialist parties into solidarity with Abyssinia. The Comintern proper, however, remained mute.[47]

At the 7th Comintern Congress in August 1935, Palmiro Togliatti alone raised the Abyssinian issue at any length. Even his call to battle was carefully given in the name only of the PCI and not the Comintern as a whole.[48] Only in September and October, as the Kremlin was forced to choose between London and Rome, did the Comintern wholeheartedly launch its anti-imperialist campaign against Italy over Abyssinia.

Would the Axis have been formed had London made its peace with Rome? Might a collective security system encompassing Moscow and Rome have thwarted Hitler's ambitions and precluded the Second World War? The questions themselves suggest the missed possibilities, missed largely in the first instance because of London's curious preference to deal with Nazi Germany and shortsighted priority to preserve its imperial integrity rather than European security. Britain was determined to avoid the Balkan and East European quagmire—even though this was where the First World War had begun only two decades before and where the Second was to begin only half a decade later.

THE FINAL BREAK

In retrospect, Italy's slide down the slippery slope into a suffocating German alliance might seem inevitable. During the mid- and late 1930s, however, the matter was not so clear. Despite its constant fears of the worst, all the way to June 22, 1941, when the Italian jackal followed the German wolf into war against Soviet Russia, Moscow tried to wean Italy from its alliance. The Kremlin in May 1936, for example, approached Rome with an offer of an Italo-Franco-Soviet accord in exchange for the removal of Soviet sanctions, now that Abyssinia had become the jewel of the Italian empire. During July rumors abounded that Mussolini had seriously studied the possibility.[49]

In the end, however, Italy broke off trade negotiations with the Soviet Union, although Ciano claimed this was for economic rather than political reasons:

Only with Russia, of all the countries with which we were in contact was it impossible to conclude negotiations successfully, because that country demanded a balance in her favour of many tens of millions and we were unable to see why such exceptionally favourable treatment should be accorded to the Soviet Union.[50]

The efforts at reconciliation after Italy's Abyssinian adventure were dashed by the onset of the Spanish Civil War in July 1936, with Italy and Germany supporting Francisco Franco's Rebels, and the USSR supplying the Republicans. For the next three years, relations between the two states degenerated into little more than vicious public attacks on one another and covert Italian submarine and air attacks on Soviet merchantmen plying the Mediterranean. In 1937 and 1938 commercial relations between the two plummeted to almost nothing.

Nonetheless, once the Spanish Republic's fate was sealed in the spring of 1939, Moscow again worked to find points of common interest against Germany. That policy seemed to have been vindicated with Italy's declaration of *nonbelligeranza* at the onset of World War II. Even after Italy's declaration of war against France in June 1940, the Kremlin still did its utmost to exploit any friction between Italy and Germany.[51]

Rationally, that policy, followed so consistently since 1933, should not have come to naught. Mussolini had represented Italy's interests quite well in the first half of the 1930s and had appeared willing to entertain the Kremlin's entreaties to work toward their common interests. Seduced by Hitler and his own vainglory, however, he ultimately rejected that policy in the months immediately preceding the German attack on Soviet Russia on June 22, 1941.

NOTES

1. Gaspare Ambrosini, "L'ingresso dell'U.R.S.S. nella Società delle Nazioni e la sua ripercussione sull'ideologia universalistica dei bolscevichi," *Rivista di studi politici internazionale* (Apr.-June 1935): 125-33; "The Struggle of the U.S.S.R. for Collective Security in Europe during 1933-1935," *International Affairs* (Moscow) (June 1963): 107-16; (July 1963): 116-23; (Aug. 1963): 132-39; (Oct. 1963): 112-20.
2. Litvinov did recognize the difficulty of achieving Italo-French cooperation in

the face of Rome's difficulties with Yugoslavia. Cerruti to Mussolini, 11/19/34; Quaroni circular, 11/26/34: AP URSS b12 f4.

3. *Pravda*, Mar. 21, 1934; Attolico to Rome, 3/28/34: AP URSS b15 f1.

4. Attolico to Rome, 4/5/34: AP URSS b15 f1. B. Lavreniev in *Vechernaia Moskva*, Mar. 16, 1934, reported on his tourist trip to Italy. He contrasted Venice with the rest of Italy, which "is modernizing rapidly and lives the fervid pace of an industrial country." Attolico to Rome, 4/5/34: AP URSS b15 f1. *Pravda*, Mar. 27, 1934, also saw Italy as having liquidated the economic crisis and as marching to a rapid tempo of economic life. *Izvestia*, June 28, 1934, however, reprinted a story from the *Daily Telegraph* describing Italy's difficult financial-economic situation; see also *Izvestia*, June 2, 1934.

5. *Izvestia*, Feb. 18, 1934; Attolico to Rome, 2/22/34: AP URSS b13 f1. *Izvestia*, May 14, 1934, also denigrated fascist Italy's musical situation as only a little better than Germany's and "provincial" when compared to the past of Verdi and Puccini. Attolico to Rome, 5/17/34: AP URSS b15 f2.

6. Attolico to Rome, 2/22/34: AP URSS b13 f1.

7. *Izvestia*, May 11, 1934; Attolico to Rome, 5/12/34: AP URSS b15 f1.

8. *Pravda*, May 12, 1934, see also May 13, 1934, and Attolico to Rome, 6/7/34: AP URSS b13 f1.

9. *Izvestia*, June 24, 1934. Meanwhile, the Soviet press did praise an article that Mussolini had written for the German press. *Pravda*, May 14, 1934; *Izvestia*, May 15, 1934. Soviet papers on June 20, 1934, reprinted an article from foreign press accounts saying that Mussolini always had wanted good relations with the USSR and was working to reduce Soviet-German tensions. On June 24 *Izvestia* reprinted part of an article from *Lavoro Fascista* insisting that the USSR be invited to the next naval conference. See *Izvestia*, May 28, 1934 and Attolico to Rome, 5/17/34, 6/28/34, 6/30/34: AP URSS b15 f2.

10. Suvich memorandum, 6/6/34: AP URSS b12 f2; see also Buti to Suvich, 5/30/34: AP URSS b14 f1.

11. Attolico to Rome, 6/29/34: AP URSS b14 f1. At the end of May and beginning of June Litvinov traveled by auto to San Remo for a vacation. Promemorial for the Cabinet, 5/26/34; MAE Cerimoniale, Uff. 3, to DGAP, 5/29/34: AP URSS b12 f2. The *Journal de Moscou*, June 27, 1934, called the description in the *Giornale d'Italia* of forced labor in the USSR a "fable." Attolico to Rome, 6/30/34, 7/4/34: AP URSS b15 f2.

12. Attolico to Rome, 7/12/34: AP URSS b14 f1.

13. *Izvestia*, July 2, 1934; *Pravda*, July 11, 1934.

14. Mussolini memorandum, 7/13/34: AP URSS b12 f3; Attolico to Rome, 7/15/34: AP URSS b14 f1.

15. Bastianini to Rome, 6/5/34: AP URSS b12 f2; Bastianini to Rome, 7/4/34: AP URSS b14 f1.

16. *Pravda*, July 17, 1934; Attolico to Rome, 7/17/34: AP URSS b14 f1.

17. Attolico to Rome, 8/1/34: AP URSS b14 f1.

18. Tamaro to Rome, 7/6/34: AP URSS b12 f3. Only four months later, Moscow nominated Shtein as plenipotentiary to Rome to replace Potemkin. Mussolini noted that Shtein was a faithful collaborator of Litvinov's and one of the better diplomats. Shtein had helped negotiate the 1924 trade treaties between Italy and the USSR. Berardis to Rome, 11/14/34; Mussolini to Pasqualini, 11/15/34: AP URSS b12 f4.

19. Rome to Attolico, 7/19/34; Attolico to Rome, 8/2/34: AP URSS b12 f3. For more on the continuing hostile Italian and Soviet presses, see Suvich memorandum, 6/6/34: AP URSS b12 f2; Attolico to Rome, 6/7/34: AP URSS b13 f1; Attolico to Rome, 6/29/34, 7/12/34; Bastianini to Rome, 7/4/34: AP URSS b14 f1.

20. *DVP* 18: p. 612.

21. Ibid., 18: no. 1.

22. Petr Alekseevich Lisovskii, *Italo-Abissinskii konflikt* (Moscow, 1935), pp. 22-26; V. I. Avershin, "Bor'ba SSSR za kollektivniu bezopasnost' v dunaiskom basseine i na Balkanakh (1933 g.-iiuni 1935)," in I.N. Chempalov, ed., *Balkany i Blizhnii Vostok v noveishee vremia* (Sverdlovsk, 1974), p. 18; Donald Cameron Watt, "The Secret Laval-Mussolini Agreement of 1935," *The Middle East Journal* (Winter 1961): 69-78; William I. Shorrock, *From Ally to Enemy: The Enigma of Fascist Italy in French Diplomacy, 1920-1940* (Kent, OH, 1988), pp. 99-116; see also *Izvestia*, Dec. 18, 1934.

23. Cedric James Lowe and Frank Marzari, *Italian Foreign Policy, 1870–1940* (London, 1975), p. 259; Mario Roatta, *Il processo Roatta* (Rome, 1945), pp. 30-31, 200-01; Franklin D. Laurens, *France and the Italo-Ethiopian Crisis, 1935-1936* (The Hague, 1967), pp. 51-54; Shorrock, *From Ally to Enemy*, pp. 117-40.

24. *Izvestia*, Apr. 4, 1935; Attolico to Rome, 4/11/35: AP URSS b18 f4. Cf. Jonathan Haslam in *The Soviet Union and the Struggle for Collective Security in Europe, 1933-39* (New York, 1984), pp. 45-46, who argues that the agreement upset the Kremlin, especially given earlier French reluctance to participate in collective security. Further, Moscow feared that "in the event of England's adherence, Mussolini, under the cloak of a new agreement, might attempt to resurrect the Four Power Pact." See *DVP* 18: p. 614. Max Beloff, *The Foreign Policy of Soviet Russia*, 2 vols. (London, 1947, 1949), 1: 132, also argues that Moscow was suspicious of the accords as seemingly heading toward a new four-power grouping and as weakening Franco-Soviet ties by providing Paris with a more socially acceptable partner. This is not unreasonable; see Mussolini's apologia, *DGFP* C, 3: no. 473.

25. Petr Alekseevich Lisovskii, *Voina v Afrike* (Moscow, 1935), pp. 26-30. Soviet press comment on the accords was quite guarded, suggesting that Laval's visit to Rome gave hope for consolidating peace in Europe, although, once again, it feared that the accords might substitute for the Eastern Pact. *Journal de Moscou*, Jan. 12, 1935. This was also the tenor of Litvinov's remarks to Laval at Geneva. The rub was, according to Litvinov, that French resolve was weakening. *DVP* 18: nos. 16, 19.

26. Attolico to Rome, 2/16/35: AP URSS b17 f2. See Haslam, *Soviet Union*, pp. 63-66.

27. *Pravda*, Dec. 16, 1934. Italy, presumably, was especially fearful of these Japanese advances because of its poor economic situation. *Izvestia*, Mar. 29, Aug. 17, Nov. 20, Dec. 10, 1934; *Pravda*, Dec. 11, 1934. Attolico to Rome, 12/20/34, 2/16/35: AP URSS b15 f2.

28. *Izvestia*, Mar. 21, 29, 1935. For Italian stories on Soviet-Japanese relations see Attolico to Rome, 3/21/35: AP URSS b18 f4.

29. After the war, *Pravda*, June 25, 1936, picked up these themes, in fact praising Italy's accomplishments of organization, maneuver, and transportation, which had made possible the operation of its modern army under primitive conditions. Arone to Rome, 6/27/36: AP URSS b22 f6.

30. In the week before the conference, Soviet interest in its possibilities grew.

For example, Karl Radek in *Izvestia*, Apr. 6, 1935, declared that peace could be stabilized "only with the collaboration of all interested powers." Given the Kremlin's exclusion from Stresa, this cry for "collective security" seems a plea for the USSR's admittance to the councils of Europe. Attolico to Rome, 4/11/35: AP URSS b18 f4.

31. "La Conferenza di Stresa ed i suoi sviluppi", *Rivista di studi politici internazionale* (Apr.-June 1935): 156-77. The Soviets later told Cerruti that Stresa had been necessary to oppose Germany. MAE circular, 6/8/35: AP URSS b16 fl.

32. *Izvestia*, Apr. 14, 16, 1935; *Pravda*, Apr. 16, 1935; Attolico to Rome, 4/18/35: AP URSS b18 f4; Suvich memorandum, 1/24/35; Suvich circular, 1/28/35; MAE circular, 6/8/35: AP URSS b16 fl.

33. *Journal de Moscou*, Apr. 27, 1935; Attolico to Rome, 4/28/35: AP URSS b16 fl. For similar ideas, see *Journal de Moscou*, Apr. 13, 1935; *Pravda*, Apr. 10, 1935; and Attolico to Rome, 4/18/35: AP URSS b18 f4. Haslam, *Soviet Union*, pp. 48-49, argues that Moscow was upset with these commitments by the French, who, encouraged by London, were attempting to evade commitments to defend the USSR. To make his point, Haslam quotes Potemkin telling Laval that "the slightest indiscretion . . . might lead to the decomposition of the front of states interested in peace in Europe." *DVP* 18: no. 166. Despite the fears of the creation of a front excluding the Soviet Union, the Soviet press responded positively to the Stresa Accords. *Journal de Moscou*, Apr. 19, 1935. Haslam explains this anomaly by suggesting that the agreements had made the Germans more interested in improving relations with Moscow.

34. Other bricks included Italy's overtures to Yugoslavia in early 1935, the Franco-Soviet and Czecho-Soviet pacts of May 2 and 15, 1935, and Soviet entry into the League of Nations on September 18, 1935. See the *Moscow Daily News*, June 15, 1935, for remarks on Italy's favorable press comments on the Franco-Soviet pact.

35. Shorrock, *From Ally to Enemy*, p. 127.

36. Vilnis Sipols and Mikhail Kharlamov, *On the Eve of World War II, 1933-1939: A Foreign Policy Study* (Moscow, 1974), p. 81. Abyssinia already, on May 5, had warned Moscow that Italy was likely to attack in collusion with France in October 1935. *DVP* 18: no. 214.

37. Nina Dmitrievna Smirnova, *Politika Italii na Balkanakh: Ocherk diplomaticheskoi istorii, 1922-1935 gg.* (Moscow, 1979), p. 277; Andrei Andreevich Gromyko, I.I. Zemskov, and V.A. Zorin, eds., *Istoriia diplomatii*, 5 vols. (Moscow, 1959-74), 3: 618; Iosif Mikhailovich Lemin, *Ugroza voiny i mirnaia politika SSSR* (Moscow, 1935), p. 66; Sergei Danilovich Skazkin, K.F. Miziano, and S.I. Dorofeev, eds., *Istoriia Italii*, 3 vols. (Moscow, 1970-71), 3: 117; Vladimir Petrovich Potemkin, ed., *Istoriia diplomatii*, 3 vols. (Moscow, 1941-45), 3: 548; Suvich memorandum, 6/26/35: AP URSS b16 fl. Haslam, *Soviet Union*, pp. 61-62, argues that when faced with Suvich's criticisms of a press campaign in Abyssinia's behalf, Shtein, "being one of those Soviet diplomats confident to act independently," took it upon himself, "evidently without explicit authorisation," to deny that his government intended to get involved in the dispute. See Suvich memorandum, 5/16/35: AP URSS b16 fl. Haslam adds that the Soviet Union had a vested interest in forestalling any Italian adventure in East Africa, because it could only weaken Rome's capacity to act against Germany. Shtein, therefore, had "unwittingly conveyed the illusion" that Moscow was indifferent. This independence, during the purges, seems doubtful; therefore, to suggest that Moscow was not "indifferent," seems equally unlikely. More probably the Soviets

just wanted the matter resolved quickly—whatever the solution—so that Italy could return its gaze to the Brenner. See *Moscow Daily News*, Apr. 10, 1935, and Attolico to Rome, 4/18/35: AP URSS b18 f4.

38. Lisovskii, *Voina v Afrike*, p. 34; Shorrock, *From Ally to Enemy*, esp. p. 123.

39. Quaroni circular, 7/29/35: AP URSS b16 f2; Haslam, *Soviet Union*, pp. 62-63.

40. *DBFP* 2nd, 14: no. 413.

41. Haslam, *Soviet Union*, p. 63, suggests that this last sentence should be taken literally and that Litvinov's opinion was hardening more rapidly than Moscow's. This seems unlikely. Deniable trial balloons are such common diplomatic ploys that claims by representatives to be exceeding their authorizations cannot usually be accepted uncritically. How much more true this was for Stalin's Russia! Finding a breathing space for Rome was the Kremlin's policy as well as Litvinov's.

42. Jane Tarbitsky Degras, *Soviet Documents on Foreign Policy*, 3 vols. (New York, 1978), 3: 142-43.

43. Ibid. p. 146.

44. Haslam, *Soviet Union*, pp. 60-61, lays the cause for the collapse of Italo-Soviet cooperation on a different table. He writes that relations between the two were complicated by their different strategies to contain German expansionism. The Soviets sought a mutual security system in East Europe but were stymied by Polish opposition. Rome was interested in forging a Danubian grouping to protect Austria, and it aimed to win Polish friendship to counterbalance Germany. Thus Rome was prepared to back Warsaw in its hostility to Soviet proposals for collective security. Throughout the spring of 1935 the Soviets tried hard to dissuade Italy from its Polonophile activities. See Suvich memorandum, 5/3/35: AP URSS b16 f1; *DVP* 18: no. 207, pp. 636-37.

45. *Journal de Moscou*, Aug. 30, 1935.

46. See Attolico to Rome, 4/19/35, 4/29/35: AP URSS b18 f12.

47. Haslam, *Soviet Union*, p. 64.

48. Ibid., pp. 64-65.

49. Cerruti to Rome, 5/22/36: AP URSS b19 f1; Vitetti to Rome, 7/18/36: AP URSS b21 f5.

50. See Ciano's speech of May 13, 1937. Beloff, *Foreign Policy*, 2: 106.

51. Mario Toscano, *Designs in Diplomacy: Pages from European Diplomatic History in the Twentieth Century*, trans. and ed. George A. Carbone (Baltimore, 1970), pp. 48-252.

Selected
Bibliography

UNPUBLISHED DOCUMENTS

Ministero degli Affari Esteri, Direzione Generale degli Affari Politici, URSS. (Rome).
Abbreviated as AP URSS.

PUBLISHED DOCUMENTS

Degras, Jane Tarbitsky. *Soviet Documents on Foreign Policy*. 3 vols. New York, 1978.
Eudin, Xenia Joukoff, and Robert M. Slusser. *Soviet Foreign Policy, 1928-1934: Documents and Materials*. 2 vols. University Park, PA, 1967.
Germany. Auswartiges Amt. *Documents on German Foreign Policy, 1918-1945*. From the archives of the German Foreign Ministry. Washington, DC, 1949-83. Abbreviated as *DGFP*.
Great Britain. Foreign Office. *Documents on British Foreign Policy, 1919-1939*. London, 1946-85. Abbreviated as *DBFP*.
Investigation of the Ukrainian Famine, 1932-1933. Washington, DC, 1988.
Italy. Ministero degli Affari Esteri. Commissione per la pubblicazione dei documenti diplomatici. *I documenti diplomatici italiani*. Rome, 1953-81. Abbreviated as *DDI*.
League of Nations. *League of Nations Treaty Series*. Lausanne, Switzerland, 1930-35.
Mussolini, Benito. *Opera omnia di Benito Mussolini*. Edited by Edoardo and Duilio Susmel. 36 vols. Florence, 1951-63.
Union of Soviet Socialist Republics. Ministerstvo inostrannykh del SSSR. *Dokumenty vneshniaia politika SSSR*. Moscow, 1970-73. Abbreviated as *DVP*.
United States. Department of State. *Foreign Relations of the United States*. Washington, DC, 1945-53. Abbreviated as *FRUS*.

NEWSPAPERS

Izvestia (Moscow)
Pravda (Moscow)
The Times (London)

ANNUALS

Toynbee, Arnold Joseph. *Survey of International Affairs.* London, 1931-35.
Wheeler-Bennett, John Wheeler, and Heald, Stephen A., eds. *Documents on International Affairs.* London, 1931-36.

SECONDARY SOURCES

Alfieri, Dino. *Due dittatori di fronte.* 2nd ed. Milan, 1948.
Alvaro, Corrado. *Viaggio in Russia.* Florence, 1943.
Ambrosini, Gaspare. *L'Italia nel Mediterraneo.* Foligno, 1927.
————. *Il partito fascista e lo stato.* Rome, 1934.
————. *I problemi del Mediterraneo.* Rome, 1937.
Amendola, Giorgio. *Antonio Gramsci nella vita culturale e politica italiana.* Naples, 1978.
Antonicelli, Franco. *Trent'anni di storia italiana (1915–1945).* Turin, 1961.
Arendt, Hannah. *The Origins of Totalitarianism.* New York, 1973.
Averbukh, Revekha Abramovna. *Italiia v pervoi i vtoroi mirovykh voinakh.* Moscow, 1946.
Bakulin, Sergei Nikolayevich. *Statistika vneshnei torgovli kapitalisticheskikh stran.* 2nd ed. rev. and enl. Moscow, 1961.
————. *Statistika vneshnei torgovli kapitalistika vneshnei torgovli kapitalisticheskikh stran.* Moscow, 1952.
————. *Nauchno issledovatel'skii institut monopolii vneshnei torgovli.* Moscow, 1934.
Bakulin, Sergei Nikolayevich, and Dmitrii Dmitriyevich Mishustin. *Statistika vneshnei torgovli SSSR.* Moscow, 1935.
————. *Statistika vneshnei torgovli SSSR.* Moscow, 1940.
————, comps. *Vneshniaia torgovlia SSSR za 20 let 1918–1937 gg. Statisticheskii spravochnik.* Moscow, 1939.
Bakulin Sergei Nikelayevich, and Arkadii Petrovich Vinokur, eds. *Vneshniaia torgovliia Soiuza Sovetskikh Sotsialisticheskikh Respublik: Za period 1918–1927/ 28 gg. Statisticheskii obzor.* Leningrad, 1931.
Baldoni, Claudio. *La Sovetà delle Nazioni: Sue funzioni e sua riforma.* Milan, 1936.
Barmine, Alexandre. *One Who Survived: The Life Story of a Russian under the Soviets.* 5th ed. Introduction by Max Eastman. New York, 1945.
Barzini, Luigi. *U.R.S.S., l'impero del lavoro forzato.* Milan, 1935.
Baskerville, Beatrice C. *What Next O Duce?* London, 1937.
Bavaj, Amor. *Il principio rappresentativo nello stato sovietico.* Preface by Sergio Panunzio. Rome, 1933.
Beloff, Max. *The Foreign Policy of Soviet Russia.* 2 vols. London, 1947, 1949.

Belousova, Zinaida Sergeevna. *Frantsiia i evropeiskaia bezopasnost, 1929-1939 gg.* Moscow, 1976.

Bertoni, Renzo. *Russia: Trionfo del Fascismo.* 2nd ed. Milan, 1937.

Bestuzhev, I.V. *Bor'ba v Rossii po voprosam vneshnei politiki, 1906-1910.* Moscow, 1961.

Boffa, Giuseppe. *Storia dell'Unione Sovietica.* 2 vols. Milan, 1976.

Braunthal, Julius, ed. *The Tragedy of Austria.* London, 1948.

Cammett, John McKay. *Antonio Gramsci and the Origins of Italian Communism.* Stanford, CA, 1967.

Cannistraro, Philip V., ed. *Historical Dictionary of Fascist Italy.* Westport, CT, 1982.

Caretti, Stefano. *La rivoluzione russa e il socialismo italiano (1917-1921).* Pisa, 1974.

Carocci, Giampiero. *La politica estera dell'Italia fascista (1925-1928).* Bari, 1969.

Cassels, Alan. *Mussolini's Early Diplomacy.* Princeton, NJ, 1970.

Catalano, Franco. *I rapporti italo-russi dal 1900 alla prima guerra mondiale.* Rome, 1970.

Chabod, Federico. *A History of Italian Fascism.* Translated by M. Grindrod. London, 1963.

Chempalov, I.N., ed. *Politika velikikh derzhav na Balkanakh i Blizhnem Vostoke (1933-1943).* Sverdlovsk, 1977.

Ciocca, Gaetano. *Giudizio sul Bolscevismo (Con il tavole fuori testo).* Milan, 1933.

Coselschi, Eurgeio. *Tre bandiere sul mondo.* Florence, 1938.

Craig, Gordon Alexander and Felix Gilbert, eds. *The Diplomats, 1919-1939.* Princeton, NJ, 1953.

D'Amoja, Fulvio. *Declino e prima crisi dell'Europa di Versailles: Studio sulla diplomazia italiana ed europea (1931-1933).* Milan, 1969.

Davis, Kathryn Wesserman. *The Soviet at Geneva: The U.S.S.R. and the League of Nations, 1919-1933.* Geneva, 1934.

Deborin, Grigorii Abramovich. *Obrazovanie dvukh ochagov voiny i bor'ba za sozdanie kollektivnoi bezopasnosti (1932-1937).* Moscow, 1947.

De Felice, Renzo. *Fascism: An Informal Introduction to Its Theory and Practice.* New Brunswick, NJ, 1976.

―――. *Il fascismo e i partiti politici Italiani: Testimonianza del 1921-1923.* Rocca San Casciano, 1966.

―――. *Mussolini il Duce: Gli anni del consenso 1929-1936.* Turin, 1974.

Deutscher, Isaac. *Stalin: A Political Biography.* Rev. ed. New York, 1966.

Dinale, Ottavio. *Quarant'anni di colloqui con lui.* Milan, 1953.

―――. *Tempo di Mussolini.* Milan, 1934.

Di Pretoro, Francesco. *Fascismo e bolscevismo nell'Europa e nel mondo.* Florence, 1940.

Dodolev, Mikhail Alekseevich. *Demokraticheskaia oppozitsiia i rabochee dvizhenie v Italii, 1922–1926 gg.* Moscow, 1975.

Donnini, Guido. *L'accordo Italo-Russo di Racconigi.* Milan, 1983.

―――. *Il 1917 di Russia nella stampa italiana.* Milan, 1976.

Efremov, Pavel Nikolaevich. *Vneshniaia politika Rossii (1907-1914 gg.).* Moscow, 1961.

Emets, Valentin Alekseevich. *Ocherki vneshnei politiki Rossii v period pervoi mirovoi*

voiny: Vzaimootnosheniia Rossii s soiuznikami po voprosam vedeniia voiny.
    Moscow, 1977.
Eubank, Keith. The Origins of World War II. New York, 1969.
Filipovic, Filipo [B. Boshkovich]. Balkany i mezhdunarodnyi imperializm. Moscow,
    1936.
————. Malaia Antanta: Sotsial'no-ekonomichesko-politicheskii ocherk. Moscow,
    1934.
————. Pered novym vzryvom na balkanakh. Moscow, 1934.
Gaetano, Ciocca. Giudizio sul bolscevismo (Con il tavole fuori testo). Milan, 1933.
Gai, Silvio. L'Italia e il petrolio. Rome, 1938.
Gayda, Virginio. La politica italiana nei Balcani: Suoi sviluppi e sue prospettive.
    Milan, 1938.
Gotlib, V.V. [Wolfram Wilhelm Gottlieb]. Tainaia diplomatiia vo vremia pervoi
    mirovoi voiny. Moscow, 1960.
Grandi, Dino. Giovani. Bologna, 1941.
Gregor, Anthony James. Fascism. Morristown, NJ, 1974.
————. The Fascist Persuasion in Radical Politics. Princeton, NJ, 1974.
————. The Ideology of Fascism. New York, 1969.
————. Interpretations of Fascism. Morristown, NJ, 1974.
————. Italian Fascism and Developmental Dictatorship. Princeton, NJ, 1979.
————. A Survey of Marxism. New York, 1965.
————. Young Mussolini and the Intellectual Origins of Fascism. Berkeley, 1979.
Gregoraci, Giuseppe. Riuscirá la Russia? Preface by Virginio Gayda. Rome, 1932.
Gromyko, Andrei Andreevich; I.I. Zemskov, and V.A. Zorin, eds. Istoriia diplomatii.
    5 vols. Moscow, 1959-74.
Haslam, Jonathan. Soviet Foreign Policy, 1930–33: The Impact of the Depression.
    New York, 1983.
————. The Soviet Union and the Struggle for Collective Security in Europe, 1933-
    39. New York, 1984.
Henri, Ernst [Henri Rostovskii]. Hitler over Europe. New York, 1934.
————. Hitler over Russia? The Coming Fight between the Fascist and Socialist
    Armies. Translated by Michael Davidson. London, 1936.
Hodson, Henry Vincent. Slump and Recovery, 1929-1937: A Survey of World Eco-
    nomic Affairs. London, 1938; reprint, New York, 1983.
Hoover, Calvin B. The Economic Life of Soviet Russia. London, 1931.
Hubbard, Leonard Egerton. Soviet Money and Finance. London, 1936.
Iakhimovich, Zinaida Pavlovna. Rabochii klass Italii protiv imperializma i militarizma
    konets XIX-nachalo XX vv. Edited by I.N. Undasynov. Moscow, 1986.
————. [Zinaida P. Jakhimovic]. I rapporti italo-russi negli anni precedenti la prima
    guerra mondiale. Rome, 1970[?].
————. Revoliutsionnoe dvizhenie v Italii, 1914-1917 gg. Moscow, 1962.
————. Zapadnaia Evrope, 1917-i: Fevral'skaia Revoliutsiia v Rossii i krizis bur-
    zhuaznykh metodov upravleniia narodnymi massami v Anglii, Frantsii, Italii.
    Moscow, 1977.
Ianson, Iakov Davidovich [J. Davidovich Yanson]. Foreign Trade in the U.S.S.R.
    London, 1934.
Iugov, Aron [A. Yugoff]. Economic Trends in Soviet Russia. Translated by Eden and
    Cedar Paul. New York, 1930.

————[A. Yugow]. *Russia's Economic Front for War and Peace: An Appraisal of the Three Five-Year Plans.* Translated by N.I. and M. Stone. New York, 1942.

Jarausch, Konrad Hugo. *The Four Power Pact, 1933.* Madison, WI 1965.

Khaitsman, Viktor Moiseevich. *S.S.S.R. i problema razoruzheniia (mezhdu pervoi i vtoroi mirovymi voinami).* Moscow, 1959.

Kim, M.P., ed. *Istoriia SSSR: Epokha sotsializma (1917-1957 gg.).* Moscow, 1957.

Kirova, Kira Emmanuilovna. *Revoliutsionnoe dvizhenie v Italii, 1914-1917 gg.* Moscow, 1962.

————. *Russkaia Revoliutsiia i Italiia: Mart-oktiabr' 1917 g.* Moscow, 1968.

————. *Zapadnaia europe, 1917-i: Fevral'skaia Revoliutsiia v Rossii i krizis burzhuaznykh metodov upravleniia narodnymi massami v Anglii, Frantsii, Italii.* Moscow, 1977.

Knickerbocker, Hubert Renfro. *Fighting the Red Trade Menace.* New York, 1931.

————. *The Red Trade Menace: Progress of the Soviet Five-Year Plan.* New York, 1931.

Kobliakov, I.K. *USSR, For Peace Against Aggression, 1933-1941.* Moscow, 1976.

Korsun, N.G. *Italo-abissinskaia voina 1935-1936 gg.* Moscow, 1939.

Lemin, Iosif Mikhailovich. *Blok agressorov.* Moscow, 1938.

————. *Mezhdunarodnyi proletariat na zashchitu SSSR.* Moscow. 1933.

————. *Obrazovanie dvukh ochagov voiny i bor'ba SSSR za kollektivnuiu bezopasnost', (1931-1938 gg.).* Moscow, 1951.

————. *Propaganda voiny v Iaponii i Germanii.* Moscow, 1934.

————. *Ugroza voiny i mirnaia politika SSSR.* Moscow, 1935.

Lemin, Iosif Mikhailovich, and A. Nikonov, eds., *Vooruzheniia kapitalisticheskikh stran v 1935 g.* Moscow, 1936.

Lopukhov, Boris R. *Evoliutsiia burzhuaznoi vlasti v Italii.* Moscow, 1986.

Lowe, Cedric James, and Frank Marzari. *Italian Foreign Policy, 1870–1940.* London, 1975.

Lozzi, Carlo. *Mussolini-Stalin: Storia delle relazioni italo-sovietiche prima e durante il fascismo.* Milan, 1983.

Lunacharskii, Anatolii Vasil'evich. *Italiia i voina.* Petrograd, 1917.

Macartney, Maxwell Henry Hayes, and Paul Cremona. *Italy's Foreign and Colonial Policy, 1914-1937.* New York, 1938.

Mack Smith, Denis. *Italy: A Modern History.* Rev. ed. Ann Arbor, 1969.

————. *Mussolini: A Biography.* New York, 1982.

————. *Mussolini's Roman Empire.* New York, 1976.

Mahaney, Wilbur Lee, Jr. *The Soviet Union, the League of Nations and Disarmament, 1917-1935.* Philadelphia, 1940.

Manacorda, Guido. *Il bolscevismo: Marxismo-mistica-meccanesimo-ateismo- morale-politica-economia-letteratura e arte-scuola e propaganda.* 3rd ed., rev., enl., updated. Florence, 1940.

Michels, Roberto. *Lavoro e razza.* Milan, 1924.

Mishustin, Dmitrii Dmitriyevich, ed. *Torgovye otnosheniia SSSR s kapitalisticheskimi stranami.* Moscow, 1938.

————. *Vneshniaia torgovlia SSSR.* 3rd ed., rev. Moscow, 1941.

Missiroli, Mario. *La politica estera di Mussolini dalla marcia su Roma al convegno di Monaco, 1922-1938.* Milan, 1939.

Mosca, Rodolfo. *Russia, 1932: Verso il secondo piano quinquennale.* Milan, 1932.

Nanni, Torquato. *Bolscevismo e fascismo al lume della critica marxista Benito Mussolini.* Bologna, 1924.

Napolitano, Tomaso. *Maternità e infanzia nell'U.R.S.S. (Saggio di politica sociale).* Florence, 1938.

———. *Maternità e infanzia nell'U.R.S.S. (Saggio di politica sociale).* Preface by Gennaro Marciano. Padua, 1934.

———. *Le metamorfosi del bolscevismo.* Milan, 1940.

———. *La politica criminale sovietica.* 2nd ed., rev. and enl. Padua, 1936.

Nobile, Umberto. *Quello che ho visto nella Russia sovietica.* Rome, 1945.

Notovich, F.I. *Diplomaticheskaia bor'ba v gody pervoi mirovoi voiny.* Vol. 1: *Poteria soiuznikami balkanskogo poluostrova.* Moscow, 1947.

———. *Ot pervoi ko vtoroi mirovoi voine: Kratkii ocherk mezhdunarodnykh otnoshenii v 1919-1942 gg.* Tashkent, 1943.

———. *Razoruzhenie imperialistov, Liga Natsii i SSSR.* Edited by E. Pashukanis and B. Vinogradov. Moscow, 1929.

———, ed. *Protiv fashistskoi fal'sifikatsii istorii: Sbornik statei.* Moscow, 1939.

Noussimbaum, Leo [Essad Bey]. *Giustizia Rossa: I processi politici nell'U.R.S.S.* Translated by Mario Bacchelli. Florence, 1938.

Nozzoli, Guido. *I ras del Regime: Gli uomini che disfecero gli italiani.* Milan, 1972.

Ovsianyi, Igor Dmitrievich. *Taina, v kotoroi voina rozhdalas' (Kak imperialisty podgotovili i razviazali vtoruiu mirovuiu voinu).* 2nd ed., enl. Moscow, 1975.

Panunzio, Sergio. *La persistenza del diritto.* Pescara, 1910.

———. *Lo stato fascista.* Bologna, 1925.

Parodi, Mario. *Il bolscevismo si confessa.* Milan, 1943.

Paryczko, Demetrio. *La situazione della classe operaia nell'U.R.S.S.: Tratta unicamente da documenti sovietici.* Florence, 1938.

Pauley, Bruce F. *The Habsburg Legacy, 1917–1939.* New York, 1972.

Petracchi, Giorgio. *Diplomazia di guerra e rivoluzione: Italia e Russia dall'ottobre 1916 al maggio 1917.* Bologna, 1974.

———. *La Russia rivoluzionaria nella politica Italiana: La relazioni italo-sovietiche 1917-25.* Preface by Renzo de Felice. Bari, 1982.

Petricioli, Marta. *L'occupazione italiana dell Caucaso: "Un ingrato servizio" da rendere a Londra.* Introduction by Rodolfo Mosca. Milan, 1972.

Pettinato, Concetto. *I Francesi alle porte d'Italia.* Milan, 1934.

———. *Nella Russia degli zar.* Rome, 1968.

———. *L'ora rossa.* Bologna, 1920.

Ponomarev, Boris Nikolaevich, et al. *A Short History of the Communist Party of the Soviet Union.* Translated by David Skvirsky. Moscow, 1974.

Pope, Arthur Upham. *Maxim Litvinoff.* New York, 1943.

Potemkin, Vladimir Petrovich, ed. *Istoriia diplomatii.* 3 vols. Moscow, 1941-45.

Renouvin, Pierre. *World War II and Its Origins: International Relations, 1929-1945.* Translated by Remy Inglis Hall. New York, 1968.

Risaliti, Renato. *Problemi dei rapporti italo-russi e della storiografia sovietica.* Pisa, 1979.

Rizzi, Bruno, *La lezione dello Stalinismo.* Rome, 1962.

Roatta, Mario. *Il processo Roatta.* Rome, 1945.

Rochat, Giorgio. *Italo Balbo: Aviatore e ministro dell'aeronautica, 1926–1933.* Ferrara, 1979.

Salata, Francesco. *Il Patto Mussolini: Storia di un piano politico e di un negoziato diplomatico*. 2nd ed. Milan, 1933.

Salvatorelli, Luigi. *Prelude to World War II*. Garden City, NJ, 1954.

――――. *Under the Axe of Fascism*. New York, 1936.

Salvatorelli, Luigi, and Giovanni Mira. *Storia d'Italia nel periodo fascista*. Turin, 1959.

Samoilovich, Rudolf Lazarevich. *Na spasenie ekspeditsii Nobile: Pokhod "Krasina" letom 1928 goda*. Leningrad, 1967.

Serra, Enrico. *Nitti e la Russia*. Bari, 1975.

S.I.A.I. ali nella storia. Florence, 1979.

Sipols, Vilnis. *Sovetskii Soiuz v bor'be za mir i bezopasnost', 1933-1939*. Moscow, 1974.

Sipols, Vilnis, and Mikhail Kharlamov. *On the Eve of World War II, 1933-1939: A Foreign Policy Study*. Moscow, 1974.

Skazkin, Sergei Danilovich, K.F. Miziano, and S.I. Dorofeev, eds. *Istoriia Italii*. 3 vols. Moscow, 1970-71.

Smirnova, Nina Dmitrievna. *Politika Italii na Balkanakh: Ocherk diplomaticheskoi istorii, 1922-1935 gg*. Moscow, 1979.

Taracouzio, Timothy Andre. *War and Peace in Soviet Diplomacy*. New York, 1940; reprint, Westport, CT, 1975.

Toscano, Mario. *Designs in Diplomacy: Pages from European Diplomatic History in the Twentieth Century*. Translated and edited by George A. Carbone. Baltimore, 1970.

Trukhanovskii, Vladimir Grigor'evich. *Peace to the Nations: Sixty Years after Lenin's Decree on Peace*. Moscow, 1977.

Ulam, Adam Bruno. *Expansion and Coexistence: Soviet Foreign Policy, 1917-73*. 2nd ed. New York, 1974.

Urban, Joan Barth. *Moscow and the Italian Communist Party: From Togliatti to Berlinguer*. Ithaca, NY, 1986.

Villari, Luigi. *Italian Foreign Policy under Mussolini*. New York, 1956.

Vinogradov, V.N, I.S. Dustian, N.V. Zuev, Iu. A. Pisare, and A.A. Iaz'kova. *Mezhdunarodnye otnosheniia na Balkanakh*. Moscow, 1974.

Volkov, Vladimir Konstantinovich. *Germano-iugoslavskie otnosheniia i rasval Maloi Antanty, 1933–1938*. Moscow, 1966.

Vyshinskii, Andrei Ianvar'evich. *Diplomaticheskii slovar'*. 2 vols. Moscow, 1948, 1950.

Warth, Robert D. *Soviet Russia in World Politics*. New York, 1963.

Weinberg, Gerhard L. *The Foreign Policy of Hitler's Germany: Diplomatic Revolution in Europe, 1933-36*. Chicago, 1970.

Wheeler-Bennett, John Wheeler. *The Disarmament Deadlock*. London, 1934.

Wiskemann, Elizabeth. *Fascism in Italy: Its Development and Influence*. 2nd ed. London, 1970.

Zuev, Fedor Grigor'evich, V.P. Nikhamin, and I.F. Ivashin. *Mezhdunarodnykh otnosheniia i vneshnei politika SSSR (1917-1957)*. Moscow, 1957.

Index

Abyssinia. *See* Italo-Abyssinian War
  (1935–36)
Aeronautica Macchi of Varese, 160 n.42
Afghanistan, 49, 105, 129, 169, 187
Agnelli, Eduardo, 36 n.64
Agnelli, Giovanni, 32, 36 n.64
Albania, 13, 127, 165, 166, 167, 168,
  172, 176–77, 178
Aloisi, Pompeo, 43, 53 n.24, 102, 109
  n.18, 124–25, 133, 177, 192
Alto Adige (South Tyrol), 39–40, 50, 65
Alvaro, Corrado, 97 n.75
Andreev, Professor, 151, 152
Ansaldo of Genoa, 29, 151–54, 159–60
  n.39, 160 nn.42, 43
anti-Semitism, 39, 46, 50, 93 n.15, 97
  n.74, 128, 135
appeasement, 41, 52 n.12
Ardemagni, Mirko, 96 n.58
Arone, Pietro, 162 n.56
Attolico, Bernardo, 13, 34 n.26, 53
  n.21, 64, 66, 92 n.3, 97–98 n.76, 108
  n.6, 110 n.39, 120 nn.21, 35, 126,
  131, 139 n.6, 143 n.63, 145–46, 147,
  151–53, 164, 174, 190; evaluates Soviet policy, 45–46, 48, 98 n.77, 136–
  37, 138, 165, 168, 169, 188; Italo-Soviet Pact of Friendship, Neutrality,

and Nonaggression (1933), 102, 113–
  19 passim; mediation between USSR
  and Germany, 42–48 passim; press
  relations, 54 n.39, 139 n.12, 186,
  187, 188
Austria, 3, 4, 13, 39, 142 n.34, 148;
  Anschluss and the German threat,
  14, 33 n.14, 39–41, 43, 48, 49–50, 55
  n.43, 56 n.64, 56–57 n.74, 63, 117,
  126, 132–33, 145, 163, 164, 165,
  170–78 passim, 181 n.49, 189; Nazi
  Putsch (1934), 158 n.18, 170, 175–78.
  See also Four Power Pact (1933),
  Austria; Rome (Italy-Austria-Hungary) Protocols (1934); Venice Meeting, Hitler and Mussolini (1934)
Avanguardia Socialista, 79
Avanti!, 79
Azienda Generale Italiana Petrolio
  (AGIP), 29

Badoglio, Pietro, 189
Balabanoff, Angelica, 79, 93 n.14
Balbo, Italo, 15–17, 35 n.40, 145–48
  passim, 157 n.5
Baldini, Alberto, 187
Balkan and Danubian areas: Italo-
  French competition, 127, 132, 140

nn.15, 19, 156, 163, 164, 177; Italo-
German competition, 50, 51, 57
n.74, 63, 177; Italo-Soviet competi-
tion, 3–4, 9, 117, 136, 138. *See also*
Austria; Balkan Pact (1934); Little
Entente; Rome (Italy-Austria-Hun-
gary) Protocols (1934)
Balkan Pact (1934), 69, 166–68, 171
Baltic States, 29, 47, 65, 71, 103, 129,
165, 167, 170
Banca Commerciale, 30, 50, 178
Banco di Roma, 30
Bardi, *I soldati italiani nella Russia in
fiame*, 140 n.23
Barduzzi, Italian consul, 97 n.74, 107–8
Barmine, Alexander, 18–19, 31–32, 35
n.51, 37 n.72
Barthou, Louis, 69, 176
Barzini, Luigi, 187–88
Bavaj, Amor, 97 n.69
Belgium, 63, 138
Beloff, Max, 197 n.25
Benni, Antonio Stefano, 32, 37 n.72
Berardis, Italian chargé, 46, 88, 96
n.65, 130
Bertoni, Renzo, and *Il trionfo del fas-
cismo nell'U.R.S.S.*, 89, 97 n.69
Bessarabia and Bessarabian Protocol
(1927), 6, 129, 165
Bordiga, Amadeo, 93 n.16
Borev Case, 104
Bottai, Giuseppe, 83, 95 n.37
Breda, Ernesto, 30
Briand, Aristide, and Briand Plan, 12,
13, 34 nn.24, 25, 66
Brochieris, Beonio, 169
Brothers in Need, 55 n.47
Brown International, 49, 50
Brunetta, Ernesto, 95 nn.43, 47
Budnenny, Semen Mikhailovich, 149,
158 n.23
Bulgaria, 13, 14, 15, 49, 117, 121 n.41,
127, 129, 132, 136, 140 n.19, 164,
165, 172. *See also* Balkan Pact (1934)

Cammett, John M., 94 n.27
Cantieri Riuniti dell'Adriatico (CRDA),
149, 151–52

Catholicism, 39, 70, 131, 133, 142
n.41, 169
Central Asia, 141 n.26, 169, 187
Cerruti, Vittorio, 11, 16, 33 nn.14, 15,
34 n.20, 39, 48, 53 n.27, 61, 63, 109
n.29, 135, 177, 185, 198 n.31
Chicherin, Georgi Vasilevich, 5, 7
n.19, 11
China, 41, 49, 52 n.12, 105, 132, 169
Ciano, Galeazzo, 53 n.24, 88–89, 97
n.74, 173, 195
Ciocca, Gaetano, and *Giudizio sul Bolscevismo*, 88–89, 140 n.23
Cipolla, Arnoldo, 187
collective security, 33 n.5, 41, 47, 60,
91, 119 n.4, 158 n.18, 168–72, 175–
78, 185, 197–98 n.30, 198 n.34, 199
n.44. *See also* Balkan Pact (1934);
Eastern Pact; Little Entente; Rome
(Italy-Austria-Hungary) Protocols
(1934); Rome (Mussolini-Laval) Accords (1935); Stresa Accords (1935)
Comintern (Communist International),
5, 10–11, 16, 33 n.10, 45, 91, 102,
109 n.29, 128, 138, 139 n.12, 193–94
commerce, Italo-Soviet, 36 nn.65, 66,
84, 88, 108 n.6, 124, 125, 195;
agreement (1921), 5; agreement
(1924), 6, 104, 196 n.18; agreement
(1930), 29–30, 36 n.59; agreement
(1931), 30, 36 n.62, 10l, 150; agreement (1933), 77, 101–5, 109 n.18,
110 n.35, 134, 146; commodities exchanged, 20–28, 29, 99, 100, 105,
107–8, 111–12, 141 n.29; credits, 17–
18, 19, 29–30, 31–32, 36 nn.59, 62,
37 n.69, 100, 103, 105, 130, 134,
137–38, 139 n.6, 152, 154, 160 n.43;
dumping, 18–19, 138; Great Depression, 19, 31, 36 n.58, 99, 100, 108
n.3, 150; institutional convergence,
99–100; Italian technical assistance,
89, 110 n.35, 111–12, 159 n.25; ruble
values, 108 n.3. *See also* Barduzzi,
Italian consul; Barmine, Alexander;
FIAT; Knickerbocker, Hubert Renfro; Levenson, Mikhail; National Fascist Federation of Industry; naval

construction; Rosengolts, Arkady Pavlovich; World Economic Conference (1933)

Communist Party of Italy (PCI), 5, 10–11, 194

Corrado, air record holder, 169–70

Coselschi, Eurgeio, 89, 97 n.73

Cot, Pierre, 119, 121 n.40, 126

Credito Italiano, 30

Cremona, Paul, 72 n.3

Critica Fascista ("Roma o Mosca?") debate, 83–87, 95 nn.43, 47, 51

Croce, Benedetto, 79, 92 n.11

Curato, Federico, 110 n.38, 137–38

Czechoslovakia, 44, 48, 49, 63, 69, 148, 165, 171. *See also* Little Entente

Daladier, Edouard, 63, 66, 67

De Felice, Renzo, 92 n.9

Definition of Aggression (1933), 44–46, 115, 116, 124, 129, 165, 166, 192, 193

Delfino, 145–46

Denmark, 140 n.19

De Vendetti, director of Villar-Peroza, 30

Dimitrov, 180 n.33

Dinale, Ottavio, 79, 80, 89, 93 n.17

dirigibles, 161 n.48, 162 nn.56, 57, 154–56; Dirizhablestroi, 154, 155, 156. *See also* Nobile, Umberto

Dirksen, Herbert von, 42–43, 44, 53 nn.23, 27, 55 n.48, 64–65, 109 n.12

Ditta Isotta Fraschini of Milan, 160 n.42

Dollfuss, Engelbert, 40, 133, 170–76 passim

Drucker, Peter Ferdinand, 92 n.6

Eastern Pact, 47, 119 n.4, 170, 197 n.25

Eden, Anthony, 192

Ehrenburg, Il'ia Grigor'evich, 181 n.49, 186

Eideman, Robert Eideman, 147, 158 n.13

Emanuelli, Luigi, 36 n.64

Engels, Friedrich, 79

Enrico, engineer, 152

Estonia, 41, 44, 104, 105, 138

feminism, 95 n.47

Ferrari, Aldo de, 145–46, 157 n.2

FIAT, 29, 30, 37 n.69, 147, 158 n.15

Finland, 41, 44, 188

Fiorini, Riccardo, 84–85, 86, 95 n.43

Five Year Plans (FYP), 17–19, 31–32, 83, 96–97 n.67, 97 n.68, 137, 149

Flaxermann, air engineer, 154

Four Power Pact (1933), 120 n.35, 166, 173, 191; Austria, 62, 65, 68, 69; France, 60–71 passim, 112, 131; Germany and Hitler, 61–71 passim, 112; Great Britain, 62–71 passim, 112; League of Nations, 59–69 passim; Little Entente, 45, 62–72 passim, 112; Litvinov, 64–66, 71, 131, 132, 136; Mussolini, 54 n.29, 59–71 passim, 112, 131, 132, 136; Poland, 63–71 passim, 73 n.41, 112, 117, 140 n.13; USSR and its exclusion, 43, 44, 45, 54 n.29, 62–72 passim, 73 n.25, 74 n.67, 77, 111–12, 124, 128, 131, 132, 137, 139 n.10, 188; World Disarmament Conference and disarmament, 59–69 passim. *See also* Italo-Soviet Pact of Friendship, Neutrality, and Nonaggression (1933); Four Power Pact (1933)

France, 15, 44, 60, 69, 166–67, 186, 198 n.33; commerce with USSR, 31, 108 n.6, 130, 152, 159 n.38; disarmament, 14, 15, 47, 59, 62, 129; Franco-Soviet Nonaggression Pact (1932), 41, 43, 53 n.23, 123, 124, 125, 129, 164; Germany, 46–51 passim, 67, 74 n.67, 109 n.27, 132, 138; Italo-Franco-British declarations (1934), 170, 176, 191; Italo-German cooperation against, 40–41, 43, 111; Italo-Soviet-German opposition, 9–15, 34 n.26; Italy, 50, 51, 65, 67, 74 n.67, 111, 132, 136, 140 n.19, 145, 148, 157 n.5, 163, 164, 168–77 passim, 179 n.5, 189, 191, 195–96 n.2, 197 n.25, 198 n.36; Italy and the

Mediterranean, 32 n.2, 115, 116; Italy and the USSR, 11, 12, 33–34 n.19, 34 n.26, 102, 112, 115–16, 117, 119 n.4, 121 n.41, 125–30, 136, 141 n.26, 159 n.28, 165, 166, 168, 170, 171, 185, 187, 188, 189, 193, 195, 197 n.24; Little Entente, 67, 163–68 passim, 188; military cooperation with Italy, 158 n.18, 175, 189; Mussolini, 10, 49–50, 51, 61, 111, 112, 116, 170, 189, 195; Poland, 42, 47, 48, 53 n.23, 69, 115, 187; USSR, 45–49 passim, 53 n.22, 67, 108 n.6, 135, 136, 145, 155, 156, 159 n.28, 170–75 passim, 189, 198 nn.33, 34; Yugoslavia, 164, 176, 196 n.2. See also Briand, Aristide, and Briand Plan; Four Power Pact (1933), France; Italo-Soviet Pact of Friendship, Neutrality, and Nonaggression (1933), France; Rome (Mussolini-Laval) Accords (1935)
Fraschini, 30, 37 n.68

Gayda, Virginio, 101, 108–9 n.8, 124, 173
Gel'fand, Leon, 121 n.40
Gallo, Luigi, 139 n.12
Gentile, Giovanni, 94 n.29
Georgia, 5
Gerarchia, 96 n.58
Germany, 4, 10, 13, 14, 59, 105, 118, 138, 141 n.26, 167, 174–75, 191–95 passim; Berlin Treaty (1926), 33 n.10, 43–44; disarmament, 59–60, 62, 129; France, 46, 48, 67, 109 n.27, 132, 138; ideology and government, 43, 46, 47, 53 n.27, 55 n.50, 102, 109 n.29, 125; Italian view of Soviet-German relations, 42–44, 128–31, 138; Italy, 49, 50, 56 n.74, 121 n.41, 138, 177, 188; Italy and France, 43, 63, 116, 126–27, 139–40 n.13, 145, 176; League of Nations, 61, 69, 129; Little Entente, 164, 165, 166; Litvinov's visit to Italy (1933), 128, 129, 131; Poland, 44, 46, 47, 48, 68, 133, 136; press relations, 42–

44, 46, 54 n.39, 140 n.23; Rapallo Agreement (1922), 5, 33 n.10, 41, 42, 48, 71, 103, 116, 128, 129, 145, 165; USSR, 17, 19, 41–44, 46, 53 n.22, 104, 112, 125–27, 129, 140 n.15, 147, 156, 193; USSR and France, 115, 121 n.40, 135, 138. See also Alto Adige (South Tyrol); Austria; Dirksen, Herbert von; Four Power Pact (1933), Germany; Henri, Ernst; Hitler, Adolf; Italian example of relations with USSR; mediation, between USSR and Germany by Italy; Rome (Italy-Austria-Hungary) Protocols (1934)
Gordovikov, General, 148
Göring, Hermann, 43, 51, 56–57 n.70, 109 n.27, 133, 140 n.23
Gorky, Maxim, 110 n.37, 161 n.53
Gramsci, Antonio, 5, 6
Grandi, Dino, 12–14, 30, 33–34 n.19, 81, 112, 113
Grazioli, General, 148
Great Britain, 14, 15, 59, 60, 107 n.3, 112, 141 n.6, 166–67, 185, 190, 192, 194; Italo-Franco-British declarations (1934), 170, 176, 191; Metro-Vicker's Trial, 104, 109 n.33; USSR, 5, 6, 19, 36, 49, 103, 104, 151, 156, 187. See also Four Power Pact (1933), Great Britain; Italo-Soviet Pact of Friendship, Neutrality, and Nonaggression (1933), Great Britain; Stresa Accords (1935)
Great Purge Trials (1936–38), 52 n.12
Greece, 13, 15–16, 117, 127, 132, 147, 164, 166. See also Balkan Pact (1934)
Gregor, Anthony James, 92 n.9
Guarneri, Professor, 31, 36–37 n.67

Halevy, Elie, 92 n.6
Haslam, Jonathan, 53 n.18, 197 n.24, 198 nn.33, 37, 199 nn.41, 44
Hassell, Ulrich von, 40–41, 63, 66, 116, 135–36, 172, 173–74
Henri, Ernst [Henri Rostovskii], 48–51, 56 n.64, 177–78, 182 n.79

Herriot, Edouard, 109 n.27, 119, 121 nn.40, 41, 124–27 passim

Hitler, Adolf, 14, 32, 33 n.14, 39–41, 49, 66, 71, 124, 125, 127, 195; USSR, 42, 46, 48, 49, 71, 127, 132. *See also* Austria; Mussolini; Venice Meeting, Hitler and Mussolini (1934)

Holtsman, Abramo, 154, 155

Hugenberg Memorandum, 54 n.39, 136

Hungary, 13, 14, 40, 49, 65, 69, 70, 94 n.31, 117, 132, 134, 142 n.34, 164, 165, 166, 178. *See also* Rome (Italy-Austria-Hungary) Protocols (1934)

Ideology, 186; Balbo, Italo, 16–17; fascism, communism, and Stalinism, 16–17, 45, 48–51, 56 n.64, 78–90 passim, 92 nn.3, 6, 94 nn.25, 27, 28, 29, 95 n.46, 96 n.58, 97 n.68, 110 n.38; and government, 13–14, 16–17, 43, 46, 47, 53 n.27, 55 n.50, 102, 103, 105, 109 nn.18, 29, 124, 125, 128, 134; Mussolini and government, 102, 109 n.29, 124; Mussolini and ideological convergence, 36 n.66, 78, 80–81, 85, 89, 90, 96 n.58; Mussolini and syndicalism, fascism, and bolshevism, 79, 80, 81, 82; syndicalism, fascism, and bolshevism, 78–82, 88, 89, 91, 92 nn.9, 10, 92–93 n.13, 93 nn.14, 15, 16, 17, 18. *See also Critica Fascista* ("Roma o Mosca?") debate; Mussolini, mediation between USSR and Germany; *and names of individual authors*

inclusion, Soviet desire for, and fears of exclusion, 34 nn.20, 25, 61, 64–65, 105, 111, 112, 129, 131–32, 136, 191, 197 n.24, 198 n.33. *See also* Four Power Pact (1933), USSR and its exclusion

India, 187, 190

Ingianni, Luciano, 86, 95 n.43

Insabato, Enrico, 10, 32 n.4, 53 n.16

Italia, 15, 35 n.42, 155, 156

Italian example of relations with USSR, 10, 43–48 passim, 53 n.27, 55 n.50, 56 n.55, 105, 121 n.41, 125

L'Italia Nostra, 80, 93 n.18

Italo-Abyssinian War (1935–36), 51, 87, 91, 92 n.9, 148–49, 156, 168–69, 177, 189–94, 195, 197 nn.21, 27, 29, 198 nn.36, 37, 199 n.41; Japan, 132, 142 n.34, 168–69, 190, 197 n.27. *See also* Rome (Mussolini-Laval) Accords (1935); Stresa Accords (1935)

Italo-Russian relations, 3–5

Italo-Soviet Pact of Friendship, Neutrality, and Nonaggression (1933), 77, 110 n.38, 120 n.35, 134, 146; Four Power Pact (1933), 111–17 passim, 123–29 passim, 140 n.15; France, 111–19 passim, 119 n.4, 121 n.41, 124, 125, 126–27, 139–40 n.13; Franco-Soviet Nonaggression Pact (1932), 123, 124, 125; Germany, 115–19 passim, 121 n.41, 124–27 passim, 134–36; Great Britain, 112, 118, 125, 127, 134, 140 n.18; Japan, 118, 119, 120 n.21, 125, 126, 141 n.26; Little Entente, 113, 117, 125, 127; Mussolini, 102, 111–19 passim, 123, 124, 127, 131; negotiations, 105, 111–19, 120 n.35; Poland, 112, 115, 117, 125, 126; terms and analysis, 123–27, 138–39 n.2, 139 nn.5, 12, 140 nn.15, 19, 20; Turkey, 115, 116, 117, 127

Italo-Soviet relations, 1920s, 5–6

Italo-Turkish War (1911–12), 4, 80, 85

Iurenev, Konstantin Konstantinovich, 6, 8 n.21

Japan, 53 n.12, 69; Italy, 41, 129, 132, 136, 142 n.34, 168–69, 188, 197 n.27; USSR, 41, 42, 47, 49, 118, 119, 120 n.21, 128–38 passim, 141 n.26, 142 n.34, 151, 165, 193. *See also* Italo-Abyssinian War (1935–36); Italo-Soviet Pact of Friendship, Neutrality, and Nonaggression (1933), Japan

Kaganovich, Lazar Moiseevich, 88, 96 n.64

Kaganovich ball-bearing plant, 88–89, 96 n.59
Kamanev, Lev Borisovich, 8 n.22
Karakhan, Lev Mikhailovich, 33 n.15
Kellogg-Briand Pact (1927), 44, 61, 63, 112, 115
Khinchuk, L. M., 41
Kmelnitskii, General, 148
Knickerbocker, Hubert Renfro, 18
Kollontai, Alexandra, 110 n.38
Krasin, 15, 35 n.42
Krasnyi Kavkaz, 145–47, 157 n.8
Krestinskii, Nikolai Nikolaevich, 11, 13, 33 n.15, 41, 44, 45, 53 n.27, 66, 103, 115, 118–19, 141–42 n.33, 169
Kukel, Admiral, 154
Kurskii, Dmitrii Ivanovich, 6, 8 n.22, 10

Labriola, Arturo, 79, 92 n.10, 93 n.16
Lancia, 29
Lanzillo, Agostino, 79, 93 n.16
Laqueur, Walter Zeev, 56 n.64
Latvia, 41, 44, 104, 105, 121 n.41, 138
Lausanne Convention, 127
Laval, Pierre, 197 n.25, 189, 191, 198 n.33
Lavreniev, B., 196 n.4
League of Nations, 12–15, 33 n.19, 41, 59, 60, 61, 69, 72 n.3, 102, 103, 112, 125, 129, 131, 132, 133, 137, 138, 142 nn.34, 38, 143 n.63, 164, 170, 173, 174, 185, 187, 191, 192. *See also* Four Power Pact (1933), League of Nations
Lenin, Vladimir Il'ich, 5, 79, 80, 81, 83, 92 n.9
Leone, Enrico, 79, 93 n.16
Levenson, Mikhail, 18, 31, 96 n.65, 104, 110 n.35, 130, 152
Libya, 65
Lisovskii, Petr Alekseevich, 189
Lithuania, 44, 65, 104, 105, 140 n.15

Little Entente, 45, 49, 112, 113, 129, 132, 136, 138, 163–77 passim, 187, 188. *See also* Four Power Pact (1933), Little Entente; Italo-Soviet Pact of Friendship, Neutrality, and Nonaggression (1933), Little Entente
Litvinov, Maksim Maksimovich, 10, 33 n.5, 41, 53 n.16, 54 n.39, 126, 141 n.24, 165, 167, 169, 174, 176, 196 nn.11, 18; anti-French tripartite co-operation, 10, 12, 33 n.6; Catholi-cism, 131, 133, 142 n.41; commercial relations, 44, 100, 102, 108 n.6, 133, 134, 136; cooperation with Italy, 11, 102, 137; France, 33 n.6, 108 n.6, 127, 129, 136, 138, 177; Germany, 52–53 n.16, 132, 134–36; ideology and government, 46, 55 n.50, 66; Italian example of relations with Ger-many, 44, 55 n.50; Italian mediation between USSR and Germany, 42, 43, 132, 133, 136; Italian view of Lit-vinov, 11–12, 33 nn.15, 16; Italo-Abyssinian War (1935–36), 192–93, 199 n.41; Italo-French relations, 177, 185, 195 n.2, 197 n.25; Italo-Soviet Pact of Friendship, Neutrality, and Nonaggression (1933), 111, 113, 118, 124, 127; Japan, 132, 135, 142 n.34; League of Nations, 129, 131, 132, 138, 143 n.63, 185, 188, 192–93; meets Grandi at Milan (1930), 12–13, 112, 113; panslavism, 132, 135, 138; press relations, 139 n.12, 186–87, 188; purported anti-German alliance of Italy-France-Britain-USSR thwarted, 142 n.42; radio propa-ganda, 110 n.39, 133–34; speech, Dec. 29, 1933, 46, 55 n.50, 71, 136–37; Soviet desire for inclusion, 129, 132, 170; United States, 128, 135, 140 n.21; visit to Italy (1933), 69, 88–89, 128–38 passim, 140 n.21, 141–42 n.33, 142 nn.41, 42, 143 n.56, 146–47. *See also* Definition of Aggression (1933); Four Power Pact (1933), Litvinov
Lloyd Triestino Company, 107, 154

Locarno (Pact) Accords (1925), 6, 63, 67, 68, 112, 116, 124, 125
Lombrassa, Giuseppe, 96 n.51
London Conventions (1933). *See* Definition of Aggression (1933)
Luchini, Alberto, 85

Macartney, Maxwell Henry Hayes, 72 n.3
MacDonald, Ramsay, 59, 63, 109 n.27
Malvezzi, Giovanni, 36 n.64
Malyghin, 154
Manevich, Lev Efimovich, 110 n.33
Markov, Ivan, 109 n.33
Marocco, Secondo, 88
Marsoni, Professor, 169
Marx, Karl, 79
Matteoti, Giacomo, 6
mediation, between USSR and Germany by Italy, 39, 42–48 passim, 54 n.39, 102, 103, 109 n.29, 111–13, 116, 119, 125, 126, 129, 132–37 passim, 139–40 n.13, 187, 188, 196 n.9
Mediterranean Sea, and Italian foreign policy, 9, 32 n.2, 132
Michels, Roberto, 79, 94 n.25
Mikoian, Anastas Ivanovich, 169, 180 n.31
military exchanges: air exchanges, 15–17, 146, 147–48, 157 n.5, 158 n.18; army exchanges, 146, 147, 148, 158 n.20; Attolico and de Ferrari tour (1933), 145–46, 157 n.2; French concerns, 11; naval exchanges, 7 n.8, 11, 15, 35 n.39, 110 n.38, 111, 145–47, 149, 157 nn.8, 9; Potemkin, 111, 146, 147, 157 n.9; significance, 77, 129, 145–49 passim, 157 n.7, 158 n.18. *See also* dirigibles; naval construction; Nobile, Umberto
Missiroli, Mario, 93 n.16
Molotov, Viacheslav Mikhailovich, 56 n.55, 90, 101, 109 n.12, 169
Mondolfo, Rodolfo, 94 n.25
Mongolia, 105
Montecatini, 29, 30

Monti, General, 148
Mosca, Rodolfo, 89
Mosely, Oswald, 50
Mussolini, Benito, 9, 36 n.66, 44, 88, 89, 97 n.69, 156, 164, 177, 178, 191; Austria, 40–41, 49–50, 132–33, 176; commercial relations, 19, 101, 104, 105, 130, 153; disarmament, 59–60, 62; France, 10, 49–50, 51, 61, 102, 111, 112, 116, 170, 189, 195; Hitler, 41, 42, 50, 53 n.22, 70, 102, 142 n.42; Hitler and Germany, 34 n.35, 39, 41, 42, 50–51, 53 n.22, 133; ideological convergence, 36 n.66, 78, 80–81, 85, 89, 90, 96 n.58; ideology and government, 102, 109 n.29, 124; Japan, 132, 142 n.34, 168–69; League of Nations, 59–60, 62, 72 n.3, 129, 131, 132, 133, 142 n.38, 143 n.63; Lenin, 80, 81, 92 n.9; Litvinov's visit to Italy (1933), 130–36 passim, 141–42 n.33, 142 n.42; mediation between USSR and Germany, 39, 109 n.29, 111–13, 116, 119, 125, 132, 133, 135, 136, 196 n.9; press relations, 111, 112, 139 nn.10, 12, 187, 188; Russia and the USSR, 5–6, 13, 195; Soviet inclusion, 111, 112, 131–32; syndicalism, fascism, and bolshevism, 79, 80, 81, 82; treaty revision, 59–61, 62, 68, 72 n.3. *See also* Austria; Four Power Pact (1933); Italo-Soviet Pact of Friendship, Neutrality, and Nonaggression (1933), Mussolini; Rome (Mussolini-Laval) Accords (1935); Venice Meeting, Hitler and Mussolini (1934)

Nadolny, Rudolf, 46–47, 48, 135
Nanni, Torquato, 82
Napolitano, Tomaso, 87, 88, 96 n.58
Nasti, Agostino, 87
National Fascist Federation of Industry, 30–31, 36 n.64
naval construction, 32, 149–54, 159 nn.29, 38, 160 nn.41, 42, 161 n.45

Neurath, Constantin von, 52–53 n.16, 61, 66, 135, 174
New Economic Policy (NEP), 81, 83
Nobile, Umberto, 15, 35 n.42, 154–56, 161 nn.47, 53
No-Force Pact, 61
Novorossiisk, Italian trade with, 106–8

October Revolution, 4, 82
Odero-Terni-Orlando of La Spezia (OTO), 160 n.42
Odessa, Italian trade with, 107, 108
Officine Galileo of Florence, 160 n.42
Olivetti, Angelo Oliviero, 36 n.64, 79, 80, 92–93 n.13
Olivetti, Gino, 36 n.66
Omodeo, Angelo, 36 n.66, 124
Orano, Paolo, 79, 80, 93 n.15
Ordzhonikidze, Grigorii Konstantinovich, 88, 96 n.64, 152
Ottico Meccanica Italiana of Rome, 160 n.42

Pagine Libere, 80, 92 n.13, 93 n.15
panslavism, 3, 45, 69, 81, 97 n.74, 132, 135, 138, 165
Pantaleoni, Maffeo, 92 n.11
Panunzio, Sergio, 79–91 passim, 93 nn.15, 16, 95 n.43, 97 n.69, 135
Papen, Franz von, 41, 42, 43, 109 n.27, 119, 132
Pareto, Vilfredo, 79, 92 n.11
Persia, 44, 104, 105, 169
Petrolea, 104, 109 n.33
Petrovskii, 146–47
Pettinato, Concetto, 94 n.31
Pirelli, 30
Poland, 41–49 passim, 53 n.23, 68, 112, 129, 133, 135, 136, 138, 139–40 n.13, 140 n.15, 147, 148, 157 n.7, 165, 168, 175, 187, 199 n.44. See also Four Power Pact (1933), Poland; Italo-Soviet Pact of Friendship, Neutrality, and Nonaggression (1933), Poland
Poppo, General, 147

Potemkin, Vladimir Petrovich, 45, 55 n.44, 70, 104, 109 n.18, 113, 120 n.21, 132–34, 135, 141 n.26, 165, 168, 172, 174–75, 180 n.33, 191, 196 n.18, 198 n.33; commercial relations, 89, 101–5 passim, 111–12, 151–52; Four Power Pact (1933), 65, 70, 111–12, 131; Italo-Soviet Pact of Friendship, Neutrality, and Nonaggression (1933), 111–19 passim, 123; military exchanges, 111, 146, 147, 157 n.9; press relations, 102, 109 nn.18, 27, 111–12, 119 n.2, 121 n.43, 186–87
press relations, 42–44, 46, 54 n.39, 70, 74 n.67, 102, 109 n.27, 111–12, 119 n.2, 121 n.43, 128, 139 nn.10, 12, 140 n.23, 180 n.26, 185–89, 196 nn.4, 5, 9, 11, 198–99 n.37
Prezzolini, Giuseppe, 94 n.25
propaganda, 141 n.23, 157 n.8
PS 8 (ship), 153–54, 160 n.42
PS 26 (ship), 153–54, 160 n.42
Purmal, head of Dirizhablestroi, 154

Racconigi Accord (1909), 4, 85
Radek, Karl Bernardovich, 43, 46, 53–54 n.28, 65, 69–70, 73 n.25, 134, 139 n.12, 186, 198 n.30
radio propaganda, 96 n.58, 110 n.39, 133–34
Rivoire, Mario, 85, 86
Rizzi, Bruno, 82, 94 n.27
Romania, 6, 15–16, 29, 44, 124, 127, 165, 166, 178. See also Balkan Pact (1934); Bessarabia and Bessarabian Protocol (1927); Little Entente
Rome (Mussolini-Laval) Accords (1935), 116–17, 168, 176, 189–90, 191, 193, 197 nn.24, 25
Rome (Italy-Austria-Hungary) Protocols (1934), 55 n.43, 69, 170–72, 178
Rosenberg, Alfred, 42, 46, 49, 52 n.15, 53 n.16, 70, 120 n.21, 129, 132, 133, 136, 167, 176
Rosengolts, Arkady Pavlovich, 30–31, 36 nn.64, 65, 66, 104, 152, 169
Rosso, Augusto, 128, 156
Rossoni, Edmondo, 93 n.18

Rudolf, N., 110 n.39
Russell, Bertrand, 56 n.64

Sadoul, Jacques, 117, 120 n.34
San Marco incident at Theodosia (1934), 143 n.60
Schuschnigg, Kurt von, 176
Settembrini, Domenico, 92 n.9
Shaumian, 146–47
Shtein, Boris, 143 n.56, 188, 191, 192, 196 n.18, 198 n.37
Silurificio Italiano of Naples, 160 nn.41, 42
Silurificio Whitehead of Fiume, 160 n.42
Simon, John, 63, 67, 143 n.63
Sirianni, Giuseppe, 151, 152, 160 n.41
Smirnova, Nina Dmitrievna, 119 n.4
Socialist Party of Italy (PSI), 5, 93 n.14
Società Rimorchiatori Napoletani, 157 n.8
Società S. Giorgio of Sestri, 160 n.42
Spampanato, Bruno, 83–84, 85–86
Spanish Civil War (1936–39), 89, 91, 149, 195
spying and spies, 42, 48, 103, 104, 109–10 n.33
Stalin, J. V., 42, 47, 78, 81, 82, 83, 90, 93 n.14, 94 n.27, 121 n.43, 142 n.38, 168
Stomonyakov, Boris Spiridonovich, 169, 180 n.31
Stoppani, air record holder, 169–70
Stresa Accords (1935), 191–93, 197–98 n.30, 198 nn.31, 33
Suvich, Fulvio, 45, 55 n.43, 63, 89, 103–4, 105, 109 n.27, 119 n.2, 120 n.21, 121 n.43, 131, 135, 141 n.26, 146, 147, 157 n.9, 167–74 passim, 180 n.22, 186–87, 188, 191; Italo-Soviet Pact of Friendship, Neutrality, and Nonaggression (1933), 105, 113, 115, 118, 119
Switzerland, 127

Tabouis, Genevieve R., 108–9 n.8
Tamaro, Attilio, 188
Tasca, Angelo, 93 n.16
Thyssen, Fritz, 49, 50, 177, 178, 183 n.85
Togliatti, Palmiro, 11, 194
Toplitz, Giuseppe, 50, 178
Tosti, Armando, 86, 95–96 n.51
tourists and exchanges, 30–31, 36 n.64, 89–90, 97 n.75, 169–70, 195 nn.4, 11
Tricheco, 145–46
Trojani, Felice, 155, 156
Trotsky, Lev, 36 n.64, 54 n.28, 82, 94 n.27, 96 n.58
Tukhachevsky, Mikhail Nikolaevich, 149, 158 n.23
Tunisia, 65, 177
Tupolev, Andrei Nikolaevich, 154
Tupolev TB–3 (ANT–6) bomber, 147, 158 n.17
Turkey, 11–16 passim, 43, 44, 45, 104, 105, 121 n.41, 127, 129, 132, 133, 136, 138, 140 n.21, 147, 151, 157 n.10, 164, 166, 180 n.22. *See also* Balkan Pact (1934); Italo-Soviet Pact of Friendship, Neutrality, and Nonaggression (1933), Turkey

Ukraine and Ukrainian nationalism, 10, 47, 49, 53 n.16, 54 n.39, 70, 121 n.43, 136, 140 n.23, 141 n.24, 175
L'Unità, 6
United States, 14, 41, 46, 49, 69, 107 n.6, 128–35 passim, 141 n.26, 168, 190
Utitskii, General, 148
Utopia, 79

Valle, Giuseppe, 147
Venice Meeting, Hitler and Mussolini (1934), 172–75, 182 n.60
Villari, Luigi, 68, 175
Villar-Peroza, 30
Voroshilov, Klementii Efrimovich, 44, 54 n.36, 90, 146, 149, 152, 153, 157 n.10, 169

Vyshinskii, Andrei Ianvar'evich, 52 n.12

World Disarmament Conference (1932–33) and disarmament, 14, 15, 46, 47, 59–60, 62, 102, 109 n.27, 115, 126, 129, 130–31, 132, 135, 173, 174. *See also* Four Power Pact (1933)
World Economic Conference (1933), 44, 54 nn.39, 40, 100, 101, 108 n.6

World War I, 4, 80, 81, 163
Wrangel Fleet, 143 n.60

Yemen, 32 n.2, 129
Yugoslavia, 29, 40, 44, 50, 62, 65, 69, 127, 129, 140 n.20, 166, 172, 176, 177, 196 n.2. *See also* Balkan Pact (1934); Little Entente
Yvetot, Georges, 93 n.16

ABOUT THE AUTHOR

J. CALVITT CLARKE III is an assistant professor at Jacksonville University in Jacksonville, Florida, and teaches courses in Russian and Soviet history, modern European history, and diplomatic history. He has published an article, "Manifestations of Cordiality," in *Naval History*.